Sport

George Caplan • Philip Smith

OCR
National Level 2

www.heinemann.co.uk
✓ Free online support
✓ Useful weblinks
✓ 24 hour online ordering

01865 888058

Heinemann
Inspiring generations

Heinemann Educational Publishers
Halley Court, Jordan Hill, Oxford OX2 8EJ
Part of Harcourt Education

Heinemann is a registered trademark of
Harcourt Education Limited

© George Caplan and Philip Smith, 2005

First published 2005

10   09   08   07   06   05
10   9   8   7   6   5   4   3   2   1

British Library Cataloguing in Publication Data is available
from the British Library on request.

10-digit ISBN 0-435-45940-6

13-digit ISBN 978-0-435459-40-6

Designed by Lorraine Inglis
Typeset by Integra

Original illustrations © Harcourt Education Limited, 2005

Illustrated by Integra (India) Ltd/Barking Dog Art

Cover design by Wooden Ark Studios

Printed by Printer Trento S.r.l

Cover photo: © Getty Images

Picture research by Liz Savery

Contents

Acknowledgements

George Caplan would like to thank the teaching team at Tresham Insitute and in particular Mr Kim Davis and Miss Lisa Irons, whose resources proved invaluable. Thank you also to the wifey, Caroline, whose support and willingness to look after our daughter seven days and seven nights a week helped tremendously. To my father Mr Ken Caplan who detests sport but always encourages me in anything I do. Finally, I am indebted to my daughter Jenny, who was willing to put up with me slaving over the computer for long spells and not playing pirates, witches, ogres and the like.

Philip Smith would like to dedicate the book to his father, for his support and inspiration through the years.

The authors and publisher would like to thank all who have given permission to reproduce material.

Central Council for Physical Recreation (page 21)
Humber Sports Partnership (page 2)
National Basketball Camps (page 28)
Sport England (page 20)
UK Sport (page 19)

Photographs

Action Plus/ Steve Bardens page 193/ Matthew Clarke page 215/ Glyn Kirk page 275/ Neil Tingle page 157
Alamy Images pages 145, 243, 256, 261
Bettmann/Corbis page 175 (top and bottom)
Corbis pages 33, 43, 46, 171, 189, 191, 194, 235, 251
Empics page 158, 190/ PA page 187
Getty Images UK/ Darren England page 44/ Photodisc pages 67, 135, 202/ Spencer Platt page 239
Harcourt Education Ltd/Gareth Boden page 224/ Trevor Clifford page 223
Reuters/Corbis page 116
Rex Features/Nicholas Bailey page 11/ Carl Fox pages 45, 166
Science Photo Library pages 64 / AJ Photo page 237/ Steve Vowles 233
Xscape page 7

Every effort has been made to contact copyright holders of material reproduced in this book. Any omissions will be rectified in subsequent printings if notice is given to the publishers.

Websites

There are links to relevant websites in this book. In order to ensure that the links are up to date, that the links work, and that the sites are not inadvertently linked to sites that could be considered offensive, we have made the links available on the Heinemann website at www.heinemann.co.uk/hotlinks. When you access the site the express code is 9406P.

Please note that the examples of websites suggested in this book were up to date at the time of writing. It is essential for tutors to preview each site before using it to ensure that the URL is still accurate and the content is appropriate. We suggest that tutors bookmark useful sites and consider enabling students to access them through the school or college intranet.

Introduction

Sport is a major industry in the UK, and many job opportunities have been created as a result of people's participation in sport or by their spending money on sports-related goods and services. The range of sporting activities and goods now on offer is ever-increasing, and these have resulted in new and varied careers in the sports industry. Sport also promotes fitness, and fitness brings social and economic benefits to the country as a whole as well as to individuals.

The majority of jobs in the sports industry require trained staff. The OCR Level 2 National Certificate in Sport will provide you with the background knowledge and skills you need to launch a career in the sports industry, and this book will help you to complete this course.

The qualification is designed to be equally deliverable by schools, colleges and private training providers.

How to use this book

Your course will be certificated by OCR, one of the country's main awarding bodies for vocational qualifications. This book covers all ten mandatory and optional units for the course. Mandatory units are those which are considered core and therefore must be completed to achieve the qualification. Optional units are likely to be chosen by the centre, based on their suitability for student group. The mandatory units for this qualification are indicated in bold. You must also complete a minimum of two of the remaining optional units.

Unit 1: **The Sporting Environment**
Unit 2: **Healthy, Safety and Prevention of Injury in Sport**
Unit 3: **Effective Sports Leadership**
Unit 4: **The Body in Action**
Unit 5: Social Issues in Sport
Unit 6: Sports Skills
Unit 7: Lifestyle and Fitness
Unit 8: Outdoor Activities
Unit 9: Career Planning for the Sports Industry
Unit 10: Work Experience in the Sports Industry

This book can be used in conjunction with the specification provided by OCR. This document follows the same format for each unit of work. An introduction is followed by a summary of the learning outcomes or main learning aims. These are further broken down into assessment objectives (AOs) for each unit. The assessment objectives detail what you must be able to do in order to show that you have acquired the underpinning knowledge and skills necessary to complete each unit. For this reason the section headings in this book mirror closely the assessment objectives contained in the specification.

Several of the units in this qualification have some content which is similar. (For example, several units refer to the process of risk assessment or identifying potential factors that could cause a person harm and minimising that risk). Where this occurs it is highlighted in this book, to aid assessment and save unnecessary duplication on your part.

Assessment

You will be assessed through a series of assignments. Each assignment is designed so that you can demonstrate your understanding and show that you can apply a number of assessment objectives. The assessment objectives for each unit may be assessed by one large or a series of smaller assignments. All units are internally assessed and externally moderated by OCR. Centres can devise their own assessments or use OCR model assignments where available. For each unit there is a pass, merit or distinction grade. Further guidance on assignments and exemplar assessments are available from OCR.

Portfolio building

Assignments for each unit will normally be collected together in a folder known as a portfolio. This folder is likely to be divided by unit and is an easy way for an OCR moderator to check your work.

There are opportunities for your tutors to develop cross-unit assessments as many of the assessment outcomes are linked. Where these exist you must clearly show in your portfolio where the unit evidence is located and provide some form of checklist or contents page.

How will this book help you?

Throughout the text there are a number of features that are designed to encourage you to reflect on the issues raised and to relate the theory to practice. These are as follows:

- *Did you know*? These sections contain interesting facts and information for further discussion.
- *Activities*: Each unit provides a range of practical tasks and activities for you to undertake. These will help contribute towards the skills you will need to pass the qualification at the level that is best for you.

- *Case studies*: Case studies are used to help explain a concept or to link the theory to practice.
- *Test your knowledge*: Each unit (except Units 9 and 10 in the Appendix) ends with a series of questions that will test your knowledge of the issues covered in the unit.
- *Glossary*: The glossary sections explain words or concepts that may be new to you.

Many of these features will help to you compile the evidence you need to complete each unit. In addition, you should try to keep your knowledge current by:

- watching television and listening to the radio for items related to the sports industry;
- reading local and national newspapers and cutting out any important sports-related articles; and
- making full use of the Internet by accessing the websites listed in the bibliography.

All this will keep you up to date about what is happening in a rapidly changing industry and should enable you to carry out your assignments so that you complete the certificate successfully.

Support from OCR

You will find a wide range of support material, particularly for assessment, on the OCR website (accessed through www.heinemann.co.uk/hotlinks and express code 9406P).

The Sporting Environment

Introduction

By studying this unit you will gain an understanding of the sports industry, at both a local and national level. You will learn that there is a wide range of sports provision in the UK provided by the government, private individuals, private companies and voluntary organisations. Each type of organisation has different objectives and receives funding from different sources, and these are explored in this unit. Sports facilities within the public, private and voluntary sectors provide opportunities for people to participate in one or many sports, and the organisations in these sectors aim to meet the needs of the people who want to take part in a particular sport.

How you will be assessed

In this unit you will be assessed by an assignment drawn up and marked by your school or college. It is likely to involve you in researching local sports facilities and their users and reporting back in the form of a written report or verbal evidence.

In this unit you will learn how to:

① Describe four different types of sporting facilities available in the local area

② Describe four different types of national sporting facilities

③ Describe the role of the private, public and voluntary sectors in providing local sporting opportunities and facilities

④ Describe the aims of three national organisations involved in sport

⑤ Describe local and national sources of funding used to support two sports at local level

⑥ List the specific needs of four different user groups which may affect their participation in sport

⑦ For each of the four different user groups identified suggest ways to increase their participation in sport

1.1 Describe four different types of sporting facilities available in the local area

This section covers

- Sport and recreation centres
- Swimming pools
- Recreation facilities
- Sports stadiums
- Outdoor recreation centres

Opportunities to participate in sport vary according to locality, but most areas in the UK have a range of provision. Where can you find out what

Leaflets often advertise sports facilities provided by local councils and other organisations

is available in your area? A good starting point is your local telephone directory or the Internet. Your local tourist information centre or library may also prove useful, and these places often have leaflets which advertise sports facilities provided by the local council.

We'll now examine the different types of facilities in more detail.

Sport and recreation centres

DID YOU KNOW?

The first purpose-built sports and leisure centre was constructed in Harlow, Essex, in 1960.

Sport and recreation (or leisure) centres are mainly provided by local authorities. There is, however, no legal obligation for them to do so. They only have a legal duty to provide sports facilities in schools, but most go beyond this to provide a wide range of provision, including multi-purpose sport centres.

Early sport and recreation centres were built in the centre of towns so that they were accessible to the local population. These tended to be small with limited facilities. However, during the 1970s, in response to a report by the Sports Council, most local authorities started to provide larger facilities that combined indoor and outdoor facilities, such as hardcourt playing areas and athletic tracks, and indoor swimming pools and multi-functional sports halls.

Some sports centres are attached to schools and operate what is known as a 'dual use' mode of provision. This means that the pupils use the facilities during the day and the wider public are able to use the facility during the evenings and at weekends. The advantage of this system is that there are no slack periods: when people are at work and thus cannot use the centre, the centre is used by the school.

GLOSSARY

Local authority: the organisation responsible for running all the amenities in an area that are mainly paid for out of council tax (education, waste disposal, sport and recreation centres, etc.).

DID YOU KNOW?

Kettering Leisure Village is a large, multi-purpose sports centre on the edge of Kettering. It contains a health and fitness club that has a swimming pool, sauna and fitness suite. The club is run by a private company who have successfully won the contract to run this from the local authority. The main building also contains a 'Kids' Kingdom' play and adventure area, a bar and a restaurant. Further facilities include a conference room and a multi-purpose sports hall that can accommodate badminton, five-a-side football, basketball, tennis and gymnastics, among other sports, and that is also used for concerts and other events. The outdoor area has a 400-metre running track and an astro-turf area for team sports.

Sport and recreation centres that are run by the local authority often provide opportunities for different sections of the community to play sport. These groups include senior citizens, children, adults, unemployed people and people with disabilities. Sports centres also try to balance their programme by providing opportunities for the following:

- Casual bookings (individuals and groups should be able simply to turn up and play).
- Learners (members of the public who want to learn a new sports skill or improve an existing one).
- Clubs (the provision of training facilities and match venues).
- Spectators (spectating facilities for important events).
- Special sessions (for example, sessions aimed at specific target groups such as women-only swimming).
- Activities for minority groups (facilities for minority sports and minority groups which are not available in the local community).

You will often find that a sports centre programme has something for everyone!

ACTIVITY

Visit your nearest local-authority-run sport and recreation centre and pick up a timetable. Is there a wide range of sports activities? Which groups are these sessions aimed at? Are there any groups that are not catered for very well?

A further type of sport and recreation centre is often called a health and fitness club. Sometimes these are run by the local authority within a major sports complex but, more often, they are standalone facilities provided by private companies. Companies that provide these facilities include LA Fitness, Esporta and Virgin Fitness. These companies continue to expand and, if they haven't already opened a facility close to your home, it is a fair bet one will do so soon.

These facilities commonly have a fitness suite with various weight-training and cardiovascular fitness equipment, a swimming pool and health and beauty facilities (sauna, sun-beds, steam room, etc.). Often there will be an exercise studio for aerobics and other exercise classes such as spinning, which is a fast-paced class on exercise bikes. These clubs often have long opening hours so that they can accommodate people who work different hours, and they have a range of membership packages to maximise the use of the facilities. Table 1.1 summarises some figures concerning leisure centres in the UK.

TYPE OF CENTRE	NUMBER
Sports centres with no pool	1,483
Sports centres with a pool	975
Private health and fitness clubs	2,200
Pools only	807

Source: Hayward (2000)

Table 1.1 *Leisure centres in the UK*

Swimming pools

Public swimming pools were first provided by local councils in the 1800s. This was largely in response to the Baths and Washhouses Act 1846, which stated that councils should provide recreational facilities as well as places for the public to bathe. It is hard to imagine a time when people did not have facilities in their own homes to keep clean, but at the time this Act was a dramatic advance. The building of both indoor and outdoor pools continued and was further stimulated by the Public Health Act 1936, which emphasised providing facilities to encourage people to participate in sport rather than simply cleanliness.

Some swimming pools exist more or less as they were first built during this period, but most have been upgraded or demolished to make way for larger, more modern pools. The traditional 25-metre pool has been retained in some places. However, other facilities have leisure pools that come in a multitude of shapes and sizes and that also have wave machines, slides and other water features. Whilst the focus of these pools is on fun, this type of pool can also be used for serious swimming – hence their popularity.

DID YOU KNOW?

Waterworld in Stoke-on-Trent is one of the largest leisure pools in the UK. It has a large, kidney-shaped pool that varies in depth to accommodate a range of groups from toddlers to serious swimmers. There are three flumes (water slides), one of which requires you to ride on an inflatable rubber ring to generate extra speed. In addition, there is an outside pool area that is joined to the main pool and water rapids. The pool also has a wave machine and is surrounded by a seated area and café, which means the facility can be hired out for parties.

Health and fitness clubs often have swimming pools, but these are usually much smaller than local council pools and tend to be a more traditional shape (rectangular). They also do not have additional features, such as wave machines and water rapids. The emphasis is to provide a facility for the serious swimmer or those wishing to use swimming to improve their fitness.

Recreation facilities

In addition to sport and recreation centres, there is a wide range of other facilities. Some provide for specific sports only, whilst others offer the opportunity to play several different sports. For example, the parks maintained by local authorities in towns and cities frequently have cricket pitches, hardcourt tennis, bowling greens and facilities for children, such as play areas.

Your local authority is also likely to provide community centres that act as meeting places for a range of voluntary sports and leisure clubs. These centres are usually run by a committee of volunteers.

Facilities for single sports include ten-pin bowling alleys. These are usually provided by private companies that operate nationally. Ice-skating is another sport where you may find a rink run by the local authority or a private company.

ACTIVITY

Visit your local park and draw a plan of the facilities it offers. List all the sports that can be played there.

DID YOU KNOW?

The Snowdome in Milton Keynes (see Figure 1.1) is a major facility for skiing as it has one of the largest indoor ski slopes in the UK. The facility makes use of the latest technology to provide real snow, and it offers slopes to challenge both the beginner and competent skier. The complex also houses various retail outlets, a climbing wall, a bowling alley and a number of themed restaurants and bars.

Other sports-specific facilities in your local area may include tennis, cricket and bowls clubs. These clubs are often registered charities but they may still employ paid staff to manage and run them.

Sports stadiums

Sports stadiums range in size from those used by local football teams that have only one small stand to accommodate a handful of spectators, to the multi-million pound Cardiff Millennium stadium that can accommodate over 50,000 spectators.

Athletics stadiums usually have a 400-metre running track and a throwing circle for the hammer, discus and other events. There will also be a jumping pit for the long and triple jumps and an area for throwing the javelin.

Figure 1.1
The Snowdome, Milton Keynes

Advances in technology have enabled the development of all-weather tracks and have also reduced the risk of injury by supplying extra layers of cushioning. This is important for the serious runner, who can notch up many miles in training. Most athletics stadiums have at least basic changing facilities, and some have additional facilities, such as a bar and social area.

Rugby and football stadiums can often accommodate many thousands of supporters. They usually have secondary facilities such as bars, fast-food restaurants and retail outlets.

DID YOU KNOW?

Luton FC once played all their home games in the First Division (now the Premiership) on an astro-turf pitch!

Outdoor recreation centres

The countryside provides many opportunities to engage in sport and recreational activities. Many of these activities, however, carry a significant degree of risk should the safety rules not be followed. Activities such as rock climbing, kayaking and surfing are often referred to as 'adventure' activities, which are increasingly popular among all age groups. Individuals may join in such activities for personal enjoyment or because of the skills they develop as a result of participation, such as improved communication skills or the ability to work as part of a team.

The training and supervision needed for such outdoor activities are provided by outdoor recreation centres. These centres are sometimes operated by charitable organisations but, usually, they are run by local authorities or private companies. They offer a range of activities and courses that cater for beginners as well as for those who wish to improve their skills.

CASE STUDY

Skern Lodge

Skern Lodge, in Bideford, Devon, is run by a private company. It offers the opportunity to participate in a range of adventure-based sports and activities. Its facilities include a high-wire course, a playing field, a restaurant, accommodation, and conference and teaching rooms. This enables the centre to deliver many teambuilding activities on site and deliver underpinning knowledge and safety information for the majority of outdoor activities which are undertaken off-site. Planning for such activities is very time-consuming for centre staff as they must take into account weather, staffing and transport issues.

The centre makes use of the extensive natural resources in the area, including local beaches for surfing and kayaking and both Dartmoor and Exmoor for hillwalking. The centre can arrange for other activities such as quad-biking and even bungee jumping!

1 What kind of activities are Skern able to deliver on-site?
2 What problems are created by being dependent on resources off-site?
3 Why is it necessary to undertake a classroom briefing prior to departure from the centre?
4 What are the advantages and disadvantages of having accommodation on-site?

ACTIVITY

Using the your local telephone directory, the Internet, your tourist information centre and library, etc., research all the main facilities and opportunities to play sport in your area. If you have students from different areas in your class it may be useful to compare maps. Does one area provide more opportunities than another? Is there a lack of facilities for certain sports?

The next step is to pick out four facilities and describe these in detail. You description should include the following:

1 The location and size of the facility (a plan may be useful in this regard).
2 The sports activities that are offered (include the different categories of people who are catered for).
3 Who runs or owns the facility (e.g. the local authority, a private company or some other organisation).

1.2 Describe four different types of national sporting facilities

This section covers
- Sports centres/recreation facilities
- Swimming pools
- Sports-specific grounds
- Athletics stadiums
- Outdoor centres

Sports centres/recreation facilities

National sports centres are provided by a government agency called Sport England, although sometimes they are managed by private companies. They provide high-quality sporting and residential facilities and focus on providing people with the opportunity to train and compete at the highest level. Each centre provides state-of-the-art equipment, support facilities and access to top coaches.

Each of the five national sports centres in England and Wales specialises in providing facilities for a particular range of sports. The five centres and the sports they serve are as follows:

1 Crystal Palace, London – athletics, swimming, basketball.
2 Lilleshall, Shropshire – cricket, football, gymnastics.
3 Holme Pierrepont, Nottinghamshire – rowing, sailing, canoeing.
4 Bisham Abbey, Buckinghamshire – squash, football, tennis.
5 Plas y Brenin, North Wales – mountaineering, rock climbing, canoeing, orienteering.

DID YOU KNOW?

The National Water Sports Centre at Holme Pierrepont, Nottinghamshire, has world-leading facilities that include a 2,000-metre regatta lake, a canoe slalom course and a water-ski lake. In addition there is a multi-purpose sports hall, a physiotherapy room and a fitness suite. Accommodation is provided for those people who have travelled across the UK to train or compete at the centre.

The facilities and layout of each of these five centres obviously differ according to the sports they provide. However, in addition to the sports areas, there are extensive support facilities, such as fitness suites, and conference and lecture rooms.

Swimming pools

There are only a small number of pools that offer the facilities to support professional swimmers. These include the Manchester Aquatics Centre, Loughborough University and Ponds Forge Swimming Pool in Sheffield. The facilities provided are different from the smaller, local council-run pools. First, they have a full-sized, 50-metre pool area with separate pools for training and diving. They also have additional facilities, such as fitness suites and treatment rooms.

DID YOU KNOW?

The Manchester Aquatics Centre was built for the Commonwealth Games. It has two 50-metre pools that can be joined together to form one pool or used separately for a variety of activities ranging from general swimming to aqua tone. There is also a specialist diving pool that can be used for water polo. The centre's extensive health and fitness facilities include a fitness suite, a sauna and a plunge pool. The centre has been designed so that it can be used to the full even when it is not being employed as a competition venue or training facility.

Sports-specific grounds

There a number of specialised stadiums that are important nationally in that they can accommodate a large number of spectators and have state-of-the-art facilities. These stadiums include Twickenham (the home of rugby in the UK) and the Millennium Stadium in Cardiff. In addition to hosting major sporting events, these stadiums are capable of hosting other large leisure events, such as concerts.

There was much debate recently over the building of a new national stadium. Various proposals were put forward for locating this in the Midlands or the north, but these were rejected in favour of the redevelopment of Wembley.

DID YOU KNOW?

The new Wembley Stadium will have a retractable roof. This is so big, the Millennium Wheel could fit under its main arch!

DID YOU KNOW?

The All England Tennis Club, in Wimbledon, London, is the national home of tennis. It hosts the Wimbledon Fortnight – one of the most prestigious tennis competitions in the world. Its extensive facilities include the Centre and Number 1 Court (which are fully enclosed stadiums) and a number of outdoor courts and training courts. There are physiotherapy rooms, social areas, fitness training facilities and a range of retail outlets. Outside Wimbledon Fortnight, these facilities can be enjoyed by club members. During the competition, the club subsidises some ticket prices so that everyone can watch the best tennis players in the world battle it out for the title 'Wimbledon Champion'.

Athletics stadiums

Another nationally important group of facilities are the large athletics stadiums such as those at Crystal Palace in London (see Figure 1.2) and Kelvin Hall in Glasgow. These stadiums have 400-metre running tracks and facilities for track and field events. They can accommodate large numbers of spectators and have additional features (such as fitness suites and treatment and conference rooms) that smaller stadiums are unable to supply.

Figure 1.2
Crystal Palace

CASE STUDY

The Birmingham National Indoor Arena

The Birmingham National Indoor Arena is not strictly speaking an athletics stadium but a multi-functional building that hosts pop concerts and other leisure events. However, the main arena can be transformed into a major venue for athletics events, and it has hosted the World Indoor Athletics Championships. The athletics track is on a hydraulic platform underneath the floor that can be raised into position for competitions and retracted when not needed. Additional seating that is normally stored flat against the walls can be pulled out to accommodate the large numbers of spectators who are a feature of major sporting events.

The size of the facility means that it must have a continuous programme of events in order to survive financially and that it is not cost-effective to be used as sports provision for the wider community.

1 What is innovative about the design of Birmingham Indoor Arena?
2 Why is the arena not bookable by the wider community to play sports?
3 Find out what other sports events have been hosted by the arena or suggest events that could be hosted by an indoor facility of this size.

Outdoor centres

There are a number of large outdoor centres in the UK, but Plays y Brenin, in Snowdonia, North Wales, is generally regarded as the UK's main facility for mountain sports. It is a national sports centre and therefore enjoys financial support from Sports England.

ACTIVITY

Using the Internet, your library and, if you can, your own reports of visits you have made to these centres, etc., research four different types of national sporting facilities.

You now need to describe these facilities in detail. You descriptions should include the following:
1 The location and size of the facility (a plan may be useful here).
2 The sports activities that are offered (include the different categories of people who are catered for).
3 Any additional features the facility has (e.g. accommodation, the ability to host events other than sports, fitness suites, etc.).

1.3 Describe the role of the private, public and voluntary sectors in providing local sporting opportunities and facilities

This section covers

- The private sector
- The public sector
- The voluntary sector
- Partnerships

There are many facilities that provide the opportunity to play sports. One way of classifying these facilities is according to who runs them. There are three different types of organisation that can operate sports venues: those in the private sector, those in the public sector and those in the voluntary sector.

If a facility is run by a national government agency or a local council, it is said to be in the public sector; if it is run by a private individual or a company, it is in the private sector; and if is run mainly by volunteers, it is in the voluntary sector.

We will now look at each of these three sectors in turn.

The private sector

The private sector is concerned with making money from the products or services it provides. Any profits that are made from the business are shared between those people who invested the money in the first place or are used to develop the business further. Private sector provision is therefore often said to be demand led. This means that private sector organisations will only provide sports activities when there is a profit to be made. For example, health and fitness clubs provide for the increasing demand among the public for fitness equipment and fitness classes. The membership fees for such clubs, however, can be expensive, and this may deter some people from joining. Facilities in the private sector are therefore unlikely to provide opportunities for minority sports or to subsidise the cost of participation. They focus on attracting those user groups (i.e. certain types of customer) from whom they will make a profit. They thus operate within specific markets and with specific user groups in mind.

CASE STUDY

Esporta

Esporta is a major provider of exclusive health and fitness clubs. The company provides sporting and fitness facilities for those people who can afford the membership fees. These people include:

- single young professional people;
- young professional couples; and
- families.

The company structures its facilities and programme of activities to cater for these groups. For example, young professional people are often influenced by fashions and trends and therefore seek out the latest sports and fitness activities. Esporta therefore constantly updates its programming to include new activities and equipment. A recent example is spinning, which is a fitness class on exercise bikes. Crèches are also provided so that young mothers and families are able to go for a swim or take an exercise class whilst their youngest children are looked after elsewhere. There are also social clubs and activities aimed specifically at single people. An organisation like Esporta responds to particular groups of people by offering facilities and opportunities tailored to their needs.

1 Why does Esporta target certain groups to use its facilities?
2 Give two examples of how it meets the needs of these groups.

Private sector businesses are involved in a wide range of sporting activities. These include sports retail (for example, clothing and equipment sales), gambling, spectator sports (such as professional football clubs) and sports you can participate in (for example, golf clubs). They also come in many forms. A private sector business that is owned and operated by one person is known as a sole trader. One example of a sole trader might be a freelance sports coach who is self-employed and who works for a number of different organisations.

Most sports facilities in the private sector, however, are run by private or public limited companies. This means many people, not just one, have shares in the business. Private companies are usually owned and operated by a small number of people, whereas public limited companies sell shares in their business which are traded on the stock exchange. There are many examples of public limited companies in the sports industry (for example, Virgin Active, Esporta and LA Fitness, which operate successful chains of health and fitness clubs). First Leisure, on the other hand, runs a chain of swimming pools and sport and recreation centres, as well as other businesses in the wider leisure industry sector. Anyone can buy shares in these companies, but the value of the shares will go up or down, depending on the company's success. You can track the share prices of these companies in the financial pages of newspapers.

The public sector

Public sector sports facilities include parks, sports centres, community halls and swimming pools. The costs of these facilities are met by central and local government through a system of national and local taxation. For example, the money that members of the public pay to go swimming only goes some way to covering the pool's running costs (i.e. the cost of staffing, heating, lighting, etc.). Therefore such facilities are subsidised with the extra money that comes from taxes.

Local authority sports facilities are provided on a discretionary basis, which means that the council does not have to provide them in the same way that it has a legal obligation to provide schools and hospitals. There is nothing to stop a local authority closing a swimming pool or sports centre if there is a shortage of money.

Public sector organisations do not have to make a profit like the private sector but they must usually break even. This means that the running costs they incur must be equal to the amount of income they receive from subsidies and admission charges. At the very least, they must be seen to be giving value for money.

The main objective of public sector facilities is not, therefore, financial but to provide sports facilities for the whole community. Thus they may, for example, provide opportunities for sport for people on low incomes by reducing admission costs. The aim is to present a programme of activities that caters for as many community groups as possible.

A sports centre could probably book out every hour of every day to five-a-side football but still not meet all the demand for this game. It would not, however, do this as it must cater for the needs of people who do not want to play five-a-side football. So instead you will often find badminton, basketball and a range of other sports appearing on the centre's timetable. Whilst this provides for the relatively small demand for these sports, it is also an attempt to promote these sports to increase participation in them.

A balance must also be achieved between casual use (i.e. individual bookings) and club sessions. Some people do not want to belong to a club and thus play a particular sport on a regular basis, but would still like to play occasionally. If a sports centre did not allocate time to such people, it would be discriminating against them.

The public sector also aims to extend the use of its facilities as much as possible. This means a centre will be open for as long as possible and will offer a range of other activities, such as fundraising marathons and classes for children during the school holidays. The ultimate objective is to provide as many sports and as many opportunities for leisure activities as possible for the local population.

The voluntary sector

Voluntary sector organisations usually exist to meet a local need, and thus they vary greatly in terms of size and aims. Often, people with a shared interest form clubs or societies (for example, a group of keen local runners might form a running club). Committees are sometimes elected by the club's members so that a more formal structure is established. A committee would comprise, at the very least, a chairperson to co-ordinate the club, a treasurer to handle money and a secretary to deal with administration.

Clubs may be run by unpaid volunteers, although sometimes people are paid expenses. In contrast, some voluntary organisations, such as the YMCA, employ paid staff and have budgets of millions of pounds. Voluntary clubs often hire facilities rather than owning their own.

Voluntary sports clubs are very important to sport in the UK. People who cannot afford the fees charged by private clubs might join a local club run by volunteers. This promotes social inclusion – all groups of people are given access to sports activities. The voluntary sector is also involved in improving levels of participation in sport. Clubs may do this via outreach programmes (for example, running sessions in such venues as schools and colleges) or by working with local authority sports development officers to promote a particular sport. Voluntary sector organisations, therefore, can be said to be engaged in community development.

ACTIVITY

Investigate the voluntary sector sports clubs in your area:

1 Make a list of the clubs according to the sports they provide.

2 Describe two of these clubs in detail. Include in your description such things as the facilities they offer, their location and their membership numbers.

Partnerships

These three sectors (the private, the public and the voluntary) are related in a number of ways. Private companies frequently manage public facilities. This means that councils will invite companies to submit a tender to run facilities. The company offering the lowest figure will normally win the contract, providing it can meet certain quality criteria (see Figure 1.3).

The link between the voluntary and public sectors is explored more fully later in this unit, but two sources of funding open to voluntary sector organisations are local grants provided by the local authority and National Lottery grants provided by central government. Voluntary sports clubs are also unlikely to be able to afford their own facilities and will therefore hire facilities from the public sector.

The voluntary and public sectors sometimes receive sponsorship (in the form of financial support) from private sector organisations. This is a very

GLOSSARY

Tender: to submit in writing an estimate of the cost of supplying a service. Once submitted, tenders cannot be changed. Tenders are kept secret – the companies submitting tenders for a particular job do not know what prices the other companies have tendered.

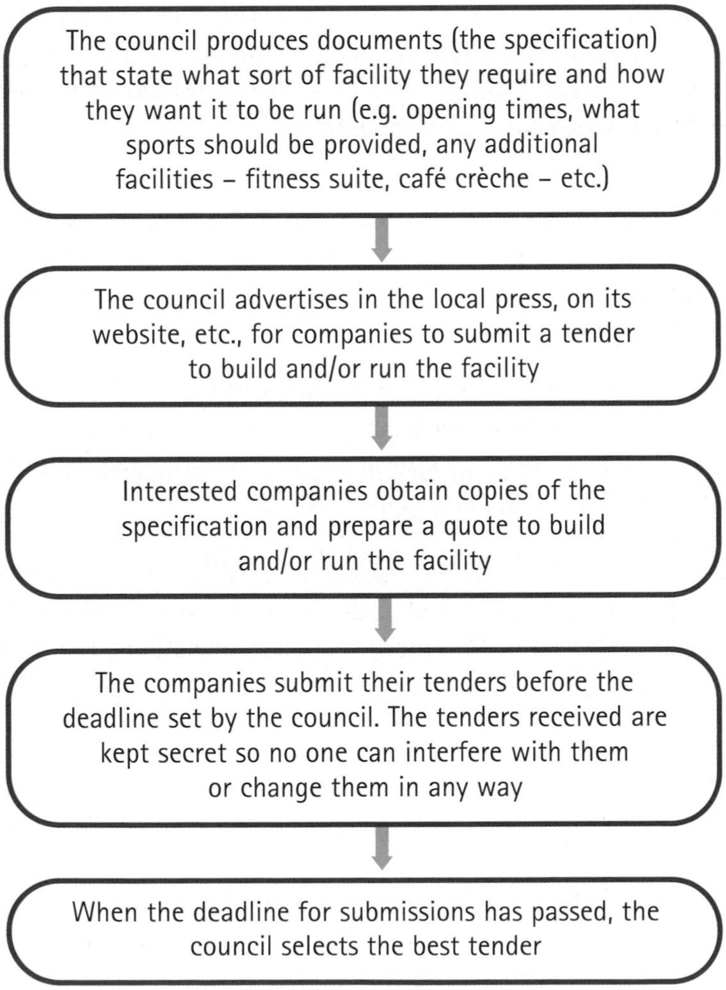

The council produces documents (the specification) that state what sort of facility they require and how they want it to be run (e.g. opening times, what sports should be provided, any additional facilities – fitness suite, café crèche – etc.)

⬇

The council advertises in the local press, on its website, etc., for companies to submit a tender to build and/or run the facility

⬇

Interested companies obtain copies of the specification and prepare a quote to build and/or run the facility

⬇

The companies submit their tenders before the deadline set by the council. The tenders received are kept secret so no one can interfere with them or change them in any way

⬇

When the deadline for submissions has passed, the council selects the best tender

Figure 1.3 *The tendering process*

important source of income as, without this money, many clubs would not survive.

One form of co-operation that exists within the same sector is the provision of dual-use facilities (see 'Sport and recreation centres' earlier in this unit). A sports facility built as part of a school or college will be run by the local education authority (in the public sector), and this organisation will work with the local council (again in the public sector) to provide a facility that is used by the school during the day but by the public in the evenings and at weekends.

While the voluntary and public sector are increasingly dependent on the private sector to fund or manage facilities in a cost-effective way. It should be remembered that the private sector is not dependent on the other sectors. As we have seen, the main objective of a private sector organisation is to make a profit. This usually means its income exceeds its expenditure and it is able to survive independently. If this were not the case then the business would not survive in the long term.

ACTIVITY

Working for the local authority, you have been tasked with reviewing the provision available locally for three sports, in order to establish whether the council could provide further facilities for these sports. Write a report in the following format:

1 An introduction that outlines the purpose of the report.

2 Definitions of the three main sectors or categories of provider with details of objectives and funding.

3 A table showing the different facilities and whether they fall into the private, public or voluntary sector.

4 A conclusion which comments on your findings. (Is there, for example a lack of provision generally, or is there more private than public provision?)

1.4 Describe the aims of national organisations involved in sport

This section covers
- UK Sport
- Sport England
- Sports governing bodies
- Central Council of Physical Recreation
- Sports Coach UK

There are a number of organisations that are involved in the co-ordination and funding of sport at a national level. These include sports n specific organisations such as governing bodies which give advice, guidance, training and funding to one particular sport. In addition there are organisations such as UK Sport that have a more overarching role in that every sport can access the services they provide.

Many national organisations are involved in sport, and each organisation has a different role to play to enable people to participate in sports. Some actively promote sports participation, whilst others provide technical advice or distribute funds to develop new sports facilities.

We will now look at a selection of these organisations and their main functions.

UK Sport

Established in 1996, UK Sport works in partnership with the home countries to drive the development of world class performance in sport. The ultimate goal is to achieve more medals and more success in all international competitions.

It is responsible for distributing over £29 million of government funding as well as funds from the National Lottery. The money is spent on a variety of key objectives aimed at boosting performance. For example, it works in partnership with the sports councils to develop elite facilities and support services. The organisation is also responsible for leading an anti-doping programme that includes random drug testing of elite performers, to ensure fairness at the highest level.

SPORT ENGLAND

ACTIVITY

Find the Sport England website (through www.heinemann.co.uk/hotlinks - express code 9406P) and describe in detail a current initiative to increase sports participation.

Sport England

Sport England, previously known as the English Sports Council, is a semi-autonomous government agency. This means that it is responsible for making its own decisions regarding policy and spending its money, but is given a budget by government and listens carefully to its advice on how to spend the funds.

The mission statement of Sport England is 'to foster a healthier and more successful nation through increased participation in sport'. The benefits of this policy are obvious. If more people take part regularly in sport, then they remain healthy and therefore will have less time off sick from school or work, benefiting the country as a whole. In order to achieve this aim, Sport England has two main objectives which are:

- to increase participation in sport; and
- to develop more sports facilities.

It is responsible for the distribution of National Lottery funds to sport, and gives help and advice to sports-related projects.

Wales and Scotland also have their own agencies that play similar roles.

Sports governing bodies

These bodies are responsible for the general administration of individual sports and the organisation of competitions, among other roles. Each governing body operates a system whereby clubs affiliate or pay a fee to join, which then enables to them to have a say on certain issues and enter competitions organised by that body. The number of clubs who join is normally related to the popularity of the sport concerned. For example, the Football Association (FA) had nearly 50,000 member clubs at the last count.

Governing bodies are also part of a hierarchy of organisations that operate at different levels within the overall structure of sports administration:

- International sports federations.
- European associations.
- National governing bodies.
- Regional /member associations.
- Local clubs.

In other words, most governing bodies will have regional divisions, and will also themselves belong to a European and/or a world organisation governing that sport.

At present there are over 300 governing bodies and their major concerns are:

- to establish and update rules and regulations;
- to organise local, regional and national competitions;

ACTIVITY

Pick one sport and check out who governs that sport at international, national and regional level. Describe the main role of each organisation.

- to develop coaching/instructing awards; and
- to select individuals and teams to represent the sport at regional and national level.

CASE STUDY

The Football Association

The Football Association (FA) is the governing body of football in England and is responsible for developing and promoting the game at every level.

Football is the nation's most popular sport with more than two million registered players and 29 million spectators attending matches every year. The FA takes the lead in providing a structure for organised football. Specific activities include:

- running international teams;
- organising cup competitions;
- youth development;
- refereeing;
- coach education;

- medical matters;
- developing the laws of the game in partnership with international bodies; and
- operating a set of rules and regulations that govern the game.

The game is controlled at local level by 43 county football associations which are affiliated to the national body and have responsibility for organising and running football activities in their area.

1 Why does the FA have such a large regional structure ?
2 The FA has many roles. Which roles are performed only at national level ?

Central Council of Physical Recreation

CCPR
One voice for sport and recreation

The Central Council of Physical Recreation (CCPR) is the umbrella body for 270 national sport and recreation organisations. Its role is to represent and promote the interests of voluntary sector sport and recreation. Most of the CCPRs membership consists of national governing bodies whose clubs contribute sporting and recreational opportunities at local level. The other newer organisations comprise groups working with youth education and local government services. Some of the recent issues and campaigns that the CCPR has been involved in include:

- the establishment of the Community Amateur Sports Clubs scheme (CASCs) which provides 80 per cent mandatory rate relief for registered sports clubs;
- helping to bring about the Government pledge that all schoolchildren by 2010 will receive two hours of physical education within the school curriculum; and

- the exclusion of sport and recreation activiies from the EU Working at Height Directive.

Sports Leaders UK

Formerly known as the British Sports Trust, this organisation was created primarily to promote leadership skills among young people who wish to work in a sports-related field. It organises various leadership awards that increase in difficulty progressively.

This includes the JSLA, aimed at 14-16 yr olds, which develops leadership and motivational skills among this age group. The more advanced CSLA, available to those over 16 years of age, involves more independent planning and development of sessions. Another widely recognised qualification is the Basic Expedition Leaders Award (BELA), which qualifies successful students to lead groups on outdoor expeditions using a map and compass.

Youth Sports Trust

The Youth Sports Trust is a registered charity established in 1994. Its mission is to work in partnership with other organisations to develop and run sport programmes for young people of all ages, from 18 months to 18 years.

Some of the specific projects it has been involved in focus on issues such as:

- inclusion of young disabled people;
- encouraging more participation among teenage girls; and
- supporting gifted and talented young sportspeople.

Sports Coach UK

Formerly the National Coaching Foundation, this organisation gives advice and technical support primarily through a range of diplomas and short courses/seminars. The courses have a reputation for being concise and informative and can be taken by prospective through to experienced coaches who do not have the time to study for a longer qualification.

SkillsActive

SkillsActive is a charitable organisation which focuses on the needs of employers in the sports and recreation sector. Its main aims are to:

- influence Government and other decision makers regarding sports-related issues;
- promote the image of the sports industry to the public;

- ensure the quality of training and qualifications;
- help the sports industry attract and keep staff; and
- Attract funding to meet employers training needs.

The organisation works in partnership with government departments and other agencies to achieve these aims. For example, they will work in partnership with the Department for Education to ensure that qualifications reflect the demands of employers and are based on adequate assessment.

1.5 Describe local and national sources of funding used to support two sports at local level

This section covers
- Local funding
- National funding

Local funding

Playing a sport costs money. Whether you participate from time to time or belong to a club, you will need to purchase or hire equipment and facilities. You may also need specialist clothing or coaching to take part. You may pay for these things yourself but, if you belong to a club, it is likely the activity will be subsidised. The club will receive money from a number of sources so that you will not have to meet all the costs of participation yourself.

We will now consider some of these sources of funding in more detail.

Grants

A club may receive money from its local authority in the form of cash or a reduction in the cost of using the local authority's facilities. There are also wealthy benefactors or local charitable organisations to which sports clubs can apply for a grant to help them with their activities. Usually, certain criteria must be met before an application can be made. For example, a local charity may have as its main aim the aiding of local community projects for children. An application from an adult football team to this charity would not receive much consideration, but an application for financial assistance from a youth football team would be welcomed.

The National Lottery

Launched in 1994, the lottery has regular draws, and the bulk of the money it receives goes to good causes. People buy tickets in the hope of winning cash prizes. Some of the money from ticket sales is retained by the lottery operators, but the majority is passed on to the government for distribution to various agencies concerned with promoting the arts, heritage or sport.

Organisations can make an application for funding but, in most cases, must 'match' the amount applied for. For example, if a local football club applied for money to build a new clubhouse and changing facilities, it would need to fund this project partly from its own finances. Therefore if the cost of the project was £50,000, the lottery fund would only be prepared to fund half this amount (i.e. £25,000).

Certain criteria must be met in order to obtain a lottery grant, however. For example, the cost of the project will be compared with the benefits it will bring to the community. If the cost seems too high compared to the numbers of people who will benefit, it may be refused a grant.

CASE STUDY

Lottery funding

Since 1998, the New Opportunities Fund has supplied grants for projects in deprived areas of the country, such as the inner cities. A total of £750 million has been spent on a number of projects, including the following:

- The building of new indoor and outdoor facilities and the refurbishment of existing ones.
- The building and modernisation of outdoor adventure facilities, primarily those for young people.
- Funding the running costs of some community facilities.

The projects aim to bring long-term benefits to these areas, such as the promotion of healthy living and encouraging participation in sports activities, especially among children.

Consequently, the funding is used to encourage participation as well as to provide facilities.

However, only a relatively small number of projects have been funded, and the government has been criticised for concentrating on only a few areas of the country.

1 In your opinion, is it right to target certain priority groups and/or certain areas for funding?
2 What impact are these schemes likely to have?
3 It is now recognised that the provision of facilities is not enough to guarantee increased participation. How might you encourage groups to use the new or refurbished facilities?

Membership

Most local clubs will charge a membership fee to join. This fee may be a single, one-off payment or an annual charge. Some clubs also charge match fees or weekly 'subs' to help with cost of equipment, kit and administration. Some clubs even have a life membership scheme, but the large injection of funds this produces must be measured against a reduction in membership income in future years.

Sponsorship

A popular way for a club to raise funds is to approach a local business for financial help. The club will receive money or goods in return for promoting the business in some way. For example, football teams emblazon the name of a sponsoring company across their shirts in return for financial support: local businesses appreciate seeing or hearing their names in the media (e.g. match reports in local newspapers or, even better, photographs). The sponsor would expect to have its image enhanced by its association with the club. For example, a club is unlikely to be attractive to a sponsor if it gains a reputation for dirty play, or if team members are known for causing trouble in pubs and night-clubs. The financial assistance a club receives from sponsorship is very important, and many clubs would not survive without it.

As well as clubs receiving financial support through sponsorship, individual sportspersons can also benefit from sponsorship through various schemes. One such scheme is Sportsaid. Sportsaid helps aspiring young sportsmen and women to develop their sporting potential.

With money from individual donors, corporate partners and other bodies, Sportsaid is able to work with national governing bodies to identify potential elite athletes. Financial support is given either through TASS, the Talented Athlete Scholarship Scheme where the individual combines their training with an academic programme of study in further or higher education, or through a more traditional grant where monies are used to fund equipment, travel to competitions and participate at training camps. This is already beginning to reap benefits in producing world class athletes.

Fundraising activities

Sports clubs may also generate funds by various activities, such as sponsored walks or car-boot sales. New and inventive ways of raising money are always being found. A club may embark on a series of one-off events to raise money for a special project, such as the redevelopment of social facilities. Such events may include knockout tournaments, races and rallies, or more social activities such as discos, themed evenings and raffles.

CASE STUDY

Sportsmatch

Sportsmatch is a government funded scheme set up to help fund grass-roots and community sports in England. They do this by matching new sponsorship money with Sportsmatch funding, on a matched funding basis. For example, if a sports club wants to build a new changing facility and can get a local business to contribute ten thousand pounds, then sportsmatch will contribute the same amount.

Applications to Sportsmatch for funding can be made from any not-for-profit organisation capable of delivering community sport. It is directed at projects which aim to increase participation in sport at grass-roots level, and/or improve basic skills.

Sportsmatch was founded in 1992, following a move by a number of people in industry to encourage businesses to invest money in grass-roots sports.

In its first 6 months of funding, Sportsmatch had £1 million to distribute and made 61 awards. Since that time, Sportsmatch has grown as an organisation and now has an annual budget of approximately £3.5 million and funds more than 400 projects a year, making Sportsmatch one of the largest vehicles for government aid to sport.

1 Why was Sportsmatch set up ?
2 How does Sportmatch funding work ?
3 Look at the Sportsmatch website through www.heinemann.co.uk/hotlinks (using express code 9406P) and describe in your own words three projects that have benefited from Sportsmatch funding ?

ACTIVITY

In small groups, complete Table 1.2 for a local sports club.

Some events are more appropriate to particular clubs than others: a marathon would be ideal for an athletics club, a knockout tournament for a hockey club and a rally for a cycling club. The money raised could be 'matched' with the lottery funding where an application for such funding has been successful.

National funding

So far we have considered funding at a local level for voluntary sector sports clubs. At a national level, clubs are much bigger and have considerably greater running costs.

SOURCE OF FUNDING	PAPERWORK REQUIRED	AMOUNT OF MONEY AVAILABLE	WHAT THE MONEY CAN BE SPENT ON	ANY CONDITIONS?
National Lottery	A large amount		Buildings and facilities. Cannot be spent on kit, etc.	
Sponsorship		Usually small amount		Must mention the company regularly in publicity material
Fundraising			Anything	Event may clash with other local events
Membership fees	Setting charges and recording payments			Different rates for different types of people
Grants	Letters to be written and sent	Various		

Table 1.2 *Sources of funding for voluntary sector sports clubs*

ACTIVITY

Investigate a professional sports club (a Premier League football team, for example). Make a list of all the costs involved in running the club. You should be able to find this information in the club's annual accounts, which you may be able to obtain by contacting the club or by investigating its website. The first two have been completed for you.

1 Players' wages.

2 Ground maintenance.

What is the most expensive item? Are there any costs you did not expect to find? Are any costs less or more than you expected? Can you explain why?

There are clearly considerable costs involved in running a professional sports club. A number of sources of funds, however, provide clubs with income to cover some or all of this expenditure.

Income from media rights/sponsorship

Many professional sports clubs sell the TV rights to screen their matches or competitions. TV companies are prepared to pay large sums – millions of pounds in some cases – to broadcast certain sports events. They do this because the popularity of certain sports events on TV means businesses will pay the TV companies large sums of money to advertise during commercial breaks.

Businesses are also prepared to sponsor professional teams directly because of the media coverage they receive. As certain sports have increased in popularity, they have attracted increasing levels of sponsorship (see Figure 1.4). Other sports find in difficult to attract sponsors. Minority sports, such as netball and hockey as well as those that do not make good TV (such as archery), fall into this category. The more media coverage a sport enjoys, therefore, the more sponsorship it will potentially attract.

Figure 1.4
Popular sports are able to attract sponsors

SPONSOR	SPORT	COMPETITION	INDIVIDUAL
			David Beckham
		The Premiership	
	Test match cricket		
	England rugby team		
		The FA Cup	
	Ferrari Formula One Team		
O_2 Mobile			
Telephone Network			
		The London Marathon	
Vodafone			

Table 1.3 *Professional sport and sponsorship*

ACTIVITY

Complete the blank boxes in Table 1.3, which lists specific *sponsors*, the *sports* these specific organisations sponsor, the particular *competitions* they sponsor and even the *individuals* within that sport they sponsor.

Advertising

Clubs may also sell advertising space in a variety of locations. These include pages in the match-day programme, signs on the playing area or advertising hoardings around the pitch. The overall income gained from advertising will vary from club to club. Some of the factors which influence the amount of money are:

- the number of spectators or players who use a facility;
- the location of the club;
- the success of the club; and
- the coverage a club obtains in the media.

Merchandising

Professional clubs have become better at merchandising in recent years. For example, considerable money is to be made from the sale of replica football shirts with the team's logo on them. Logos can be put on just about anything, and therefore we can talk about creating a 'brand image' – a range of products that all have the same logo, the same colours, the same 'look'. Manchester United, for example, put their logo on bags, clothing, stationery, toys, DVDs, credit cards, etc. The list goes on and on. Some of these items are related to their core activity of playing football; others rely on people buying into the Manchester United 'brand image'.

Admission charges

Another source of funding is admission charges. This is the amount paid to watch a professional team play or the entrance charge to a sports event such Wimbledon. The amount of money a club makes from admission charges depends on the size of its stadium and other facilities and on how good it is at attracting spectators. Successful teams usually benefit from the large numbers of spectators they can attract. Some successful football clubs in the Premier League are developing new stadiums with increased capacity so that they can accommodate the large numbers of spectators who want to see them play.

ACTIVITY

Work out how much it costs to go to see your favourite team play or to attend a sports event your are interested in. Include such costs as transport and food. In your opinion, is this expensive?

Lottery funding

Professional sports clubs in the private sector are unlikely to attract lottery funding, but there are sources of funding in the public sector private sector organisations could benefit from. As we have already seen, the national sports centres (e.g. Crystal Palace in London and Holme Pierrepont in Nottinghamshire) are funded in part by government. Other one-off projects, such as the new National Stadium at Wembley, have also been partly funded by the government (in this case by lottery money).

CASE STUDY

Wembley Stadium

Wembley Stadium has been totally redeveloped to become the national stadium. At the planning stage there was much debate about where to site such a stadium. Some politicians and sports officials argued that the national stadium should be sited in a central accessible location such as the Midlands. Eventually it was decided to build a new stadium on the Wembley site despite problems with parking and access.

Some of the money for the building of the new Wembley has come from private sources and some from the government via the lottery fund. The design was changed several times before eventually construction started on the project.

The delays in deciding where to build the facility and in planning the construction of the new stadium has resulted in the project being substantially overbudget although once finished it will be one of the largest and most innovative stadiums in the world.

1 What are the main sources of funding for the new Wembley Stadium?
2 Is London the best place to site a new national stadium? List the advantages and disadvantages.
3 Look at the Wembley Stadium website through www.heinemann.co.uk/hotlinks, express code 9406P. Describe in your own words both the facilities and activities that can be hosted at the new national stadium.

ACTIVITY

You are working for a local sports club and have been tasked with investigating sources of funding for development of new facilities at the club. These may include a new clubhouse with bar and changing facilities.

1 Explain how you could use fundraising and other local activities organised by the club to part-fund the facility.
2 Describe the main national sources of funding that might fund the building of a new facility.

1.6 List the specific needs of four different user groups which may affect their participation in sport

This section covers
- Ethnic minorities
- Retired people
- Families with young children
- Single parents
- Children
- Teenagers
- Disabled people
- Unemployed people
- Working singles/young couples

If you were asked who uses sports facilities, you might answer 'The public, of course'. This is true, but everyone is an individual and 'the public' is made up of individuals of different ages, gender, race and social backgrounds. We can categorise people according to the characteristics they have in common. These categories or 'user groups' have particular needs that will have to be met if they are to take part in sport.

We will look at some of these user groups in more detail.

Ethnic minorities

People from ethnic backgrounds often have customs or traditions that differ from the population as a whole. These include such things as eating at only certain times of the day, different languages, rituals or routines associated with their religion and customs concerning dress and clothing. The opportunities for these people to take part in sport may be limited if such things are not taken into consideration.

Another barrier to participation may be stereotyping. This is dealt with in more detail in Unit 5. Basically this is when someone holds a fixed impression about a group of people based on poor information and generalises about them. If the person responsible for programming a sports centre makes such generalisations, then there may be a lack of appropriate provision for certain groups.

Retired people

The number of retired people is increasing in the UK, and some of these people may now have the time to enjoy a variety of sports. Some retired people have enough money left over after they have paid their bills to afford the membership fees of private sector facilities. Some retired people, however, find it difficult to survive on a pension and cannot afford to spend large amounts of money on sport or leisure. The cost of participating in sport is therefore an important consideration for some retired people.

Some retired people may have health problems that prevent them from becoming involved in sport, and some may consider they are now too old to take part. Whilst health problems must always be taken into account if someone wishes to become involved in a sport, negative attitudes to involvement can be changed (see Figure 1.5).

Figure 1.5 *Negative attitudes to involvement in sport can be changed*

Families with young children

Parents and their young children have different needs. Parents, for example, will need childcare facilities if they are to leave their children for a while to play a sport. Young children, on the other hand, are unlikely to have developed sufficient ability to take part in sport on their own, but they may be able to join in specially devised, adult-led sessions.

Single parents

For single parents, childcare facilities may be more of a problem as they are unable to rely on a partner to look after the children, and some may not have enough money to pay for such facilities. Cost and the provision of childcare are therefore major considerations for single-parent families.

Children

Children may be dependent on their parents for transport to sports facilities, and cost may also be a factor that prevents some children from participating in sport. When they enter competitions, they must compete with children of their own age. Thus they are reliant on specialist sessions being provided. They will also need smaller or specially adapted sports equipment, depending on their size, physique and ability.

Much research has shown that there is a lack of fitness and increasing obesity among children. Children often need to be persuaded to join in sport rather than pursue more sedentary activities, such as computer games.

Teenagers

Between the ages of 13 and 19 there is a noticeable decline in sports participation, particularly among girls. Sport needs to be made both appealing and accessible to this group. A concern of many teenagers is to build up a network of friends. Sport can help address this need.

As their bodies change and develop, teenagers often become concerned about their physical appearance. This can also prevent their participation in sport, as young people may be self-conscious about showing their bodies in public.

Disabled people

People with disabilities may find it difficult to participate in sport for a variety of reasons. Those with restricted mobility will need help getting in and out of sports facilities. Visually impaired people will need specially adapted equipment, and those who are hearing impaired will need to be given information in writing or by a signer.

Disabled people must be treated in a manner that is not condescending, patronising or dismissive. Sometimes it is the fear of being treated differently that prevents such people from participating in the first place.

Unemployed people

This group of people may have the time to join in sport but are unlikely to have the money. They may also lack of confidence, which will affect them negatively.

Working singles/young couples

There is an increasing number of people who are single or who are in a relationship but have chosen not to have children. These people often have the money to spend on sports and leisure activities but lack the time to do so as a result of work commitments. The time they do have available is usually late in the evening or at weekends. Social networks are also important to this group – a need that can be addressed through sport but is more often met by more unhealthy means (i.e. drinking with friends!).

CASE STUDY

Barriers to participation

Richborough has a diverse population, ranging from high-income professionals to socially disadvantaged groups. The main sports provision in the area is managed by the local authority which aims to provide sports opportunities for all of the local population.

The centre has recently recruited a new management team. The general manager has established that there is a large demand by clubs for five-a-side football in the local area. He has proposed to stop sessions where the public can turn up and play badminton and tennis and instead hire the main hall out to clubs for football. In this way he will increase the income to the centre.

1   What barriers are being created by the new policy of the general manager?
2   What should be the MAIN objective of a public sector sports centre?
3   Is it possible to maximise both income and user numbers?

ACTIVITY

Investigate provision at a local sports centre. Get hold of a copy of the programme for the centre and undertake the following:

1 List all different activities and describe what target group they are aimed at.
2 Compare your list with the list of user groups in this section of the book and highlight any lack of provision.
3 List any barriers to participation (e.g. cost of activities/poor transport links).

1.7 For each of the four different user groups identified suggest ways to increase their participation

This section covers
● Increased promotion
● Using role models
● Changes to cost
● Changes to timings
● Lowering the physical demand
● Providing assistance and support
● Improving access to facilities

As you have seen, different user groups have specific needs that must be addressed if they are to participate in sport on a regular basis. We will now consider some of these.

Increased promotion

One of the reasons why people do not participate in sport is that they are often unaware that particular sessions exist which meet their needs. For example, teenagers may be aware there is a local swimming pool but not that it operates a session involving a swim and social activities afterwards. Organisations need to advertise such sessions in a way that 'targets' these groups and persuades them to take advantage of the opportunities available.

Using role models

A role model is an individual with whom another individual can identify because he or she has similar physical characteristics or a similar social background. A local authority, therefore, might send a sports development officer of Asian or Afro-Caribbean origin into a school or college in order to persuade students of a similar background to engage in sport.

Changes to cost

As we have seen, the costs of playing sport can be considerable if we take into account transport to and from the venue, the hire or purchase of equipment, specialist clothing and admission charges. This is a major constraint for some groups such as the unemployed, but can be overcome by subsidising the cost of activities. Therefore a facility might provide a discounted rate of admission or free equipment hire for certain groups.

Changes to timings

The timing of sessions for sports activities is also a major factor in determining whether people can take part. Sessions for working singles or couples need to be in the evening or at weekends. Family sessions might be best programmed for weekends when parents and children can enjoy time together in such sports as swimming.

Lowering the physical demand

This means adapting a sport to make it suitable for particular groups. For instance, there are different versions of many popular sports for the visually impaired. One example is a football game that uses a specially adapted ball that is larger than normal and that has a distinctive sound so that players are able to track its movement. Some such sports have become increasingly popular in their own right as spectator sports. Wheelchair basketball is one example.

In a similar way, sports can be adapted for children. For example, 'short tennis' uses foam balls, a smaller court, a lower net and smaller, lightweight rackets. In this way, children learn the basic techniques of the game before moving on to the adult version.

Providing assistance and support

Some user groups will require additional facilities if they are to take part in sport (for example, the provision of a crèche and baby-changing facilities for single parents). Some ethnic groups will need extra support and assistance. The language barrier can be overcome in a number of ways. Leaflets can be produced in various languages, or maps and symbols can be used in place of written words to show the location of various sports areas.

Some people may be put off by the fact that they are beginners. A facility could provide sessions for different abilities and/or specialist coaching to help break down this barrier.

Improving access to facilities

For some groups, improving physical access is very important. Ramps and lifts will help the physically disabled by enabling them to move freely round the building. Wider car parking spaces near the entrance will improve access to the building from the outside. Other adaptations may include the following:

- Specially adapted changing rooms and toilets.
- Low-level fittings (wheelchair height).
- Lifts into pools.
- Adapted weight-training equipment.
- Special and regular disabled events.

A lack of suitable transport to and from the building or a lack of staff specially trained to deal with particular user groups will also affect access to the facility.

ACTIVITY

You have been asked to look at how a local sports centre can improve participation rates in sports activities. This might include physical measures such as the adaptation of facilities, or other strategies such as reducing charges.

1 Suggest a range of measures that have helped increase participation elsewhere in the local area.

TEST YOUR KNOWLEDGE

1. Give one example of each of the main types of sports provision.

2. Describe one national sports facility.

3. What are the main objectives of a private sector organisation?

4. What is council tax and how is this used to fund sports provision?

5. What are the main factors which influence the decision to give out lottery funding to a sports project?

6. Give three examples of sponsorship.

7. What is meant by the term 'user group'?

8. Identify three barriers to participation for people with disabilities.

9. Suggest three strategies for increasing participation among young people (aged 16–24 years).

10. Explain the main function of a governing body of your choice.

Health, Safety and Prevention of Injury in Sport

Introduction

Sports are fun and enjoyable, but any sporting activity carries an element of risk. This is a mandatory unit for this qualification and is concerned with learning to participate in sports in the safest way possible. When you have completed this unit you will have the knowledge, understanding and practical skills you need to ensure you can conduct sporting activities in a safe environment with the minimal risk of accidents and injury. You will also learn how to respond to any illnesses, injuries and emergency situations that may arise.

How you will be assessed

For this unit you will produce a portfolio of work that shows you have met all the assessment objectives for the unit. Your portfolio could contain risk assessments, session plans, information leaflets or reports of observations, etc., you have prepared or witnessed, and records of practical sessions you have devised and conducted (e.g. coaching sessions) that may be videotaped and reviewed by your assessor.

This unit links with Units 3, 6 and 9. Evidence collected in those units can be used to meet some of the assessment objectives for this unit and vice-versa. For example, a knowledge of sports skills, rules and regulations (as described in Unit 3 Assessment Objective 1) is essential when supervising an activity. In addition, an evaluation of the performers during the activity (as described in Unit 6 Assessment Objectives 3 and 4) is essential.

In this unit you will learn how to:

① Examine personal factors associated with health and fitness and describe how they contribute to injury prevention in sport

② Identify hazards in the sports environment and conduct risk assessments

③ Produce and implement a set of guidelines to ensure a safe and secure working environment

④ Devise and deliver a minimum of two appropriate warming up/down routines to help prevent injury

⑤ Recognise and demonstrate how to respond to injuries and illnesses within a sporting context

⑥ Investigate the importance of suitable equipment/clothing to safety in sport and provide appropriate equipment for sports activities

2.1 Examine personal factors associated with health and fitness and describe how they contribute to injury prevention in sport

This section covers

- Strength
- Speed
- Suppleness
- Stamina
- Ability
- Other factors affecting health, fitness and risk of injury

Fitness is an individual's ability to perform all the activities of daily living and to indulge in leisure pursuits without becoming overtired. It is important to realise, however, that sports fitness is specific to a particular sport. For example, a weight lifter needs a different kind of fitness from a sprinter or a ballet dancer. Fitness also depends on the individual's ability (natural and learned) and personal characteristics. Fitness is also one of the most important aspects of injury prevention. If an athlete is not fit to perform he or she will almost inevitably become injured, or will not be able to repeat his or her performance throughout a tournament or season, for example. Whatever the kind of fitness, however, every athlete needs the four basic components of fitness – strength, speed, suppleness and stamina (the four Ss of sport): each of these will help to prevent injuries in a specific way.

Strength

Strength is the ability to apply force. The more force you can summon up, the stronger you are. Strength is developed through weight-training regimes that must be designed individually for each athlete.

Weight training is used to:

- increase muscular strength;
- increase muscular endurance;
- increase speed; and
- develop muscle bulk or size.

Strength is important in injury prevention since joints rely on muscles to give them stability, particularly during sporting movements. Also, if the athlete has insufficient strength to resist force applied to the body then injuries, such as sprains, strains or even broken bones, may occur.

There are different types of strength: static strength (or isometric strength) and dynamic strength (or isotonic strength). Both types of strength depend on the contraction of the muscles in your body.

Isometric contraction

An isometric contraction occurs when the muscle contracts but neither lengthens nor shortens. For example, when you are carrying a bag, the muscles in your arm contract isometrically to hold the weight up. Isometric contraction also occurs during a rugby scrum when one side tries to hold its position whilst the other side tries to push it out of the way.

Isotonic contraction

An isotonic contraction occurs when the muscle contracts and creates movement (for example, during a dumb bell curl – Figure 2.1 – or when you are running or walking).

The development of strength is important in the prevention of injury in two ways: firstly the stronger the muscles around a joint are the more stable that joint will be and so it will be better able to resist any stresses and strains on it; secondly the stronger a muscle is the more easily the athlete can perform. This means that the risk of injury due to overloading of the muscle itself (a pulled or torn muscle) during the activity is reduced.

Strength is developed by weight-training programmes that use either weight machines or free weights. Weight machines (Figure 2.2) include such things as multi-gyms, whereas free weights include such things as dumb bells and weight-lifting bars. Both have their advantages and disadvantages (see Tables 2.1 and 2.2).

ACTIVITY

Think of two examples of isometric muscle contraction and two examples of isotonic muscle contraction that occur in different sports.

Figure 2.1
The dumb bell curl involves isotonic muscle contraction

Elite athletes tend to use free weights because of their versatility, but you do need to know how to use them properly and, for safety reasons, you need spotters in case you lose control of the bar (see Figure 2.3). This means you cannot safely use them on your own.

Figure 2.2 *Weight machines have their advantages and disadvantages*

ADVANTAGES	DISADVANTAGES
Safe	Expensive
Convenient	Require regular servicing and maintenance
Technologically advanced	
Beginners find them easier to use than free weights	

Table 2.1 *Advantages and disadvantages of weight machines*

ADVANTAGES	DISADVANTAGES
More versatile than weight machines; permit greater variety of exercises	Requires good technique
Uses explosive strength (i.e. very fast muscle contraction as in throwing or jumping)	Spotters needed for safety
Less expensive than weight machines	

Table 2.2 *Advantages and disadvantages of free weights*

Figure 2.3 *If you use free weights, you will need a spotter*

ACTIVITY

In groups, think of a range of sports where strength is important. Next, think of a situation where increased strength in a particular sport would be an advantage, giving the reasons why.

Speed

Speed is the second necessary component of fitness. It can be divided into two areas: speed of movement and reaction speed. Both types of speed are also important in injury prevention as they enable the athlete to react to a potentially harmful situation through movement, for example dodging a rugby tackle or a punch in boxing.

Speed of movement

Speed of movement is the length of time it takes an individual to perform a movement or cover a distance. The speed of movement of sprinters in a race (see Figure 2.4) is measured in metres per second. For example, a sprinter who runs 100 metres in 10 seconds has a speed of 10 metres per second.

Figure 2.4 *The speed of movement of sprinters in a race*

Reaction speed

Reaction speed is the time taken to react to a stimulus and perform an action. An example is the time taken between the sprinter hearing the starting pistol and leaving the blocks at the start of race.

Speed is an essential ingredient of all sports and can sometimes make up for lack of skill in other areas.

In many sports speed and, in particular, reaction speed is a vital part of injury prevention for without both speed and speed of movement it is impossible to avoid collisions with an opponent or an object. For instance, a cricketer receiving a 'bouncer' (a ball aimed at the head or body) from a fast bowler will have to both react and move his or her body in time or risk being hit by the ball, which may result in serious injury.

Hold a ruler vertically so that its bottom end is just above your partner's hand

ACTIVITY

For this activity you need to work in pairs. First, set up a sprint course of 20 metres and then see who of the two of you can run it the faster. Next, measure each other's reaction time (see Figure 2.5) and see how they compare. Does the faster runner have the faster reaction time?

Drop the ruler and see how far it falls before your partner catches it. The farther it falls, the longer your partner's reaction time

Figure 2.5
Measuring reaction time

Suppleness

Suppleness is also known as flexibility and can be defined as the range of movement possible at a joint. Therefore the more a joint can move, the suppler or more flexible an individual is said to be. Suppleness is developed by stretching, and there are four main types of stretching used in sport:

- static;
- dynamic;
- PNF stretching; and
- ballistic.

Static stretching

Static stretching consists of a slow gradual stretch, which can be done either individually or with a partner. Because the stretch is held for a long time – between 15 and 20 seconds – the tension in the muscle relaxes as the fibres that make up the muscle begin to move apart. As a result the muscle lengthens, allowing an increased range of movement.

Dynamic stretching

Dynamic stretching improves flexibility. The athlete performs a repetitive action at a moderate speed until no more movement is possible around the joint being exercised.

PNF stretching

PNF (proprioceptive neuromuscular facilitation) stretching is fairly new to fitness theory, but has been shown to be the most effective way of stretching. This type of stretching is performed in pairs. One of the pair (who must remain still and not move) stretches the other's muscle. The person whose muscle is being stretched then contracts his or her muscle against the resistance (i.e. his or her partner) for 6 seconds. The resistance partner then stretches the muscle further.

PNF stretching works because, during the contraction phase, the muscle is fooled into relaxing, and this means that the muscle can be stretched further. PNF stretching should only be attempted after the body is warm, as this is when the muscle is at its most elastic.

Ballistic stretching

Ballistic stretching comprises quick, bouncy movements done when the joint is either fully bent or fully straightened. This type of stretching is not recommended as it triggers a powerful stretch reflex action in the muscle, which leads to increased tension in the muscle. Because of this increased tension, there is a risk of injury – the muscle could be damaged, resulting in a decreased range of movement.

Suppleness (or flexibility) is one of the most important elements of fitness, and greater flexibility can lead to:

- improved posture;
- improved sports performance;
- improved functional capacity (in daily life);
- a reduced risk of injury; and
- stress management.

Suppleness or flexibility is particularly important in injury prevention as the more easily a joint can move through its normal range the more it can cope with the forces put onto the body during sport. For example, a good range of movement can avoid damage to the joints and surrounding soft tissues, such as ligaments, when landing from a vault in gymnastics.

ACTIVITY

Think of examples of different sports that require different degrees or types of flexibility, e.g. weight lifting, running and gymnastics.

Stamina

Stamina is also known as endurance. It is your ability to exercise continuously for a long period of time or to repeat the same exercise a large number of times. Stamina depends on your body's anaerobic and aerobic capacity, and both of these can be increased by different types of exercise. (You will learn more about the anaerobic and aerobic processes in your body in Unit 4.)

Stamina is another important factor in injury prevention since the greater the athletes stamina the less prone they are to fatigue or exhaustion, which leads to mistakes in technique and as well as a reduction in both reaction speed and speed of movement. This means that the risk of injury is greatly increased.

Anaerobic capacity

Anaerobic capacity is your body's ability to exercise whilst not taking in oxygen. Anaerobic capacity is used by sprinters and throwers, etc. It lasts for about 40 seconds, after which the body must take in oxygen.

To increase your anaerobic capacity, you must work above your current anaerobic endurance level, which means working at more than 80 per cent of your maximum heart rate (maximum heart rate = 220 minus your age). This is usually best achieved with sprints or other short bursts of activity, which are repeated many times.

Aerobic capacity

Aerobic capacity is your body's ability to exercise with oxygen, and your level of fitness will depend on your aerobic capacity.

GLOSSARY

Aerobic training zone: activity that uses your aerobic system only to provide your body with energy.

To increase your aerobic capacity, you should work in your aerobic training zone. This means working at between 60 and 80 per cent of your maximum heart rate for more than 20 minutes continuously.

Stamina, or endurance, is an important, even the most important, aspect of fitness in terms of injury prevention as it delays the onset of fatigue and allows the athlete to perform better for longer. If an athlete is tired then he or she will tend to make more mistakes and have a longer reaction time. This means that his or her body cannot meet the demands of the activity and becomes physically overloaded, resulting in injury.

Another important factor in injury prevention is the ability of the individual to perform that sport. Generally speaking, it can be shown that the more skilled an individual the less likely he or she is to become injured during a sporting activity. Also, it is important to match abilities, especially in contact sports where a less skilled individual may perform clumsily (in a mistimed tackle, for instance) and so injure him or herself and or each other.

Ability

How good or not you are at something depends on your ability – your skills in performing a particular activity. Ability is natural (i.e. something you are born with), and an athlete's skills are largely determined by the level of his or her natural ability. Athletic skills, however, can be improved through practice. There are two types of ability:

1 *Mental ability*: How able you are to process information and to respond to it appropriately in a sporting situation. This includes such things as your reaction time and your ability to co-ordinate your limbs.
2 *Physical ability*: How able you are to perform the various movements required in your sport. This depends on some of the components of fitness listed above (e.g. strength, speed and suppleness).

As you learn, your ability improves. There are three stages in this learning process:

The beginner or novice stage:

- The sportsperson makes a large number of errors.
- He or she is unable to screen out irrelevant information.
- His or her performance is inconsistent.
- His or her movements are slow, jerky and unco-ordinated.

The intermediate or practice stage:

- The sportsperson makes fewer errors.
- His or her anticipation develops – he or she can read the game better.
- He or she learns to monitor his or her own feedback.

The advanced or fine-tuning stage:

- The sportsperson's performance becomes 'second nature'.
- As his or her confidence increases, strategy comes to play an important role.
- Gains in performance become slower.

For example, when you begin to learn to ride a bike, there seems a great deal to do. You have to keep your balance, pedal, steer, change gear and use the brake – five different actions all at the same time.

An absolute beginner will use stabiliser wheels so that he or she doesn't have to balance and will practise on a bike with no gears. Eventually the stabilisers can be taken off, and perhaps a bike with three gears can be used, but it is still too dangerous to ride on the road because the learner still has to concentrate on riding the bike.

Finally, the cyclist doesn't have to think about what he or she is doing and so can now cycle safely on the road as he or she can concentrate on the traffic rather than on steering, balance, etc.

ACTIVITY

Look at a video of two performers in the same sport: one a novice and one an elite performer. Compare the ways both perform the same tasks. Select three features that show most clearly the elite performer's greater level of skill.

In the advanced stage, performance is second nature

Generally speaking the higher the individuals level of skill the less their risk of injury. This is because they can react and adapt to the demands of the activity without having to consciously think about the technical aspects of their sport. This enables them to react both more quickly and appropriately than beginners and so avoid injury.

Other factors affecting health, fitness and risk of injury

As well as the topics covered above there are several other factors that will either increase or decrease your risk of injury:

- gender
- age
- height
- weight
- heart rate
- body composition.

Gender

It is often said that women are at greater risk of sports injuries than men, but recent research has begun to question this. There are, however, physiological differences between men and women that may mean women who play, for example, football may get injured more than men who play the same sport. Some of these differences are as follows:

- *Strength*: In general, women have about 70 per cent of the muscular strength of men. This means that in strength-based events such as weight-lifting, etc., women are more prone to injury than men when lifting the same weight. This may also be true in contact sports such as rugby where women are less able to stand the impact of a tackle.
- *Aerobic capacity*: Women have between 15 and 25 per cent lower aerobic capacity than men and so are less able to cope with extreme endurance events (such as long-distance cycling or ultra-marathon running) as they fatigue more quickly.
- *Body composition*: Women have a greater level of body fat (22–24 per cent) than men (14–17 per cent).
- *Osteoporosis*: Women have a four times greater risk of developing osteoporosis than men.
- *Heat/temperature regulation*: Women lose heat more readily in cold conditions and gain heat more readily in hot conditions than men due to their greater surface area to weight ratio.

GLOSSARY

Osteoporosis: a disease of the bones. The bones lose calcium, become thinner and break more easily than normal bone.

Age

As people get older they begin to lose their aerobic capacity and muscle mass. Also, both men and women's bones get thinner and weaker, and tendons and ligaments become less flexible and more likely to tear. It is generally said that as you get older your risk of injury increases, but some studies have shown that in fact the opposite is true. This may be because participation rates drop with age and also because older people tend to play non-contact sports rather than contact sports such as rugby, football or judo.

Height

Height in itself does not appear to be a risk factor in sports injuries in adults. There can be problems with children, however, if they either exceed or fail to meet the normal heights for their age. For example, adolescent athletes often suffer muscle aches and pains during puberty when they undergo growth spurts – i.e. gaining several inches in height very rapidly.

Heart rate

Heart rate (both at rest and during exercise) is an indicator of an athlete's overall fitness. Your heart rate also determines your aerobic and anaerobic capacity (see 'Stamina' above). In general, the lower your resting heart rate and the faster it returns to normal after exercise, the greater your fitness level.

Body composition

The human body is made up of body fat (its fat mass) and lean body tissue (its fat-free mass). When your body composition is assessed, your weight is divided into lean weight and fat weight: everything that is not fat is lean.

Generally speaking people can be divided into three main body types, known as somatypes, according to their body shape.

These are:

Ectomorphs
Ectomorphs tend to be tall and long-limbed with relatively low levels of body fat. They tend to have fast metabolisms and find it difficult to gain muscle and fat. Examples would be long-distance runners such as Paula Ratcliffe.

Mesomorphs
Mesomorphs tend to have wide shoulders and narrow waists. They gain muscle easily and exhibit the classic athletic 'V' shape. Power athletes such as boxers and sprinters tend to be mesomorphs.

Endomorphs

Endomorphs tend to have slower metabolisms than the other two body types and so gain body fat (and muscle) easily. They tend to be suited to strength and power events such as weightlifting or throwing. An extreme example of a sporting endomorph would be a Sumo wrestler.

The three basic somatotypes

Mesomorph   Ectomorph   Endomorph

Body composition can be measured in different ways, such as:

Circumference method

One method uses measurements waist to estimate the amount of body fat.

- *Method*: Measure the circumference of the waist at the umbilicus (the belly button) – a measurement of more than 100 centimetres (40 inches) for men or 90 centimetres (35 inches) for women indicates they are obese.

Body mass index (BMI)

Too much fat results in obesity, which is detrimental to the health. Obesity is most commonly measured by using the body mass index (BMI), which is calculated according to the following formula:

Body weight in kilograms $\div$ Height in metres^2

For example, a man weighing 100 kilograms and 2 metres tall would have a BMI of $100 \div 4 = 25$. A BMI of below 18 is considered underweight; between 19 and 25 normal; between 25 and 29 overweight; and over 30 obese (see Figure 2.6).

Obesity is a factor in injury prevention as it is one of the elements that determines overall fitness. People who are obese tend to have less stamina, strength and speed than the general population and considerably less than

DID YOU KNOW?

- Nearly two thirds of men and half of women in the UK are overweight, and one in five are obese.
- The level of obesity in the UK has tripled in the last 20 years.
- Only about 50 per cent of the UK population take 30 minutes exercise daily.
- Obesity is already estimated to cost the health service about £0.5 billion a year, and the UK economy as a whole a total of £2 billion (2004 figures).
- It is estimated that one third of the UK population will be obese by 2020.

sporting individuals. This means they are less able to perform well and are at greater risk of injury than their leaner counterparts. In addition, the extra weight puts more load on the heart and increases the risk of a heart attack or stroke.

Your weight in kilograms

	52	54	57	59	61	63	66	68	70	72	75	77	79	82	84	
6'4"	14	15	15	16	16	17	18	18	19	19	20	21	21	22	23	190
6'3"	14	15	16	16	17	17	18	19	19	20	21	21	22	22	23	187.5
6'2"	15	15	16	17	17	18	19	19	20	21	21	22	22	23	24	185
6'1"	15	16	16	17	18	18	19	20	20	21	22	22	23	24	24	182.5
6'0"	16	16	17	18	18	19	20	20	21	22	22	23	24	24	25	180
5'11"	16	17	17	18	19	20	20	21	22	22	23	24	24	25	26	177.5
5'10"	17	17	18	19	19	20	21	22	22	23	24	24	25	26	27	175
5'9"	17	18	18	19	20	21	21	22	23	24	24	25	26	27	27	172.5
5'8"	17	18	19	20	21	21	22	23	24	24	25	26	27	27	28	170
5'7"	18	19	20	20	21	22	23	23	24	25	26	27	27	28	29	167.5
5'6"	19	19	20	21	22	23	23	24	25	26	27	27	28	29	30	165
5'5"	19	20	21	22	22	23	24	25	26	27	27	28	29	30	31	162.5
5'4"	20	21	21	22	23	24	25	26	27	27	28	29	30	31	32	160
5'3"	20	21	22	23	24	25	26	27	27	28	29	30	31	32	33	157.5
5'2"	21	22	23	24	25	26	27	27	28	29	30	31	32	33	34	155
5'1"	22	23	24	25	26	26	27	28	29	30	31	32	33	34	35	152.5
5'0"	22	23	24	25	26	27	28	29	30	31	32	33	34	35	36	150
	8,2	8,6	8,9	9,3	9,6	10	10,4	10,7	11,1	11,4	11,8	12,1	12,5	12,9	13,2	

Your height in feet and inches (left axis) / Your height in centimetres (right axis)

Your weight in stone and pounds

Figure 2.6
Body mass index

ACTIVITY

Calculate your own BMI using the formula outlined above. Then calculate your body fat percentage using the circumference method, and compare the two. From these findings think about how accurate the BMI method is as a means to calculate body composition.

Write a report that outlines the personal factors that may lead to an athlete having an increased risk of injury whilst playing sport. You should include such things as the following:

1 Strength.

2 Speed.

3 Suppleness.

4 Stamina.

5 Ability.

6 Any other factors, such as gender, age, height, etc.

2.2 Identify hazards in the sports environment and conduct risk assessments

This section covers
● Hazards
● Risks

Hazards

A hazard is anything that presents a risk to one athlete, to athletes in general, to the general public or to the environment. In sport, hazards come in many shapes and sizes and can range in severity from a slippery floor to faulty equipment to hazards in the environment itself (e.g. extremely cold or hot playing conditions). In order to coach and train effectively, you must learn how to identify and eliminate hazards to yourself and others.

Some examples of hazards in sports would be:

● wet floors;

● trailing leads and wires;

● worn pitches; and

● worn-out trainers/running shoes.

Risks

A risk is the chance that someone will be injured by a hazard, and a risk assessment is a way of checking whether that risk is high or low (i.e. likely or unlikely to cause injury).

The Health and Safety Executive lists five steps to risk assessment in any situation:

1 Look for the hazards.
2 Decide who might be harmed and how.
3 Evaluate the risks and decide if existing precautions are adequate or if more should be done. If more needs to be done, make sure this is carried out at the earliest opportunity.
4 Record your findings and any action you have taken to minimise the risk.
5 Review your assessment and revise if necessary.

In Unit 3 you will learn in detail how to conduct a risk assessment before you lead a specific coaching session. For now we will take the example of the wet floor and record our assessment of this risk, using the steps listed above. The results are shown in Table 2.3.

The level of risk is determined by multiplying the potential for an accident by the severity of the damage caused by that accident. For example in the case above there is a very high chance that people will slip on the wet area and that by doing so they may break a wrist by falling on the floor. This means that the risk is high. (See also Table 3.1).

ACTIVITY

Look at a sports hall and try to identify any potential hazards it may contain. Conduct a risk assessment like the one outlined above, listing the hazards, the degree of risk and the suggested action.

HAZARD	RISK: WHO MAY BE HARMED? HIGH OR LOW RISK?	CURRENT PRECAUTIONS ADEQUATE?	ACTION TAKEN	REVIEW NEEDED WHEN?
Water on floor	Everyone is at high risk of injury due to the slippery surface	No	Warning sign placed in area; floor mopped to remove excess water and left to dry	Check if floor is dry in 30 minutes

Table 2.3 *Risk assessment*

In sport, some hazards may be less obvious. For example, one reason there are weight categories in sports such as judo is to reduce the risk of injury as the players are evenly matched for size and strength. Another example are the age categories in sports: some sports have different rules for children (e.g. tag rugby) to reduce the risk of injury. Similarly, certain actions may be forbidden (such as the tackle from behind in football) to reduce the risk of injury.

ACTIVITY

Visit your local sports centre to find out how they have reduced the risks to children and adults by altering the rules for certain sports or activities. Then conduct a risk assessment for a sporting activity of your choice, taking account of the factors listed in this section.

2.3 Produce and implement a set of guidelines to ensure a safe and secure working environment

This section covers
- Safety guidelines
- Risk control: managing the environment
- Emergency procedures

Safety guidelines

For a sporting activity to run safely, the person organising the session should set guidelines to ensure the safety of all the participants. These guidelines may vary a little from sport to sport, but they are all designed so that everyone involved in the session (coach, participant or spectator) is as safe as possible.

Unit 3 looks in detail at the guidelines you need to follow to run a sports session safely. The following, however, are a few examples of the guidelines all sports leaders or coaches should follow in any session:

1   The session should be lead by a coach who is qualified to teach that activity. If not, a qualified coach should be present to take overall responsibility.

2   An adult trained in first aid must be on hand.

3   The coach must assess whether the participants are capable of taking part in the activity; must make sure all the participants are fit enough to join in; must abide by all the safety rules; and must make sure the participants remove any loose clothing or jewellery that may cause injury to themselves and/or other participants, secure their hair if necessary and cut or tape long fingernails.

Management of the activity

All sessions must be planned for and managed carefully. In particular, when leading any activity, you should plan for or include the following:

1   Appropriate warm-up and warm-down activities.

2   Instruction in the rules, safety procedures and skills necessary for the activity before you start the session.

3   Activities that build up the players' skills.

4   A well thought-out training and coaching programme, and clear selection criteria for choosing teams.

5   The game should be adapted so that it matches the skill and fitness levels of the players.

6   The players should be grouped according to age, ability level, strength and body size, and any other special needs they may have.

Location

The location should be suitable for the session you are about to take – there is little point organising a roller-skating session if all that is available at the time is an outdoor hardcourt tennis area. You should also make sure first-aid equipment and any equipment necessary for the session are available.

The location should be safe – it should not be near other buildings, pedestrians and traffic. You should make sure the playing area is free of obstacles and loose objects, such as stones, leaves and litter, etc. If possible, you should provide facilities for locking away unneeded equipment and the players' personal belongings. Unit 3 looks again at these issues in relation to a specific coaching session you must undertake.

Equipment

The equipment you provide should be appropriate for the activity and should be in good order. For example, for field games, all the participants should wear the correct footwear. Boots should be sturdily made, should protect the feet and should have non-slip soles. You should also inspect boots before each match. Do not allow any that have sharp edges or worn studs to be worn. You should also make sure that any obstacles on the field (such as goalposts and corner flags) are padded or made of materials that will not injury the players should they collide with them.

Risk control: managing the environment

You must make sure all the participants understand the safety rules for the sport, and you must insist that they obey them. This may mean laying down the rules clearly before you start the session. If you are organising a competition game, you should make sure all the officials understand what is required of them (i.e. they understand the rules of a competition match).

Teams should be chosen fairly: you should select players for particular positions according to their ability and suitability. Finally, it is your job to resolve disputes in an impartial and professional manner. Again, Unit 3 looks at these issues in relation to a specific coaching session you must undertake.

Emergency procedures

You must have clearly defined emergency procedures, and you must keep a lookout for anyone who may be injured. If you think a player is injured, remove this person immediately from the playing area. It is particularly important to know what to do if someone receives an injury to the head.

Do not allow any injured players to return until their injuries have completely healed. If there is any doubt, insist on a doctor's certificate.

DID YOU KNOW?

- In 1996/97, 947 major injuries were reported by employees in local authority sports facilities. This accounted for 5 per cent of all local authority injuries reported to the Health and Safety Executive.
- In the same period, 1,077 members of the public suffered major injuries whilst using local authority sports facilities, and this accounted for 94 per cent of all injuries to the general public reported by local authorities.
- In the sports industry the biggest number of injuries resulted from a slip or a trip (35 per cent), followed by a fall from a height (28 per cent).
- Some 78 per cent of injuries resulted in a fracture.
- One third of minor injuries were strains and sprains incurred whilst playing sport.

ACTIVITY

Using the guidelines given above, draw up your own set of rules for one indoor and one outdoor activity. If they are different, what are the differences between them, and why are they different?

2.4 Devise and deliver a minimum of two appropriate warming up/down routines to help prevent injury

This section covers

- Components of a warm-up
- Physiological changes resulting from a warm-up
- Cool-down

It is important that all exercise sessions begin with a warm-up. This will reduce the risk of injury and prepare you, psychologically and physically, for the activity that is to follow. You should also end the session with a cool-down to return your body to its normal state.

Components of a warm-up

All warm-ups should contain the following routines and procedures:

- Exercises that slowly increase your heart rate and your body temperature.
- Exercises that take your joints through their full range of movement.
- Stretching, if applicable.
- Exercises to warm your body further and to bring your heart rate up to workout level.

The warm-up should be gentle and should aim to raise your heart rate to between 50 and 60 per cent of maximum. Passive warm-ups that use hot showers, baths or massage only raise body temperature.

Physiological changes resulting from a warm-up

As your body temperature gradually increases, there is an increase in the rate of exchange of oxygen from the blood to the tissues. Your blood vessels widen as blood flow increases. Blood flows from less active tissue to the muscles that are now working. Your heart rate and respiratory rate, etc., are raised. Your muscles become warmer, which makes them firmer, and all the ligaments, tendons and connective tissue become more pliable. As a result of all these changes, the range of movement in your muscles is increased and they are now ready for the exercise.

Overall, therefore, a warm-up prepares your body for the main activity by making it more physically efficient. Your chances of injury are also dramatically reduced.

Cool-down

The components of a cool-down are as follows:

1 Exercises that gradually lower your heart rate and reduce your body temperature.
2 Short maintenance stretches for all the muscle groups that have been used.
3 Developmental stretches for the appropriate muscle groups.
4 Relaxation exercises to reduce tension.
5 Re-mobilisation exercises so that the activity finishes on a psychological 'high'.

ACTIVITY

Create a warm-up and cool-down for two different performers in two different sports. What differences are there between the two, and what is the same in the two routines? Would you change these routines for a team or not?

ACTIVITY

Devise an appropriate warm-up and cool-down for: (a) a badminton player; and (b) a football player.

2.5 Recognise and demonstrate how to respond to injuries and illnesses within a sporting context

This section covers
- Treatment of soft-tissue injuries
- Treatment of fractures
- Common medical conditions

As we saw earlier in this unit, every coach should have clearly defined emergency procedures for every session. A major part of these procedures will be an action plan that covers any likely injuries or illnesses that may occur as a result of the session. This action plan, therefore, should take all the following into consideration:

- *The personnel involved*: This will include coaches, the team doctor or first-aider, school or club administrators, facility managers, etc.

- *The equipment needed*: First-aid kit, basic life-support equipment, bandages, etc.

- *A communication system to summon care*: Where the nearest telephone is or who has got a working mobile phone; emergency contact numbers for all participants; details of the nearest accident and emergency department; the venue's full address (including the postcode).

- *Access for the emergency services and an escape route in case of evacuation*: Where the fire exits are and that these are not locked or blocked with equipment; the procedure for evacuation in the event of an electrical failure (particularly for evening or night-time events), a gas escape and for emergencies involving people other than yourself and the participants (pitch invasions by fans, etc.). The evacuation procedures may be different for different emergencies (for example, the route to a fire exit may pass beneath a fractured gas main or there may be limited or no emergency lighting on stairways).

Although an action plan is vital, accidents do happen, and it is important that you know how to deal with minor injuries and when to refer an injured athlete to a professional therapist or doctor for

ACTIVITY

Create an emergency action plan for a sports hall you know in the event of a fire and a gas escape. Clearly identify the personnel involved and what their roles and responsibilities would be to ensure that all people are safely evacuated.

more appropriate treatment. Amongst the most common injuries are strains and sprains of soft tissues such as ligaments, as well as other soft-tissue injuries such as bruises and 'dead legs'. A strain is a stretching or tear of a muscle or tendon (commonly known as a pulled muscle), whilst a sprain is a stretching or tear of the ligaments around a joint. Another common sports injury is a fracture of one or more of the bones.

Any of these injuries may need professional help from a physiotherapist or sports therapist for them to heal properly and to enable the athlete to return to play as soon and as safely as possible.

Treatment of soft-tissue injuries

Soft-tissue injuries, such as a sprained ankle (Figure 2.7), should be treated immediately, according to the RICE principle.

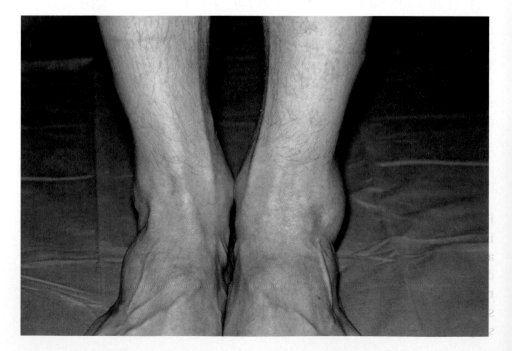

Figure 2.7
A badly sprained ankle can be relieved by the RICE method

Rest from:
- the activity during which the injury occurred;
- sport generally; and
- as many normal daily activities as possible.

(Depending on the extent and severity of the injury.)

Ice

An ice pack should be applied to the injury according to the following guidelines:

- The sooner the pack is applied the better. (*Note*: Ice and ice packs must not be placed directly on the skin as this could cause ice burns. They should be wrapped in a towel or cloth first.)
- If possible, the injured area should be raised up.
- It helps if the injury is compressed at the same time as the ice pack is applied (see below).
- The pack should remain in place for 10–20 minutes.
- Repeat this procedure every 2 hours for the first 24–48 hours.
- Crushed ice wrapped in a towel and oil applied to the skin to protect it from burns is the safest and most effective method.

Compression

Compression (i.e. applying gentle pressure to the injury) helps to:

- limit the amount of swelling;
- encourage the drainage of fluids from the injury; and
- reduce the amount of pain and keep the injured person comfortable.

Elevation

Elevation (i.e. raising the injured area) is important because it helps to support the limb in a comfortable position and also because it allows fluids to drain back to the heart away from the site of injury. The limb must be raised above the level of the heart and kept there if possible, or at least as high as is comfortable.

Treatment of fractures

Fractures must be splinted or put in a sling, if possible (i.e. supported in some way so that the fractured bone is prevented from moving), and the patient taken to the nearest accident and emergency department for medical treatment. If you suspect a fracture to the neck or back, you must not move the injured person. Call the emergency services immediately and, if necessary, abandon the activity or at least suspend it until the emergency services have removed the patient.

ACTIVITY

Devise an action plan to cope with injuries or illness during a sporting activity. This must include a plan to cope with soft-tissue injuries and illnesses where the patient can be safely moved, and injuries and illnesses where he or she cannot be moved for safety reasons.

Common medical conditions

Everyday medical conditions (such as asthma, diabetes and epilepsy) should not mean that people are automatically barred from taking part in a sporting activity, but certain precautions should be taken:

- The sports leader must be informed of any existing medical conditions team members may have.
- The person with the condition is responsible for ensuring emergency medication is available, e.g. an inhaler, insulin (or glucose) or anti-epileptic drugs.
- People with such conditions must be allowed to 'drop out' of the session if they feel unwell without seeking permission, but they must make the leader aware they are no longer participating.
- It is a good idea to nominate a 'buddy' – someone who can supervise a participant if he or she feels unwell. (See also Figure 3.4).

2.6 Investigate the importance of suitable equipment/clothing to safety in sport and provide appropriate equipment for sports activities

This section covers
- Protective clothing and the correct equipment
- Ensuring the equipment is safe and in order

Protective clothing and the correct equipment

So far in this unit we have talked about making sport safer by changing the rules, by providing good equipment and so on, but how can we prevent injury in contact sports (such as rugby or boxing) and in sports such as cricket and ice hockey where a hard object travels at speed? One answer is protective clothing and equipment (see Figure 2.8):

- It is compulsory in both amateur and professional boxing to wear a mouth-guard or gum shield. Professional boxers, however, do not

Figure 2.8
Protective clothing and equipment, such as goggles, helmets and kneepads, help reduce the risk of injury

wear head guards, whereas amateur boxers do to minimise the risk of head injuries.

● Cricketers wear protective helmets, gloves and shin pads when batting in order to prevent head isnjuries and fractures to the hands or legs.

● Crash mats are used in gymnastics and judo. These are large floor mats that reduce the risk of injury when a competitor falls.

When you are considering protective clothing, etc., it is important to take into account:

● the nature of the sport; and

● the age of the participants.

If we look at cricket again, one way to reduce injuries in children is for them to play with a larger, softer ball. This has two effects: a larger, softer ball is slower and easier to see and so the players have more time to make a shot or catch; and, if the ball does strike a batter or a fielder, there is less risk of injury because this ball is softer than a standard cork ball.

DID YOU KNOW?

● A fast bowler in cricket delivers the ball at over 87 miles per hour, and the fastest ever ball was bowled at 100 mph.

● An ice hockey puck travels at over 100 mph every time it is struck.

ACTIVITY

For two different sports, make a list of the safety clothing needed.

Ensuring the equipment is safe and in order

To reduce the risk of injury even further, it is important to ensure not only that the right equipment is used but also that this equipment is in good condition. In practice this usually means the coach will take responsibility for the equipment, or the referee or umpire will check the equipment is in order before it is used. Before play begins, referees will also check such things as the length of the studs on boots (no more than half an inch

ACTIVITY

Devise a procedure for issuing portable five-a-side goalposts and for setting them up safely. You should also include a procedure for removing them and for storing them appropriately in a safe place.

in American Football), whether the ball is pumped up properly and whether the goalposts and nets are secure.

The equipment provided by leisure or sport centres (table-tennis tables and trampolines, etc.) must also be stored safely, must be well maintained and must be set up correctly by the staff. It is also advisable that there is a formal procedure for the issue, set up, removal and return of all equipment so that any damage or loss can be checked and reported.

A final consideration is that only equipment appropriate for the activity must be used – you cannot do gymnastics or judo on a concrete floor.

ACTIVITY

As part of a consultation team for a new leisure centre, you are asked to recommend types of flooring for the following activity areas:

1 An aerobics studio.

2 An indoor badminton court.

3 The gymnasium.

State which type of flooring you would recommend for each, justifying your choice, and outline the potential hazards and risks involved in each activity.

TEST YOUR KNOWLEDGE

1 What are the four elements of physical fitness?

2 What is the difference between ability and skill, and what are the different stages of learning a skill?

3 What factors other than physical fitness may affect your chances of getting injured?

4 What is a hazard?

5 How is a hazard different from a risk?

6 How can a coach ensure his or her session is safe for the participants?

7 Why do we need to warm up and cool down?

8 What would you do immediately someone suffered a soft-tissue injury during a sports session?

9 Why do some sports need protective clothing?

10 Why is it important to check equipment before a session?

Effective Sports Leadership

Introduction

In this unit you will learn about the practical skills and knowledge you need to be an effective sports leader. Becoming a sports leader is the first step to developing coaching skills. Whilst a qualified sports coach will be able to plan and supervise independently, as a sports leader you will be able to deliver practical sessions receiving support, guidance and supervision from a tutor or other more experienced and qualified person.

You will come to understand that there are certain qualities a sports leader must possess or be willing to develop. As you saw in Unit 2, a sports leader must operate according to safety guidelines and will need to plan ahead in order to work safely and deliver enjoyable sessions. This unit looks at these issues again as they relate specifically to sports leadership. Successful sports leaders are always willing to learn from the feedback given to them by the participants or outside observers.

How you will be assessed

For this unit you will produce a portfolio of work that shows you have met all the assessment objectives for the unit. Your portfolio could contain case studies of sports leaders you have observed, log books and plans of sessions you coached or led and of those you have officiated over, notes on sessions you have observed, videos of sessions you have run and witness statements of your performance in coaching and officiating sessions.

In this unit you will learn how to:

① Describe, using examples, the key characteristics of an effective sports leader

② Demonstrate safe practice and appropriate emergency procedures in sports leadership/coaching situations

③ Demonstrate effective officiating skills in four practical activities to include refereeing, timekeeping and scoring

④ Plan, organise and lead two sports activity sessions to improve the personal skill, technique and sporting awareness of a selected group of participants

⑤ Evaluate own performance as a sports leader and suggest improvements

3.1 Describe, using examples, the key characteristics of an effective sports leader

This section covers

- Knowledge of sports skills
- Knowledge of rules and regulations
- The ability to lead effectively
- Understanding the ability and aspiration of participants

There are certain characteristics all successful coaches and other sports leaders share. However, there is much debate about whether these characteristics are inborn (i.e. the person was born with these characteristics) or are acquired as a person grows older. Some people believe, therefore, you are born with these charactcristics and that, if you do not possess these at birth, you will never become an effective leader. The other view is that certain skills can be learnt over time, through education and through the social experiences you have. Whatever your view on this subject, it remains the case that there is a body of knowledge and a range of skills you must possess.

Knowledge of sports skills

A sound knowledge of the sports you are coaching is crucial if you are to be a good sports leader. You should know about the skills that are needed to play the sport and the tactical aspects that are important to performance.

Most sports involve the development of movement or motor skills. Basically, your brain sends a message via your nervous system to the relevant muscles to produce the required movement. The muscles send back information to the brain, which acts on this feedback to make slight adjustments to that particular movement.

A coach will need to identify the skills that are needed to play a particular sport. For example, some of the skills that need to be developed in football are:

- short passing;
- long passing;
- tackling;
- shooting;
- heading;
- dribbling with the ball; and
- turning with ball.

In addition are more general skills that will make use of the above techniques:

- attacking;
- defending; and
- learning how to create and move into space.

A sports leader also needs to be aware of the various types of sports skills. These include the following:

- *Fine motor skills*: Those that use small muscle groups to produce intricate movements, such as controlling the angle of the bat in table tennis.
- *Gross motor skills*: Those that use large muscle groups, such as the kicking action in football.
- *Open skills*: Skills that are affected by the environment and that must be adapted to suit the circumstances of the moment. For example, a canoeist on a river must continually adjust his or her paddle movements to take into account changes in the water's currents and speed.
- *Closed skills*: Those skills that are not affected by the environment or by other players, such as the free throw in basketball.

You should understand how the skills necessary for a particular sport develop. A participant must first learn the basic skills and then how to apply these (this is especially important for open skills) (see Figure 3.1).

In your role as sports leader, your first step is to learn the various practice drills you will need to know in order to teach a participant a basic skill, and then the more complicated drills necessary to develop this individual's skill in competitive situations. As you become more experienced as a sports leader, you will start to develop your own drills and practice routines but, if you are starting out, it is better to look at a coaching manual to research and plan suitable practices.

ACTIVITY

In a small group, identify what skills are needed to play the following sports. (You may need to refer to Unit 6 to look at the definitions of skills.)

1 tennis
2 rugby
3 golf
4 hockey.

STAGE 1
Learning what is required

A player will first need to learn where to stand in relation to the ball, the necessary foot-eye-ball coordination and movement pattern to pass the ball.

In the first stages a player may make many mistakes, but through good coaching will be able to break down the skill into parts and put all the parts together to strike the ball cleanly.

STAGE 2
Practice

Our footballer may now be able to adjust his or her position within a game and be accurate at passing the ball most of the time.

Repeated practice will enable the player 'feel' the pass and recognise errors.

STAGE 3
Mastery

The advanced footballer who has mastered the passing movement will be able to pass from any position and also be aware of where his or her opponents are and where the position of the ball is likely to be.

The focus will be on the environment rather than the movement itself.

Figure 3.1 *The development of passing the ball in football*

Knowledge of rules and regulations

You will need to have a sound knowledge of the basic rules of the sport you are going to lead. For example, how is play started? How are points scored? What is considered foul play? You are not expected at the outset to be aware of every minor rule – a greater awareness of the rules and their application will come with experience.

CASE STUDY

Swimming rules

The rules below are some of those that have been set by FINA, the international governing body for swimming, and they apply to competitions:

SW 10.1   A swimmer swimming over the course alone shall cover the whole distance to qualify.

SW 10.2   A swimmer must finish the race in the same lane in which he or she started.

SW 10.3   In all events, a swimmer when turning shall make physical contact with the end of the pool or course. The turn must be made from the wall, and it is not permitted to take a stride or step from the bottom of the pool.

SW 10.4   Standing on the bottom during freestyle events or during the freestyle portion of medley events shall not

CASE STUDY

Swimming rules (Contd.)

----

disqualify a swimmer, but he or she shall not walk.

SW10.5 Pulling on the lane rope is not allowed.

SW10.6 Obstructing another swimmer by swimming across another lane or otherwise interfering shall disqualify the offender.

SW 10.7 No swimmer shall be permitted to use or wear any device that may aid his or her speed, buoyancy or endurance during a competition (such as webbed gloves, flippers, fins, etc.). Goggles may be worn.

1 Can you give a reason for each of the above rules?
2 For a sport you know well, find out if there are rules for competitions. Again, try to work out the purpose behind these rules.
3 Design a poster that illustrates some of the main competition rules for this sport.

As you learnt in Unit 2, each sport also has its own set of regulations that relate to such areas as equipment and clothing. The purpose of these regulations is to make the sport safe and enjoyable.

The ability to lead effectively

As we have seen, the ability to lead a group effectively may be a reflection of both inborn factors and social experiences which help develop the following skills:

- Organisational skills (planning and delivering training sessions, completing paperwork, evaluating sessions, time management skills).
- Communication skills (using language that can be understood by the group, being able to demonstrate techniques).
- Motivation skills (showing enthusiasm and being able to motivate the group through praise, criticism and the use of rewards).
- Management skills (being able to control the participants, assert discipline, build rapport with the group).

Not all leaders operate in the same way. Different types of leader suit different situations, and different aspects of your own personality will have an effect on your style of leadership. The main leadership styles are described below.

ACTIVITY

In small groups, think about the leaders you work with. You may be a leader yourself in a youth group or in a group at your school or college. What skills do these people have that identify them as good leaders?

Autocratic

The autocratic leader does not involve the participants in making any decisions – the leader expects the group to carry out his or her instructions without question. This style is sometimes used when coaching children because it is easier for the leader to keep control of the session. It can, however, be inflexible and may not bring out the full potential of participants as they are not encouraged to make decisions for themselves.

Democratic

This style is generally considered to be the opposite of the autocratic style. Participants are consulted in making decisions. For example, participants may be allowed to choose which practice drills they do in a specific session. However, this style can be time consuming as everyone must be consulted before a decision is reached.

Laissez-faire

The laissez-faire leader gives advice but has no role in making decisions. This means the participants choose what they want to do and the leader is on hand to offer the benefit of his or her experience, if required. For example, sportsmen and women at an elite level may have developed such a good understanding of their sport that they need very little direction. However, this is likely to be the only circumstance where this style is preferred as, generally, most participants need clear direction from sports leaders and coaches.

Personal leadership qualities

Leading sports sessions presents many challenges. As the leader you will be responsible for the health and safety of the group and for the development of their skills. You will need, therefore, good organisational skills, good communication skills, flexibility in your approach, a willingness to accept responsibility and bags of enthusiasm.

To prepare yourself for leadership, you must be aware of your own strengths and weaknesses. To help you recognise these, complete the questionnaire given in Figure 3.2 by ticking the appropriate box:

1 = I do not have this skill at the moment
2 = I am trying to develop this skill

3 = I am OK at this skill
4 = I am good at this skill
5 = I am very good at this skill

Adaptability	1	2	3	4	5
I can respond well to timetable changes at school or college					
I can respond well to last-minute changes at work, school or college					
I cope well in new and unfamiliar situations					
When new information is given to me I incorporate it immediately into what I already know					
If I am given something new to do I do not complain, I simply do it to the best of my ability					

Communication	1	2	3	4	5
I perform well in presentations					
I am good at role plays					
I say what I mean and mean what I say					
I can communicate to a range of people from a variety of backgrounds					
I always listen to what others say to me					
I have a good attention span					
I am familiar with and use electronic communication methods					
I can give effective talks or demonstrations to groups					
I can provide constructive feedback to individuals					
If I don't understand something I will ask questions					
If I know that I am struggling I seek help					

Figure 3.2 *Personal leadership qualities: questionnaire*

Responsibility	1	2	3	4	5
When something is my fault I admit it					
I volunteer for tasks that I don't have to do					
I understand that when I say I'll do something it means I have to do it					
I do not shirk my duties by making excuses as to why things aren't done					
I keep a firm hold on tasks that I am jointly responsible for with others					
In group tasks I understand that the responsibility I have is for the whole task, not just my bit of it					
I do not let other things distract me from my responsibilities					

Organisation	1	2	3	4	5
I always take to college, school or work everything that I need					
I arrive on time at college, school or work					
I plan time to complete work I am given to do at home					
I sort and file all of the information I receive as soon as I receive it					
If I am asked for a piece of information I usually know where to find it					
I always meet set deadlines					

Enthusiasm	1	2	3	4	5
I try to be enthusiastic about a task even when I do not want to do it					
I do not moan or complain about tasks I am given					
I encourage others to be enthusiastic					
I give the same time and attention to tasks I don't like as I would with tasks I do like					

Figure 3.2 *Continued*

Assertiveness	1	2	3	4	5
I feel able to say no if I don't want to do something					
If I am in a leadership role I feel comfortable expressing my authority					
I am not easily intimidated by others					
I speak up if I disagree with something					
I will intervene if I see someone being bullied or abused					

Conflict resolution	1	2	3	4	5
I am able to avoid conflict by being professional and not personal					
When two of my fellow students disagree I am able to help them reach a compromise					
I do not take sides in the conflict of others					
I do not cause conflict by being rude or aggressive					
I do not bring my emotions into conflicts					

Consistency	1	2	3	4	5
I am not 'moody' with my fellow students					
I do not let my personal problems interfere with how I treat people					
I am always professional and approachable					
I do not treat some people differently than others					

Figure 3.2 *Continued*

Assessing your results

Calculate your results for each section by adding together the numbers 1–5 that you ticked for each question and entering the results in the chart below. The last step is to add up your section scores to make a grand total.

Section	Max score	Your score
Adaptability	25	
Communication	55	
Responsibility	35	
Organisation	30	
Enthusiasm	20	
Assertiveness	25	
Conflict resolution	25	
Consistency	20	
Total score	235	

Making Sense of your Results	
Score 47–84	Your leadership skills are undeveloped at present. There are many areas for you to begin to improve and work on if you hope to lead groups of individuals.
Score 85–122	Your leadership skills are beginning to develop but there are still many areas for you to work on if you want to be effective as a sports leader.
Score 123–138	Your leadership skills are beginning to establish and your weaknesses are fairly evenly balanced by your strengths. This is a good foundation to build upon and improve.
Score 159–196	Your leadership skills are developed and your strengths outbalance your weaknesses. You have the makings of a sound sports leader if you continue to develop these skills.
Score 197–235	Your existing leadership skills are of a very good standard and although you may have a couple of weak areas you are well suited to a leadership role. However, you need to build on these skills with practical experience, which will enable you to identify your weaknesses and overcome them.

CASE STUDY

Leadership style

Amanda is 11 years old and enjoys playing football. She belongs to a local youth football team and also plays for the school side. Amanda has shown some potential and would like to progress to develop her footballing skills.

She trains once a week with her local team and plays games on Saturday. Training normally consists of a warm-up, jogging and then five-a-side. The manager usually sits chatting with parents and occasionally comes and asks the girls if they are alright. Amanda has made good friends with rest of the team and they can often be seen together at the local youth club.

At the school, the PE teacher is keen to develop girls' football and has planned a series of sessions that he has put on the noticeboard in the sports hall. He has stated that anyone not prepared to attend these sessions will not be considered for the school team.

His sessions have a clear structure with a group warm-up, a range of practices focusing on the development of a different technique each week, small-sided games that are stopped and analysed and a cool-down at the end of each session.

Amanda also has other commitments, including music lessons and an increasing amount of homework, and she has decided that she has to give up one of her football sessions, but cannot decide which one.

1   What leadership style is being shown by:
    a   the local youth team coach?
    b   the PE teacher?
2   Discuss the advantages and disadvantages of giving up:
    a   participation in the local youth team; and
    b   participation in the school football team.

Understanding the ability and aspiration of participants

Knowing your group in terms of their needs, physical ability and levels of motivation is extremely important to becoming an effective sports leader. Often within the same group you will have different abilities, and you must therefore devise a range of activities that cater for both the beginner and the more advanced. This is known as 'differentiation'.

Participants have their own learning styles. For example, some people learn a sports skill through verbal instructions, whilst others will need a visual demonstration. You must, therefore, incorporate both a verbal introduction and a visual demonstration of each activity into your session plan.

Some people will require a lot more praise and encouragement than others to keep them motivated, particularly if they are not very good at the sport or are having trouble learning a skill. You will find that some people are better at developing movement skills, such as co-ordination, kicking, throwing, catching and so on. You will also need to make regular checks on the progress of all your participants, and you must not move at too fast a pace whilst, at the same time, devising appropriate activities for those who have already mastered a skill.

ACTIVITY

You work for Sports Leaders UK and are in charge of a campaign to raise the profile of sports leadership training. Your research has revealed that there are many people working in a voluntary capacity who do not have all the characteristics needed to be an effective sports leader. Your organisation believes that people can develop these qualities over time. The first step in this process is to make people aware of the skills and knowledge required of them.

Design a leaflet that shows the main characteristics needed to be an effective sports leader. You should include the following:

- Knowledge of sports skills.
- Knowledge of the rules and regulations.
- Leadership skills.
- An understanding of the abilities and needs of the participants.

3.2 Demonstrate safe practice and appropriate emergency procedures in sports leadership/coaching situations

This section covers
- Safety requirements
- Emergency procedures
- Risk analysis
- Maintaining safe working areas

As you learnt in Unit 2, you need a thorough knowledge of health and safety requirements before you plan any coaching session. You will also need to produce certain documents, such as the risk assessment plan, before you are allowed to carry out your session.

Safety requirements

Depending on the session you are to lead, you will need to check the venue/areas to make sure they are suitable and safe. For example, if you were to use an indoor sports hall, you should check that all fire prevention measures are in place and that fire doors are not obstructed. You should check the flooring for any trip hazards or for greasy areas where someone might slip. The lighting must be working properly and be appropriate for the activity. If you do notice anything that is not right, you should report to the manager immediately.

The equipment you intend to use should be appropriate to the group's age and ability level. For example, you would use junior-sized tennis rackets with children. All equipment should be checked before it is used (you looked at the example of boots in Unit 2) and again, if appropriate, at the end of the session. Equipment that needs assembly (such as goals, nets and climbing frames) should be checked before it is set up and then again just prior to use.

You will need to think about the ability and potential behaviour of your group and plan accordingly. A group of young children or those with behavioural difficulties will need much closer supervision than other participants. Remember also that too complicated or too

ACTIVITY

In small groups, discuss what you would need to check before setting up the following pieces of equipment:

1 a trampoline

2 a volleyball net

3 collapsible football goals.

easy practices for the group's ability level will be a safety hazard, as participants switch off or try to gain attention in other ways.

Emergency procedures

As a sports leader you will need to be aware of the different emergency situations that could arise. What if there is a fire in another part of the building? Or what if a participant is injured? You will need to find out about:

- first-aid procedures; and
- fire and evacuation procedures.

ACTIVITY

What are the signs and symptoms of the following injuries/conditions:

1 a sprained ankle;

2 an epileptic fit; and

3 a damaged knee ligament?

First aid

Even if you are not a qualified first-aider, it is useful to know the common signs and symptoms of a range of conditions you might encounter.

You should never attempt first aid yourself unless you are fully qualified, but, as you saw in Unit 2, you must make sure there is someone qualified on-site during your session to carry out any first aid, should this be necessary. A fully equipped first-aid box should also be available (see Figure 3.3).

Procedures will vary according to the venue, but there is likely to be a central point of contact (such as reception) where you can locate the first-aider who will then administer the appropriate treatment.

Fire evacuation procedures

You will need to know what to do in the event of a fire. You should never attempt to tackle a fire but should sound the alarm and then escort the group via the nearest fire exit to a fire assembly point. There may also be other circumstances where an evacuation is needed, such as a gas leak or bomb threat. You may find that the participants panic in such situations. You should keep calm and use clear, assertive language to take control and to lead people to safety.

Organisation of the group

If an incident takes place, you will need to consider how you will supervise the rest of the group whilst you attend to those involved. This should form part of your contingency planning. For example, if a participant sustains an injury, you could provide an alternative activity (such as practice drills) for the remainder of the group rather than continue with the game. In this way the group can carry on whilst you

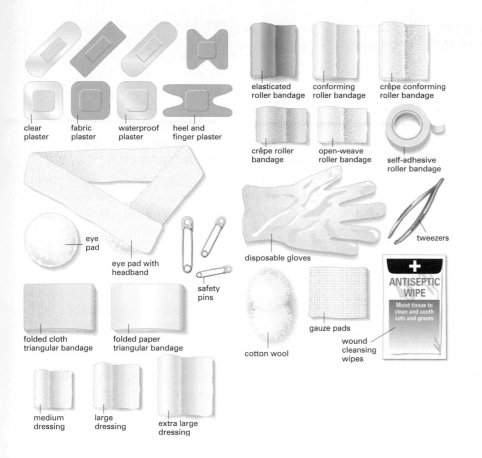

Figure 3.3 *The contents of a first-aid box*

give first aid to the injured party. Of course, if the player's injuries were serious, then you would probably not continue with the session, although you would still need to identify someone who could supervise and close the session for you.

Documentation

When first aid has been carried out, it is important that as many details as possible are recorded of the treatment given, as these may be needed at a later date. This includes the time of the incident, where and in what context the injury was sustained, who was in charge, who administered the first aid, what treatment was given and if there were any witnesses to the incident. Often, a leisure centre or other facility will have its own form that must be completed when first aid is administered. An example injury report form is given in Figure 3.4.

The responsibility for filling in this documentation is the first-aider's. There will also be an incident log book for evacuations, and such incidents should be recorded even if they were false alarms.

Injury Report Form

Date and Time of injury: *05/05/2005 2.00 pm*
Venue: *Barracks Lane Sports Ground*
Session Leader: *Lewis Brown*
First Aider: *Milly Smith*
Time of Observation: *2.01 pm*

Pulse: *85 bmp*
Breaths per min: *23*
Breathing: *quiet*

	General Information	Details of the Injured Party	Additional Comments
1	Name and age of injured	*Nathan Murray - 14 yrs*	
2	How did the injury occur/cause of the injury	*Two football players went to head the ball at the same time. Collision of heads*	*Nathan fell to the floor clutching his head*
3	The injured party's symptoms, for example a) Numbness b) Blurred vision c) Severe pain d) Mild pain, etc.	*He is conscious but is complaining about severe blurred vision, dizziness and a throbbing headache*	*Nathan feels scared*
4	Visual signs, for example a) Swelling b) Bleeding c) Dislocation d) Discoloration e) Redness f) Bruising g) Breathing difficulties h) Unconsciousness i) Concussion j) Others	*A lot of swelling at the front and side of the head*	
5	Speeech a) Respond well to questions b) Confused c) Other	*Confused*	
6	First-aid treatment given	*Ice pack for head* *Kept calm and warm*	
7	Ambulance/medical help sent for	*Ambulance called*	*2.04 pm*
8	Referred to hospital	*Yes*	*Parents contacted - minor*
9	Resume play	*No*	
10	Advice given	*Reassurance, kept talking/ kept awake, felt sleepy*	
11	Home treatment plan	*N/A*	*Referred to hospital*
12	Witness(es) Name(s) Address(es) Telephone number(s)	*N/A*	

Figure 3.4 *An injury report form*

Risk analysis

It is a legal requirement that you produce a risk assessment prior to leading a coaching session. As you saw in Unit 2, this is a document that looks at potential risk factors and makes sure you have put in place adequate solutions or control measures for the most significant hazards. The following are the stages involved in conducting a risk analysis:

1 Identify all the hazards. These include the physical features of the location itself (such as the electrical supply, floors and walls), the equipment (nets and goals) and the participants themselves (e.g. a group may have behavioural difficulties).

2 Calculate the potential likelihood of each hazard causing an injury. This is usually done on a scale (e.g. 1 – not all (low risk) – to 10 – very likely (high risk)).

3 Calculate the potential severity of the injuries that could be caused. Would the injuries sustained be minor or more serious? Again, you can use a sliding scale (e.g. 1 = minor to 10 = very serious).

4 Multiply both scores (i.e. from steps 2 and 3 above) to obtain an overall risk factor: Likelihood multiplied by Severity.

5 Describe what you have done in an attempt to control these risks. This means things you can do to minimise the risks. For example, to reduce the risk of serious injury, you could brief the group's leader about all the health and safety issues and make sure a first-aid kit and a first-aider are available.

You must address all hazards but must pay particular attention to those that have a high score as these are the ones most likely to cause injury. A risk assessment is useless unless it is acted upon and the control measures are in place. This is your responsibility. A risk assessment for a coaching session, therefore, might look something like Table 3.1.

Maintaining safe working areas

You may have checked the facility/area before commencing your session, but you will need to make regular checks during the session. Are there any greasy areas on the playing surface caused by spilt drinks or sweat? Has anybody sustained a minor cut where blood is visible? It is important to keep the environment clean in order to reduce the risk of injury and disease, and you should always act if you notice such things.

Look for obstructions and hazards. Are there any drinks bottles left around from a break that may constitute a trip hazard or that may damage the walls and floors, leaving sharp corners or jagged plasterwork? Remember to keep vigilant!

Appropriate signs should also be used in the event of spillage or other incident so that no one comes into the area until you have cleared up or dealt with the incident.

POTENTIAL HAZARD	LEVEL OF RISK (1 – LOW TO 10 – HIGH)	SEVERITY OF INJURIES THAT MIGHT BE SUSTAINED (1 – MINOR TO 10 – VERY SERIOUS)	RISK FACTOR	ACTION TAKEN
Appropriateness of the session to the group's abilities				
Equipment and clothing (list as appropriate): 1 2 3 4 5 6 7				
The environment (floors, lighting, obstacles, etc.)				
Supervision requirements (are there enough qualified adults to supervise the session safely?)				

Table 3.1 *A risk assessment for a coaching session*

POTENTIAL HAZARD	LEVEL OF RISK (1 – LOW TO 10 – HIGH)	SEVERITY OF INJURIES THAT MIGHT BE SUSTAINED (1 – MINOR TO 10 – VERY SERIOUS)	RISK FACTOR	ACTION TAKEN
First-aid procedures				
Emergency evacuation procedures				

Table 3.1 *Continued*

CASE STUDY

Following health and safety guidelines

Tom is excited to be carrying out his first coaching session. He produces a plan for the session and other relevant documentation such as a risk assessment. The session is based on his favourite sport of badminton and will last approximately one hour.

Tom sets up the sports hall and checks all the appropriate equipment. He puts up four badminton nets across the sports hall. Under normal circumstances the hall can accommodate three, but he decides to squeeze in another, marking out the areas with cones.

Initially, six participants arrive ready for the session. He gives them a safety briefing and, after a warm-up activity, they start the practices he has devised. The remaining two participants turn up late and he tells them to go quickly to the end court and start the practice. One of them is wearing inappropriate footwear but he decides that enough time has

been wasted and allows the individual to continue.

Towards the end of the session the player with shoes on rather than trainers slips and bashes into a heating grill, which is torn from its mountings and lands on the floor. Luckily the player does not sustain any injuries and so he carries on playing. Tom removes the grill and places it at the back of the sports hall. Another player over-reaches for a smash and falls on to the grill, which gashes his leg. Tom stops the play and sends someone to reception to get a first-aider who then gives the person appropriate treatment. The injury is not major but could have been a lot nastier. Tom has certainly learnt a lot from his first session in charge.

1 What mistakes did Tom make in his first coaching session?
2 What positive points can Tom take away from his first coaching experience?

ACTIVITY

For this assessment you must demonstrate safe practice and appropriate emergency procedures in sports leadership situations.

Produce a health and safety booklet for the facility you are using for your coaching practice. Your booklet should include the following:

- Safety checks relevant to the sports you are going to coach.
- The emergency procedures for the facility.
- A risk assessment for the sport(s) you are coaching and for the facility.

Remember, when you are carrying out your coaching sessions, you will need to get your tutor to provide written testimony that you carried out your sessions with due regard for health and safety issues.

3.3 Demonstrate effective officiating skills in four practical activities to include refereeing, timekeeping and scoring

This section covers
- Refereeing
- Timekeeping
- Scoring

When leading sports activities you must be able to officiate. You will need to show that you are able to time keep, to keep the score and make decisions on rules and regulations.

Refereeing

You will need to know the main rules and regulations for four practical activities. All sports have rules which are written down by the governing body for that sport. These rules are required for a number of reasons:

1 They decide the format of the game. For example, in football you are not allowed to use your hands to move the football but you are in rugby. In netball, you must take one step, pivot and release the ball whilst in football you can run with and dribble the ball.

2 They cover aspects such as the duration of game, the size of the playing area and how many substitutions are allowed. For example, in football a limited number of substitutions are allowed which is not the case for other sports.

3 They ensure that the sport is played in a safe manner. There are rules and regulations that cover equipment and the protective equipment that must be worn. For example, in hockey, goalkeepers must protect certain areas of their bodies with pads and must wear helmets.

Use Table 3.2 as a checklist for each of your four activities. This way you can make sure you have covered the basic rules for each one.

AREA	RULE/REGULATION
Minimum/maximum size of playing area	
Duration of game	
Start/finish of play	
Scoring	
Number of players	
Number of substitutions	
What constitutes foul play	
Minimum playing equipment required	

Table 3.2 *Checklist for sports rules and regulations*

Consistency

It is important that you apply the rules of your sport consistently. This means that you apply the same rule to all participants in all situations. You should not bow to pressure from players or observers, and you must have the confidence to carry out your duties fairly.

Accuracy

Obviously, you need to be accurate in the decisions you make. Remember that even experienced officials make mistakes.

Don't worry if you make the wrong decisions, but do learn from the experience.

Communication

Officials need to communicate with colleagues, players and coaching staff in order to officiate effectively. Figure 3.5 gives a few examples of the sorts of communications officials might have to make.

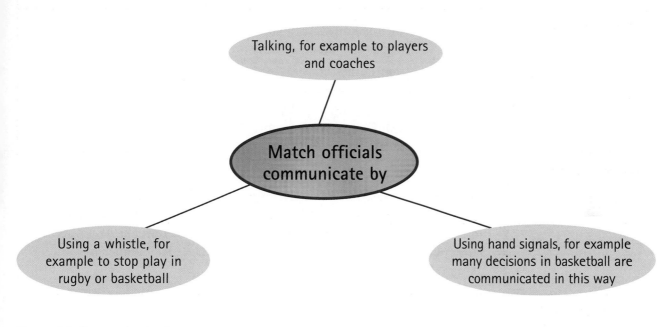

Figure 3.5 *Communication in sport*

Timekeeping

You will need to be familiar with the timing regulations for your sport. There are several key areas to consider:

- The start/finish times of the game (including quarters or halves).
- Whether play can be stopped by coaching staff (for example 'time out' in basketball).
- Whether time is added at the end of the session or game for any stoppages.

In practice, you must remember to make a mental (or written) note of any breaks in play so that time can be added. In some sports the time may be displayed elsewhere and you will need to communicate with other officials in order that the display shows the right time remaining.

Scoring

All sports have scoring systems. This refers to all the ways that points can be scored within that activity. In some sports this may be relatively straightforward, such as in football: if the whole ball crosses the line within the posts and under the crossbar, a goal is scored. However other sports have more complicated scoring systems:

- *Rugby*: Four points are scored for touching the ball over the goal line. The try can then be converted by a kick between the posts, which is known as a conversion. This is worth two points. In addition, points can also be scored through penalty kicks.

- *Badminton*: Points are only scored when you are serving. If the shuttle hits the ground in your opponent's half or is hit outside the playing area by the other player(s), then a point is scored. The first player to score 21 points is deemed to be the winner of that game.

Other scoring systems are not so clear cut and depend on people's personal opinions. For example, in gymnastics and ice skating, the winner is selected through the scores awarded by a panel of judges. In other sports the person or team with the least number of points is the winner (e.g. in golf the person with the least number of shots wins the match).

The score may also be displayed to the spectators, such as is the custom in cricket, so you will need to make sure you communicate effectively with other officials so that the score is updated regularly.

ACTIVITY

Find out how points are scored in the following sports:

1 fencing
2 bowling
3 squash.

CASE STUDY

Officiating

Tom has been asked by his tutor to referee a volleyball match during a lunch hour. The match is part of a lunchtime league at the college which, although relatively informal, is still very competitive. Tom decides that he knows enough about the rules of the sport from a brief introduction he was given by his tutor in a PE lesson. A more detailed copy of the rules is available, but he decides not to read it. He goes straight from a lesson and forgets to take a whistle or notebook.

Together with a friend, he sets out the court and the game commences. At first all goes well, but he allows a point to stand where a player touches the net. Next, he cannot decide whether a ball

CASE STUDY

Officiating (Contd.)

has landed in or out of court through a crowd of players. No one else is officiating so he cannot seek a second opinion. At times Tom's voice is too quiet to be heard and he is reliant on hand gestures to indicate his decisions. Not surprisingly, the game ends with one team complaining about the poor officiating shown by Tom.

1 Outline the main mistakes made by Tom whilst officiating in the match.
2 What factors should you take into account before agreeing to officiate?
3 List the various factors you must consider when you are preparing to officiate in any sport.

ACTIVITY

Select four sports and explain the main rules and regulations relating to each of these. Use Table 3.2 to help you do this.

You must now officiate in each of these four sports and must include a record of the feedback you receive from your tutor or other observers. To record this feedback, you could give the observers a copy of the observers' sheet shown in Table 3.3 overleaf and ask them to fill this in as soon as possible after the session. Once you have obtained this feedback, you will need to analyse it to improve your performance the next time you officiate. Table 3.4 overleaf includes the same questions as the observers' form but has spaces for you to add your own comments about the feedback. Use these spaces to make notes about how you intend to improve your officiating skills.

QUESTION	YES/NO	EXAMPLES
Did the student apply the rules consistently?		
Did the student make accurate decisions?		
Were timing regulations applied according to the rules?		
Were scoring regulations applied according to the rules?		
Was the student's communication understood by the other players and/or officials?		
Were venue/equipment checks carried out?		
In the event of any emergencies, were the relevant procedures followed?		
Were control measures in place to reduce the risk of significant hazards?		
Was the area kept clean and free from obstructions and hazards at all times?		

Table 3.3 *Observers' sheet: officiating*

QUESTION	HOW I COULD IMPROVE MY OFFICIATING SKILLS IN THE LIGHT OF THESE COMMENTS
Did the student apply the rules consistently?	
Did the student make accurate decisions?	
Were timing regulations applied according to the rules?	
Were scoring regulations applied according to the rules?	
Was the student's communication understood by the other players and/or officials?	
Were venue/equipment checks carried out?	
In the event of any emergencies, were the relevant procedures followed?	
Were control measures in place to reduce the risk of significant hazards?	
Was the area kept clean and free from obstructions and hazards at all times?	

Table 3.4 *Comment form for observers' feedback on officiating skills*

3.4 Plan, organise and lead two sports activity sessions to improve the personal skill, technique and sporting awareness of a selected group of participants

This section covers

- Objectives for the session
- Equipment needs
- Supervision needs
- Timing of activities
- Introduction/warm-up
- Skills and technique development activities
- Setting up small-sided games, competitions and teams
- The cool-down
- Session review
- Structuring the session

You will need to write a session plan before you can carry out your role as a sports leader. This is important for two main reasons. To make sure that:

1 the session is structured in order to maximise the participants' learning and enjoyment; and

2 you operate within health and safety laws and guidelines.

Several factors need to be considered when writing the plan. We will now look at each of these in turn.

Objectives for the session

Before you can set the objectives or aims for this session, you must research the group thoroughly. You will need to look at the following:

- The *size* of the group. (You may need assistance, and there are also guidelines as to the ratios of staff to participants that must be followed.)

- The *age range* and *gender mix*. (You will need to chose appropriate practice activities for the group's age range, and you may need separate activities for males and females, depending on age and the activity which is being undertaken.)
- The *ability level* of the participants. (Again this will effect the complexity of the practices that you deliver.)
- The *cultural background* of the participants. (There may be a language barrier you must overcome if people are going to understand what is expected of them in your session.)
- The *medical background* of the participants. (You must be aware of anyone in the group who has a medical condition such as asthma so that you will know if he or she needs to take medication or in case someone has to administer first aid.)

Once you have established all these factors you can set the objectives for the session. These should focus on what you want the participants to learn or achieve by the end of the session. For example, for a tennis coaching session, the main objectives may be to give the participants an awareness of the main parts of the tennis serve, and to improve the accuracy and consistency of each participant's serve. In reality this may take a number of sessions, so a series of lessons would be needed to work towards these objectives.

It is usual to use the SMART principle when setting goals or objectives for a session. SMART stands for Specific, Measurable, Agreed, Realistic and Timed:

- *Specific*: Objectives should be specific to your chosen sport and the player's position if it is team sport. For example, a sprinter should not need to work on developing his or her stamina but should do lots of practices to develop his or her speed and reaction time.
- *Measurable*: Objectives should be measurable. For example, improving the accuracy of a tennis serve could be measured by the percentage of serves that make the service box.
- *Agreed*: You should agree the objectives with the participants to make sure they are relevant.
- *Realistic*: Goals should be realistic: the participants should be able to achieve them within the session. A balance needs to be achieved between objectives or goals that are challenging and those are easy. If the objectives are too easily achieved or not sufficiently challenging, the participants will soon become de-motivated.
- *Timed*: Participants should be given deadline to achieve each goal or objective. This helps to motivate the participants and means you can track progress more easily.

Within a mixed-ability group you are likely to set individual targets. This may be done informally as you establish each person's ability level. Being able to set targets in this way is an advanced skill; it is sufficient at this stage for you to set group objectives for each session.

Equipment needs

We have already discussed the need for you to check all your equipment. In addition, you should make sure that you have sufficient equipment for the group and some spare in case you acquire extra participants. If there is not enough equipment you may need to adapt or rethink the task. You will need to ensure that the equipment is used correctly during the session to reduce the risk of injury. The equipment you will need for any coaching session may be as follows:

- *Markers*: Cones or something similar to mark out areas for practice drills or small-sided games.
- *Bibs*: Coloured bibs are essential to indicate who is on which team or who is performing a particular role in a practice session.
- A *whiteboard* or *flipchart*: These are handy for explaining practices but are not always needed if you can demonstrate the task yourself effectively.
- A *watch*: To keep track of the session.
- A *whistle*: Necessary for officiating.

In addition you will need equipment that is specific to the sport and to the group's age range and ability level (for example, smaller footballs for children or a foam ball for novices at volleyball).

You will also need to consider whether you can gain access to the equipment easily or whether you need to obtain a key from the site supervisor or another member of staff. It can take a considerable amount of time to set up equipment, so you should take this into account when planning your session.

Supervision needs

If you carried out sufficient research on the needs of your group and on the health and safety guidelines, you will know how much assistance you will need to supervise the group.

Timing of activities

After you have established the length of your session, you will need to plan how much time each practice or activity should take. Your time plan will be a guide only, and experience will tell you the rough amount of time to devote to a particular practice – so don't worry if you're slightly out with your timings. It is better to spend more time on a practice and not rush things.

ACTIVITY

Find out how many staff you would need to lead a session of 20 participants for the following sports:

1 Climbing.
2 Trampolining.
3 Rugby.

Introduction/warm-up

After introducing the aims of the session, you must warm up the participants. Warming up serves the following purposes. To:

- prepare the person mentally for the physical effort to come;
- raise the pulse and respiratory rate and to get blood to the working muscles;
- raise the body temperature; and
- increase the mobility of joints and to stretch muscles ready for exercise.

There are two main stages to warming up:

1 *Cardiovascular work*, to increase the pulse and breathing rates. Jogging and skipping are commonly used for this. You should start slowly and then gradually speed up. An imaginative leader will introduce games (such as tag) to make the activity more enjoyable for the participants.

2 *Stretching exercises*, which must be carried out smoothly (see Figure 3.6). Normally you will work from head to toes, stretching each muscle group in turn and also mobilising the joints as you go. Each stretch is normally held for between 10 and 20 seconds.

Skills and technique development activities

These activities will take up the largest part of your session, and this is where the real coaching occurs. You will need to select appropriate practices or drills for your group's ability level. Other factors that need to be considered include the following:

- The number and size of the group (i.e. the smaller the group, the more people will get a chance to practise).
- The most effective use of space (i.e. using the space available in the most efficient way by marking out grids or areas).
- The sequence of activities (i.e. you would not introduce defender-to-passing practice in football until you were happy that the participants had mastered the basic technique).

a

b

c

d

Figure 3.6
Stretching exercises for the thighs: (a) Front of thigh lying; (b) front of thigh standing; (c) back of thigh lying; (d) back of thigh standing

During each practice you will need to analyse each individual's technique, stop the activity if necessary and demonstrate the correct procedure. Diagnosing what is wrong with an individual's technique is difficult but gets easier with experience.

ACTIVITY

There are four main types of pass in basketball:

1 The chest pass.
2 The bounce pass.
3 The overhead pass.
4 The javelin pass.

Using the chest pass as an example, the main technical points to look for in this pass are as follows:

1 The ball should be held in two hands with fingers spread apart.
2 The ball travels from chest to chest.
3 The arms are extended and the fingers point to the target after releasing the ball.
4 The player should try to step into the pass.
5 The pass should be flat and fast.

Working in groups of three, take it in turns to analyse each other's technique for the chest pass in basketball. Using the above guide, make a list of any faults you observe.

Setting up small-sided games, competitions and teams

Small-sided games can be used in a number of ways to develop the participants' skills and technique. For example, you could impose rules (such as a one-touch pass in football) that are designed to improve the skills the participants have already learnt. You will need to keep the numbers low so that all the players are involved for as much time as possible.

You will also need to adapt adult versions of certain games for children or for those with special needs. Consider, for example, the following:

- *Football*: You may need a smaller pitch, smaller goals, a smaller ball and to reduce the number of players.
- *Tennis*: You may need a smaller court, junior rackets and a reduced net height.

When dividing players into teams, be careful with the selection process you use. Allowing teams to self-select has disadvantages in that, inevitably, people will select their friends or those who are better at the sport, and therefore they will create an imbalance. Use a numbering system or combine groups from previous practices. This could be done in a humorous way. For example, get the participants to stand on a bench, and then get them to swap places without touching the floor until they are in alphabetical order of surname. This is an activity that causes much amusement, especially if it is performed against the clock!

Part of the appeal of sport is the competitive element and, therefore, a league or mini-tournament is always a good way to end a session. Dividing the group into small teams may seem like a good idea, but it will lead to long periods of inactivity for some participants. Therefore you should give careful thought to the number of groups and/or games to be played. Basically, there are three main types of format:

1   A league or 'round robin' tournament were everyone plays everyone else at least once.

2   A knockout competition where only teams that win each game move into the next stage of the competition.

3   A league or group stage where the top teams play off in further knock-out rounds.

> **ACTIVITY**
>
> How many games would you need to play in order for a winner to emerge from 32 teams in a knock-out competition?

The cool-down

The cool-down is similar to the warm-up you undertook at the start of the session. The body needs to cool down gradually in order to return to its normal state and to avoid the risk of injury. You should instruct the group to carry out a mixture of cardiovascular work and light stretching so that the muscles relax and the heart and breathing rates return to normal levels.

Session review

You should recap on the main objectives of the session and state how these have been achieved. You could take the opportunity to discuss what people liked or disliked about the session or to gain more detailed feedback on how the session went.

Structuring the session

You should now be in position to structure your session. The session should have a clear beginning, a middle and an end. Each stage should have its approximate time allocation. For example, a one-hour session for a football practice might be structured as shown in Table 3.5. A blank form for structuring a session is shown in Table 3.6.

STAGE	TIME (MINUTES)
Introduction Brief details of the aims of the session, e.g. by the end of the session you will be able to . . . Then a runthrough of the format for the session, e.g. warm-up followed by individual practices and then small side-games, and finally cool-down and review	2
Warm-up Cardiovascular warm-up activity Stretching and mobility exercises	6
Skills practice Brief description, e.g. practise in pairs basic passing technique over distance; introduce a defender to add to challenge/level of difficultly	10
Small-group practice Brief description, e.g. passing exercise based on grid with defenders in the centre and players outside passing across the grid	10
Game (whole or part group) Brief description, e.g. one-touch passing within small-sided game	15
Cool-down Cardiovascular cool-down activity Stretching and mobility exercises	6
Session review Recap on learning outcomes Were these achieved? Feedback from participants	5

Table 3.5 *A one-hour session for a football practice*

STAGE	TIME (MINUTES)
Introduction	
Warm-up	
Skills practice	
Small-group practice	
Game (whole or part group)	
Cool-down	
Session review	

Table 3.6 *Form for structuring a session*

QUESTION	YES/NO	EXAMPLES
Were the objectives of the session explained clearly to the participants?		
Did the objectives follow the SMART principle?		
Were the timings accurate?		
Was the plan flexible enough to deal with unforeseen circumstances?		
Did the session meet the participants' needs?		
Was there an end-of-session review and was this effective?		
Were the activities appropriately selected and delivered?		
Were health and safety measures followed?		
Were there warm-up and cool-down activities and were these appropriate?		
Was the student's communication effective?		

Table 3.7 *Observers' sheet: coaching*

QUESTION	HOW I COULD IMPROVE MY COACHING SKILLS IN THE LIGHT OF THESE COMMENTS?
Were the objectives of the session explained clearly to the participants?	
Did the objectives follow the SMART principle?	
Were the timings accurate?	
Was the plan flexible enough to deal with unforeseen circumstances?	
Did the session meet the participants' needs?	
Was there an end-of-session review and was this effective?	
Were the activities appropriately selected and delivered?	
Were health and safety measures followed?	
Were there warm-up and cool-down activities and were these appropriate?	
Was the student's communication effective?	

Table 3.8 *Comment form for observers' feedback on coaching skills*

ACTIVITY

For this assessment you must produce two plans for two separate coaching sessions you will then go on to deliver and evaluate. Each plan must include details of the following:

- The target group.
- The objectives for the session.
- The equipment required.
- Supervision requirements.
- The timing of the activities.
- Details of the warm-up/cool-down.
- Details of practices/activities.
- Details of small-side games.
- How the session will be reviewed.
- A list of safety considerations and a risk assessment.
- Details of emergency procedures.

For each session you will need to obtain feedback on your performance from your tutor or other observers. As you did for the officiating sessions earlier in this unit, you could use the observers' form given in Table 3.7 to collect this information. As you also did for your officiating sessions, you will need to analyse this feedback to see which areas of your performance require improvement. You could use the form given in Table 3.8 to do this.

3.5 Evaluate own performance as a sports leader and suggest improvements

This section covers

- Feedback
- Evaluation

Feedback

It is important to get feedback from the participants and other observers, such as teachers and coaches. The feedback you receive is invaluable in planning future sessions. You could ask the participants the following questions:

- What did you enjoy and/or dislike about the session?
- Did you find the session challenging?
- Did the session move along at the right pace?
- What skills did you develop through this session?

Other observers are likely to give valuable feedback on such aspects of your performance as communication skills, command and control of the group, the structure and effectiveness of practices and your ability to diagnose participants' shortcomings.

CASE STUDY

Session feedback

Rebecca has delivered a netball coaching session to a mixed group of male and female students, all of whom were aged over 16. At the end of the session she asked for feedback from the participants and gave them each a blank sheet of paper. They were asked to write down what they liked and what they disliked about the session.

CASE STUDY

Session feedback (Contd.)

Some of the comments made were as follows:

- 'Netball is boring. We should have been allowed to play football. This session was mainly for girls.'

- 'A well organised session. Good practices with many skills that could be transferred to other sports, and an entertaining match, although the lads messed about a bit too much.'

- 'I liked the match, but didn't see the point of the practices.'

- 'I could already do most of things that were being practised, but enjoyed the match.'

1 Rebecca is disappointed by both the quantity and quality of the feedback she has received from the other students. Discuss how you might obtain more detailed feedback from a coaching session.

2 From the limited feedback obtained, suggest two improvements Rebecca might make for future sessions.

Evaluation

Once you have obtained sufficient feedback, you can begin to evaluate your own performance. It is useful to break your evaluation down into the areas shown in Table 3.8. You could use the second column of this table to make notes about how you would improve the session the next time you run it.

You need to answer questions like these to see what improvements you could make the next time. The improvements you may need to make could include:

- changes to activities;
- changes to objectives;
- using different equipment or bringing in extra resources;
- using additional coaches;
- altering the timings; and
- a plan to increase your leadership skills.

AREA	COMMENTS
Planning Was the plan effective in meeting its objectives? Were the timings accurate? Did the plan allow for enough resources, e.g. equipment? Was the plan flexible enough?	
The group's needs Were the activities pitched at the right level for the participants' abilities? Did the participants understand the instructions given to them? Did the participants' technique improve as a result of the practices and advice you give them?	
Leadership skills Did you allow enough time to set up the equipment? Did you motivate the participants? Did you communicate effectively?	
Session feedback Did the participants enjoy the session? What did the participants dislike about the session? Did the participants feel that their technique improved as a result of the session? What did you learn from the feedback given by any observers?	

Table 3.9 *Evaluating a session*

TEST YOUR KNOWLEDGE

1. Give two reasons why a knowledge of the rules of a game is important to a sports leader.

2. What facility/area checks should be undertaken before you start a coaching session?

3. List the main items a first-aid box should contain.

4. Describe the main factors a risk assessment should take into account.

5. Explain three types of scoring systems that are used in sport, and give examples of each.

6. Describe the main components of a warm-up.

7. What are the main things you must take into consideration when you are deciding on the practice routines to include in a coaching session?

8. What is meant by the terms: (a) a 'round robin' tournament; and (b) a knock-out competition?

9. Describe in detail how two sports can be adapted for children.

10. What sort of feedback would a tutor or other outside observer give you after a sports session?

The Body in Action

Introduction

Sports leaders and coaches must understand how the human body works if they are to devise sessions that improve the participants' strength, suppleness and technique. In this unit you will learn about those aspects of the human body that have a direct impact on an athlete's performance: his or her muscles, skeleton and cardiovascular and respiratory systems. All these components of the human body affect how well athletes move, exercise and recover after taking part in sport.

How well we exercise and perform, however, is influenced by other factors apart from our physical make-up. An athlete needs to be motivated, to have confidence and to concentrate. It is a sports leader's or coach's job to encourage all these traits in the sportsmen and women he or she trains.

How you will be assessed

This unit is assessed by an assignment drawn up and marked by your school or college.

In this unit you will learn how to:

① Describe how an appreciation of the human body systems can assist in an understanding of the body in action

② Outline the structure and function of the musculoskeletal system and its role in producing movements in sport and exercise

③ Outline the structure and function of the cardiovascular and respiratory systems and their role during exercise

④ Investigate and illustrate the short-term and long-term effects of exercise on body systems

⑤ Describe a range of psychological factors that affect a performer before and during sporting activity, and outline how these factors may influence performance

4.1 Describe how an appreciation of the human body systems can assist in an understanding of the body in action

There are three systems in your body that work together to provide the fuel, energy and force we all need if we are to move and exercise:

- The respiratory system.
- The cardiovascular system.
- The musculoskeletal system.

Each of these systems works with one or both of the other systems to burn fuel (using oxygen – your respiratory system), to distribute it around your body (via blood – your cardiovascular system) and to use that fuel to produce movement (via your musculoskeletal system).

Your respiratory system consists of your mouth, nose, trachea and lungs; your cardiovascular system of your heart, arteries, veins and capillaries; and your musculoskeletal system of your muscles, tendons, ligaments and bones.

It is important to understand that these systems work together in an integrated way to promote good health. For example, if you cannot breathe in and out properly (i.e. your respiratory system is not working well), then there is less oxygen for your muscular system, and so your ability to exercise will be reduced. Similarly, if your circulation is sluggish, waste products cannot be removed from your muscles, and so you could develop such conditions as cramp and delayed onset muscle soreness (DOMS).

Another example of the systems working together is that of a tennis player. During a match the muscles must repeatedly contract in order to move the limbs through their actions on the skeleton. They therefore have to be constantly supplied with oxygen contained in the blood via the circulatory system and this oxygen is taken in by the lungs. So that the player's body can function at a high level it needs more oxygen and so the respiratory rate increases (the player breathes in and out more) and the circulation increases (the heart beats faster and stronger). This increase in oxygen supply means that the muscles can contract more often and faster and so the player can move more quickly around the court.

DID YOU KNOW?

The average human body contains enough iron to make a three-inch nail, enough sulphur to kill all the fleas on an average dog, enough carbon to make 900 pencils, enough potassium to fire a toy cannon, enough fat to make seven bars of soap, enough phosphorus to make 2,200 match heads and enough water to fill a ten-gallon tank.

CASE STUDY

Promoting good health

John is 45 years old. He works in an office, smokes five cigarettes a day and does no exercise. About six months ago, he started to feel breathless when climbing stairs, and his legs were aching after he had walked more than about 500 metres. When he went to see his doctor, his doctor told him that he was 10 kilograms overweight, had slightly high blood pressure and that his respiratory function was poor. He advised John to stop smoking, to diet and to take some regular exercise.

John cut down his food intake by about 500 calories per day and started to walk for 30 minutes every day. He also stopped smoking over a period of two weeks.

After four months his weight had decreased by 15 kilograms and he could now climb stairs without getting out of breath. He also felt more alert during his working day and had more energy at home. His blood pressure had also returned to normal and his legs had stopped aching.

1 Why do you think John's legs were aching?
2 What effect would stopping smoking have on his respiratory function?
3 Why has his blood pressure returned to normal?

4.2 Outline the structure and function of the musculoskeletal system and its role in producing movements in sport and exercise

This section covers

- The skeletal system
- The muscular system

Your musculoskeletal system, as its name suggests, is made up of your skeleton and muscles, and each has a different part to play in making your body move.

The skeletal system

Your skeleton has various functions:

- *Support*: Your skeleton supports both your muscles and your organs. It is your skeleton that gives your body its shape.
- *Movement*: Bones provide the attachments for your muscles. They work as levers to create actions, such as walking, running or jumping, etc.
- *Protection*: The bones in your protect your body's vital organs. For example, your brain is protected from injury by your skull.
- *Blood formation*: Your long bones, such as the femur (thighbone), contain marrow. Blood cells are manufactured in marrow before they are passed into your veins and arteries.

The structure of the skeleton

There are usually 206 bones in the adult human body. These belong either to the axial or the appendicular skeleton (see Figure 4.1).

Axial skeleton:
- The cranium (skull) – 29 bones.
- Vertebral column (spine) – 26 bones.
- Thorax (ribs and sternum) – 25 bones.

Appendicular skeleton:
- Pectoral girdle (the scapula (shoulder blade), etc.) – 4 bones.
- Upper limbs – 60 bones.

- Pelvic girdle (hips and pelvis) – 2 bones.
- Lower limbs – 60 bones.

DID YOU KNOW?

- Babies are born with 300 bones, but by adulthood we have only 206 in our bodies.
- Your feet account for one quarter of all your body's bones.
- The only bone in the human body not connected to another is the hyoid, a V-shaped bone located at the base of your tongue between the mandible and voice box. Its function is to support your tongue and its muscles.

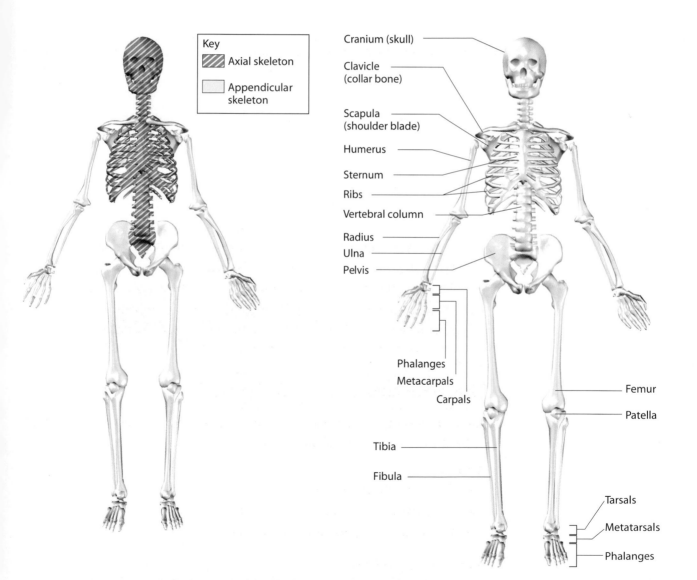

Key
- Axial skeleton
- Appendicular skeleton

Cranium (skull)
Clavicle (collar bone)
Scapula (shoulder blade)
Humerus
Sternum
Ribs
Vertebral column
Radius
Ulna
Pelvis
Phalanges
Metacarpals
Carpals
Femur
Patella
Tibia
Fibula
Tarsals
Metatarsals
Phalanges

Figure 4.1 *The human skeleton*

The axial skeleton is your body's core since virtually all movement takes place around it: it provides a stable base for the rest of your body. Your appendicular skeleton consists mainly of your limbs, and this is where movement actually occurs. For example, imagine a footballer taking a penalty (see Figure 4.2). He has to:

1   balance on one foot; and

2   kick the ball with the other foot.

His axial skeleton allows him to balance whilst the levers in his appendicular skeleton allow him to kick the ball and, hopefully, score the penalty.

Types of bone

There are different types of bone (see Table 4.1), and these are usually classified according to their shape:

- long
- short
- flat
- irregular.

Bone tissue is made up of *compact* bone and *cancellous* (or spongy) bone.

Compact bone

Compact bone comprises units of cells called osteons, and these osteons are in turn contained within a sheet or layer called a lamella (see Figure 4.3). Each

Figure 4.2 *Taking a penalty kick*

TYPES OF BONE	EXAMPLE FOUND IN THE BODY	EXAMPLE OF FUNCTION
Long bones	Femur Humerus	Large movements: long bones act as levers within the body to move large joints such as the knee and elbow Cell production: long bones produce blood cells in the marrow, a jelly-like substance in the centre of bones
Short bones	Carpals Metatarsals	Small movements: short bones act as levers within the body to move small joints such as those in the fingers
Flat (or plate) bones	Pelvic girdle Cranium	Protection: flat bones of the skull join to provide a hard shell to cover and protect the brain Attachment of muscle: flat bones in the pelvis provide points of attachment for the large thigh muscles of the legs
Irregular bones	Vertebrae	Support: irregular bones of the spine form the spinal column which supports the body Protection: the spinal column also provides a protective tube around the spinal cord

Table 4.1 *Types of bone in the human skeleton*

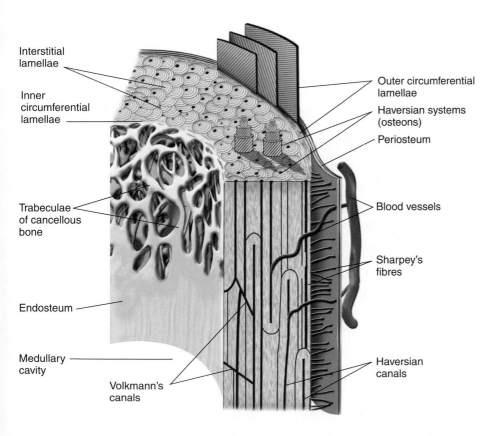

Figure 4.3 *The structure of a long bone*

osteon also has a central canal (known as the Haversian system) and canals that link one osteon with another (Volkmann's canals). These bone canals contain blood vessels, lymph vessels and nerves.

Cancellous bone

Cancellous bone is found in the inner layers of your long bones. The spaces within cancellous bone are filled with bone marrow, as is the cavity at the centre of the bone itself. Cancellous bone is made up of trabeculae. It is less dense than compact bone but it is also less brittle, which is why it is also called spongy bone. On impact, cancellous bone will bend rather than break.

The structure of bones

Your bones are surrounded on the outside and the inside by connective tissue – the outside layer is called the periosteum and the inside layer the endosteum. The periosteum is made up of two layers: a fibrous (outer) and an osteogenic (inner) layer (see Figure 4.3). These are attached to your bones by fibres (Sharpey's fibres). The endosteum surrounds the medullary cavity – the large cylindrical channel that runs the length of your bones.

Both layers of tissue (the endosteum and the inner layer of the periosteum) contain cells called osteogenic cells. These are also known as stem cells, and it is in these cells that two other types of cell are made:

1   osteoblasts, which make new bone; and
2   osteocytes, which help to maintain bone density.

Your bones also contain cells called osteoclasts. These cells dissolve bone. Together, these three different types of cell enable your body to replace its bones throughout the course of your life – a process known as remodelling.

Remodelling is important because it:

- removes old bone and replaces it with new bone, thus getting rid of damaged bone;
- extracts the calcium from your old bones that your body can use elsewhere; and
- keeps your bones in good working order.

Bone is remodelled by teams of about 10 osteoclasts and several hundred osteoblasts that work together in basic multicellular units (BMUs). In a normal, healthy person, these BMUs replace about 5 per cent of compact bone and 25 per cent of cancellous bone each year. Remodelling is also the way bones heal following a fracture – a process that takes about four months.

Bone starts out as cartilage, a more flexible tissue than bone. However, as your body grows, some of this cartilage is turned into bone – a process known as ossification. Ossification begins in the womb and continues until about the age of 25 years. When this process is complete, your body is harder, firmer and more resilient to physical stress than it was when you were younger.

Joints

You saw in the last section that bone itself is inflexible. The movement you observe when you bend your arms or kick with your feet occurs as a result of one bone moving in relation to another bone. Your bones, therefore, are joined together but not necessarily joined rigidly: some joints (the sites where two or more bones come together) are flexible to permit the movement of one bone in relation to another. There are two main types of joint: fibrous and cartilaginous.

Fibrous joints

Fibrous joints are joints where little or no movement is possible, for example the suture joints of the skull. There are three types of fibrous joints:

1 *Sutures*: Some flat bones are fused together to form a rigid structure. The joints where these bones are linked are called sutures. Sutures are found throughout the body but mainly in the skull. No movement is possible in these joints as this would weaken the structure.

2 *Syndesmosis*: This is a joint held together by ligaments, and some movement is possible here. These joints are found in the wrist and ankle.

3 *Gomphosis*: A gomphosis is a rigid joint formed where one bone is inserted into another and fixed into place by a 'peg'. The best example is your teeth. Your teeth are secured into your jaw by 'pegs' (their roots).

Cartilaginous joints

Cartilaginous joints are flexible, and they are usually protected by a surrounding layer of fluid (synovial fluid) which lubricates the joints to keep them supple (see Figure 4.4). Cartilaginous joints are classified as:

* gliding;
* hinge;
* pivot;

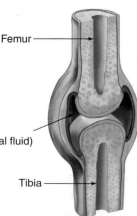

Femur

Joint cavity (contains synovial fluid)

Tibia

Figure 4.4
A simplified cartilaginous joint: the knee joint

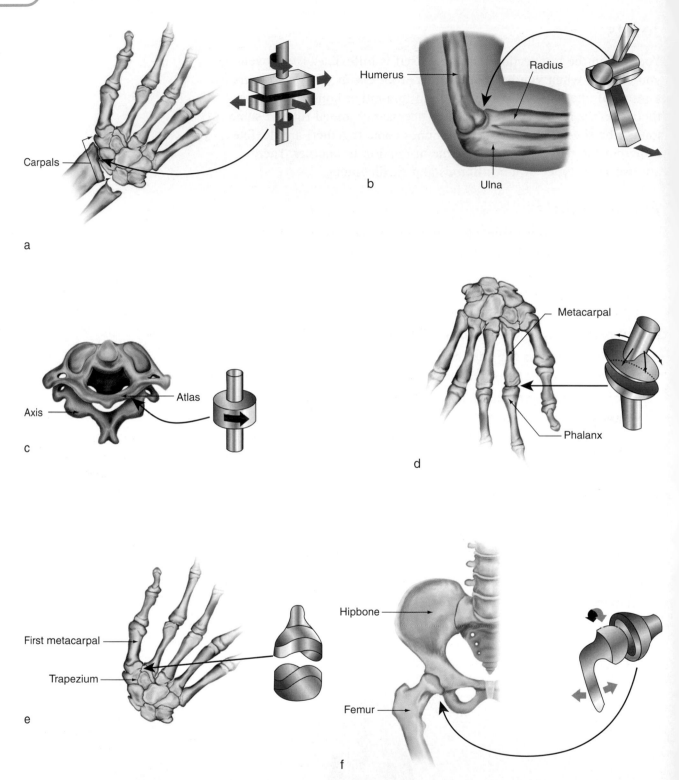

Figure 4.5 *Cartilaginous joint movements: (a) gliding (the wrist); (b) hinge (the elbow); (c) pivot (the neck); (d) condyloid (the fingers); (e) saddle (the thumb); (f) ball and socket (the hip)*

- condyloid;
- saddle; and
- ball and socket.

These joints are capable of the following movements:

- Gliding joints rotate and twist (e.g. the wrist joint).
- Hinge joints bend and straighten (e.g. the elbow). Anatomically, this is called flexion (bending) and extension (straightening).
- Pivot joints rotate (e.g. the atlas bone on the axis bone in the neck).
- Condyloid joints glide and twist (e.g. the finger joints).
- Saddle joints glide, twist and rotate (e.g. the thumb joint).
- Ball-and-socket joints bend, straighten, rotate and move sideways (e.g. the hip joint). These joints can therefore flex and extend, abduct (move away from the body sideways), adduct (move towards the body sideways) and circumduct (rotate in a circle)

Figure 4.5 (opposite) illustrates these movements.

ACTIVITY

Look at the joints in the arms and legs of your fellow students. How many movements are there at each joint? Try to classify as many joints as you can according to the list given in this section.

Joints rarely work on their own. For example, when you kick a ball, your hip, knee and ankle joints all move so that you can stay upright and, at the same time, kick (see Figure 4.6). The sequence of movement is as follows:

1 Your hip flexes so that your knee can also flex to bend your lower leg backwards.
2 Your toes plantarflex.
3 Your knee extends (straightens).
4 Your ankle dorsiflexes.

ACTIVITY

Using the example of kicking given above, look at someone throwing a ball. Now describe the movements of the shoulder, elbow and wrist.

GLOSSARY

Abduction: movement away from the body.

Adduction: movement towards the body.

Circumduction: circular movement.

Extension: the angle between two or more bones increasing, which results in a straightening movement.

Flexion: the angle between two or more bones decreasing, which results in a bending movement.

Dorsiflexion: the turning upwards (towards the head) of the foot or toes or of the hands or fingers.

Plantarflexion: the turning downwards (away from the head) of the foot or toes.

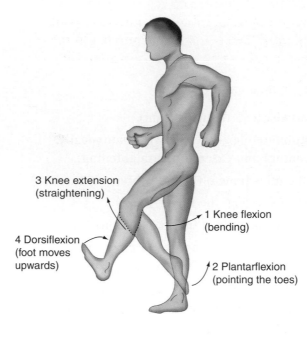

Figure 4.6 *The movements involved in kicking*

The muscular system

It is your muscles that permit movement in your body. They are connected with your bones, cartilages, ligaments and skin either directly or through fibrous structures called tendons. They work by shortening: when they contract, they pull on your bones, thus creating movement about your joints.

There are three types of muscle: cardiac, smooth and skeletal:

1 *Cardiac* muscle is found in the heart only and it contracts spontaneously (i.e. without any stimulus from the nervous system).

2 *Smooth* muscle is sometimes called involuntary muscle. It is found in such organs as the bladder. Smooth muscle contracts automatically – you have no conscious control of it.

3 *Voluntary* (or *skeletal*) muscle is the muscle that produces movements you usually have some control over (for example, the muscles in your leg). It is this type of muscle that we are mainly going to consider in this section.

Muscle structure

A muscle comprises bundles of fibres known as fascicles (see Figure 4.7). The fibres in each fascicle are themselves made up of minute filaments called fibrils. A fibril is a multi-nucleate cell that is usually cylindrical in shape, and it runs the whole length of the muscle.

Each fibril is divided into yet smaller units called sarcomeres. It is the sarcomeres in your muscles that contract to produce movement.

Muscle fibre bundles (fascicles) are surrounded by a connective tissue called the perimysium (see Figure 4.7). This tissue is connected to the tendons at each end of the muscle. The entire muscle is surrounded by a sheath called the epimysium.

DID YOU KNOW?

- Muscles can only shorten – they cannot lengthen.
- Muscles only contract when stimulated by nerve impulses.
- Muscles are generally always in a state of tension – that is, they are rarely relaxed.

Your voluntary muscles vary in shape and function, and each has evolved to perform a particular job. However, no matter what their shape, all voluntary muscles contain the same types of fibres, as outlined above. These fibres can be further classified as follows:

- Type 1: slow-twitch fibres (aerobic).
- Type 2: fast-twitch fibres (anaerobic). These fibres are further divided into Type 2a and Types 2b fibres.

About 53 per cent of muscle is made of slow-twitch fibres, the rest being either Type 2a (34 per cent) or Type 2b (13 per cent). Only Type

GLOSSARY

Aerobic: a process or chemical reaction that takes place in the presence of oxygen.

Anaerobic: a process or chemical reaction that takes place in the absence of oxygen.

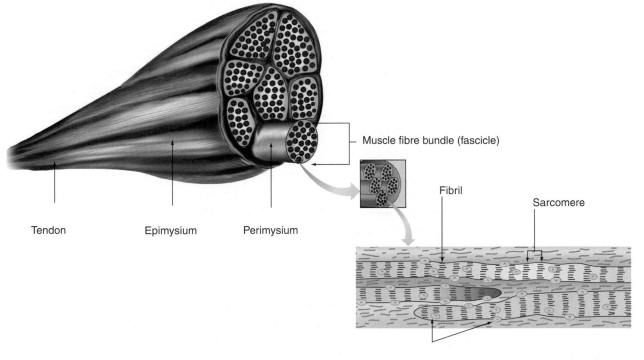

Tendon   Epimysium   Perimysium

Muscle fibre bundle (fascicle)

Fibril   Sarcomere

Nuclei

Figure 4.7 *The structure of a muscle*

2a fibres are trainable and can be developed with exercise, but some Type 2b fibres can be converted to Type 2a, depending on the demands a particular sport places on the muscle fibres.

ACTIVITY

Find out how many differently shaped muscles there are in your body and where they are located. Discuss in small groups why you think they are the shapes they are.

How do voluntary muscles work?

When there is a need for one of your muscle to contract, your brain sends an impulse down your spinal cord and via your nerve cells to the muscle in question. The impulse passes through the muscle fibres, causing them to secrete calcium ions. It is these calcium ions that initiate muscle contraction.

As mentioned above, muscles work by contracting (they *pull* – they do not push). As you also saw above, it is the sarcomeres in each muscle fibre that perform this job of contracting. A sarcomere has a striped appearance because it is composed of two types of protein filament: thick filaments of myosin and thin filaments of actin. It is these filaments that work together to create muscular contraction.

The calcium ions formed when the impulse passes through your nerve cell cause the myosin filaments to slide over the actin filaments, rather as the sections of a collapsible telescope slide one over the other. When thousands of filaments slide past each other in a single muscle cell, and thousands of muscle cells contract together, your muscle finally produces the required contraction. Once this process starts, all the fibres in the muscle contract to their maximum extent, resulting in a muscle twitch that lasts a fraction of a second.

The strength of a muscle contraction can be controlled in one of two ways. By:

1   the number of muscle fibres that are stimulated to contract at any one time; and
2   the frequency with which a number of muscle fibres are stimulated to contract.

Muscles work in pairs to create a movement. When one muscle contracts (known as the agonist muscle), another muscle (the antagonist) must relax for the movement to occur. Figure 4.8 shows the bicep curl. As the biceps (the agonist muscle) contracts to lift the forearm, the triceps (the antagonist muscle) relaxes, thus permitting the movement of the forearm upwards. This process is called reciprocal innervation.

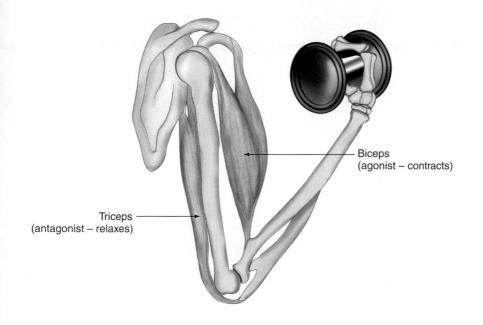

Biceps
(agonist – contracts)

Triceps
(antagonist – relaxes)

Figure 4.8 *The bicep curl*

DID YOU KNOW?

- Your body has over 600 muscles, which comprise 40 per cent of your body's weight.
- The longest muscle in your body is the sartorius. This narrow thigh muscle runs across the front of your thigh. It helps rotate your leg so that you can sit in a cross-legged position. Its name comes from the word 'sartorial', the cross-legged position tailors (or 'sartors') once assumed when working.
- Your jaw muscles can provide about 90 kilograms of force. This force is used to bring your back teeth together for chewing.

ACTIVITY

Explain the structure and function of the musculoskeletal system.

4.3 Outline the structure and function of the cardiovascular and respiratory systems and their role during exercise

This section covers
- The cardiovascular system
- The respiratory system

The cardiovascular system

The cardiovascular system is also known as the circulatory system. It consists of:

- the heart
- the arteries
- the arterioles
- the veins
- the venules; and
- the capillaries.

The heart

Your heart lies between your lungs and is basically a pump, although probably one of the most efficient pumps known. This pump works from before you are born until the moment you die, and it is so powerful that if the main artery, the aorta, were cut, a stream of blood two metres high would be released. The main role of your heart in the cardiovascular system is to ensure that your blood circulates and reaches every part of your body.

As you saw in Unit 2, everyone has a maximum heart rate, and this is calculated according to the formula: maximum heart rate (MHR) = 220 minus your age. It is important you establish your MHR as, during exercise, your heart rate is a good measure of both your fitness and your aerobic capacity.

Structure

Your heart is composed of four chambers (see Figure 4.9):

1 the right atrium;
2 the right ventricle;

> **GLOSSARY**
>
> **Aerobic capacity:** the amount of oxygen you can use per minute.

DID YOU KNOW?

- There are 60,000 miles of blood vessels in your body.
- In an average lifetime, the heart beats more than two and a half billion times.
- Your pulse per minute changes as you age. At 3 months it is 130 beats per minute (bpm). For adults it is 60–100 bpm.
- The average heartbeat is 72 beats per minute. In one day your heart beats over 100,000 times.
- On average, your heart pumps 7,200 litres of blood every day, which is almost 184,086,000 litres by the time you have reached 70 years of age.
- An average heart pumps 5 litres of blood every minute.

3   the left atrium; and

4   the left ventricle.

The right side of your heart is completely separate from the left side. The division between the two sides is called the septum.

The atria have thin walls and the ventricles have thick walls. The walls of the left ventricle are also thicker than the right, because this chamber

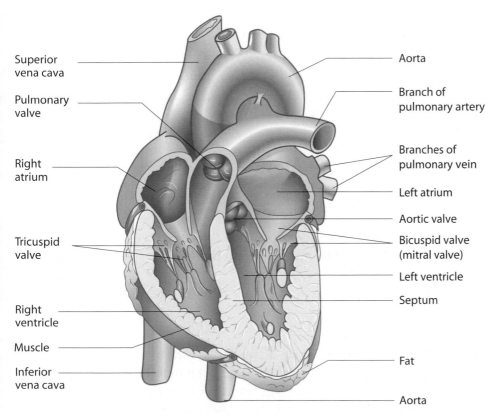

Superior vena cava

Pulmonary valve

Right atrium

Tricuspid valve

Right ventricle

Muscle

Inferior vena cava

Aorta

Branch of pulmonary artery

Branches of pulmonary vein

Left atrium

Aortic valve

Bicuspid valve (mitral valve)

Left ventricle

Septum

Fat

Aorta

Figure 4.9
A cross-section of the heart

pumps blood to your whole body. To make sure that blood flows through your heart in the correct direction, there are four valves:

1 the tricuspid valve;
2 the mitral valve;
3 the pulmonary valve; and
4 the aortic valve.

Each of these valves consists of two or three small flaps of tissue, called cusps. To stop the valves from turning inside out, cords connect the valves with the ventricle walls.

Your heartbeat is caused by the alternate contraction and relaxation of the muscular walls of the ventricles. As your heart beats, it makes a *lub-dub* sound as the valves open and close. There are two phases to each heartbeat:

1 *Systole*: This is where the muscles of your heart are contracting, or your heart is 'squeezing' itself.
2 *Diastole*: This is where the muscles of your heart are relaxing, or your heart is 'refilling' itself.

> ### GLOSSARY
>
> **Stroke volume (SV):** the volume of blood pumped out by a single contraction of the ventricles (typically 75 cm^3 by each ventricle when your body is at rest).

The sequence of events that occurs during the filling and emptying (systole and diastole together) of your heart is known as the cardiac cycle and, at 70 beats per minutes (bpm), the complete cycle takes about 0.86 seconds.

Cardiac output is the amount of blood pumped into the arteries by the contraction of the ventricles in a given time. It is calculated by multiplying your stroke volume by your heart rate per minute.

Because the right and left sides of your heart are separate, your heart is actually a double pump, and so there are two types of circulation in your body.

The pulmonary circulation

Blood flow between your heart and lungs is known as the pulmonary circulation. This operates at a lower pressure than the main circulation. Blood flows from the right ventricle, through the pulmonary arteries into your lungs, and then through the pulmonary veins into the left atrium.

The systemic circulation

Systemic circulation is the name given to the flow of blood around your body. Bloods flows out of the left ventricle, through the arteries and to the capillaries in all parts of your body, and then back through the veins to the right atrium.

How your heart works

Although the sides of your heart are separate, they work together. The right side of your heart pumps deoxygenated blood to your lungs where it collects oxygen (pulmonary circulation) whilst, at the same time, the left side pumps oxygenated blood from your lungs to other parts of your body (systemic circulation), where oxygen is released.

Once blood leaves your heart, it moves through a network of blood vessels around your body, starting with the arteries. The arteries close to your heart have thick walls to cope with the high pressure of the blood. They are elastic so that they stretch when blood is pumped through them, and then they recoil when your heart relaxes (this rhythm is the pulse).

These large arteries then branch into smaller arterioles, which lie further from your heart. Arterioles penetrate all tissues of your body and connect to beds of finely branching capillaries. Capillaries have the smallest diameter of all blood vessels (0.007 mm – the same as red blood cells). Capillary walls are just one cell thick, which helps the diffusion of oxygen into surrounding tissues. There are so many capillaries in your body that they cannot be supplied with blood at the same time. For this reason, blood is shunted to different parts of your body according to your body's needs.

From the capillary beds, venules join together to form veins, which return blood to your heart. There are more veins than arteries, and veins are generally wider than arteries. To prevent the back flow of blood as a result of gravity, the veins in your legs have one-way valves. The muscles surrounding the veins squeeze blood through the veins as they contract, so helping the return of blood to your heart. This is known as your body's muscle pump.

The coronary arteries run through your heart itself, which they supply with oxygenated blood. When these arteries are narrowed by disease, less blood is able to get through to them to supply the heart muscle with oxygen. This can cause angina or a heart attack.

> ## GLOSSARY
>
> **Angina:** a temporary shortage of oxygen supply (due to exercise, emotion, etc.) to the heart muscle causing no long-term damage.
>
> **Heart attack:** a coronary artery becomes blocked so that part of the heart muscle has no blood supply and so eventually dies. Usually, only a small part of the heart is affected.

> ## DID YOU KNOW?
>
> - A woman's heart beats faster than a man's.
> - An individual blood cell takes about 60 seconds to make a complete circuit of the body.
> - Each square centimetre of your skin contains two metres of blood vessels.

The effects of exercise on the cardiovascular system

As you get older, your cardiovascular system becomes less efficient. Although your resting heart rate (HR) and stroke volume (SV) do not change greatly with age, your maximum heart rate and therefore your exercise heart rate reduces by 5–10 beats per decade. Your exercise stroke volume remains the same but, because cardiac output = heart rate multiplied by stroke volume, your exercise heart rate decreases as you get older. In addition, your blood vessels (arteries, veins, etc.) cannot expand as much and so there is a greater resistance to the blood flowing through your body.

As a result of all these changes, less oxygen is delivered to the tissues so that your muscles can do less work. If you take regular exercise, however, these effects can be lessened, as regular exercise helps to maintain the health of the cardiovascular system.

In the short term, exercise increases cardiac output by increasing both your heart rate and stroke volume. As much as five times more blood can be pumped around your body in this way than when your body is at rest. Venous return (that is, deoxygenated blood returning to your heart) is also improved because of increased muscle pump action (particularly in your legs). Blood is also diverted from your organs, such as your stomach, to your muscles and skin. As much as 71 per cent of the blood in your body can be shunted to your muscles in this way.

The long-term benefits of exercise include the following:

- Decreased cardiovascular disease. Inactive people are twice as likely as active people to develop coronary artery disease and/or high blood pressure.
- Decreased cholesterol levels. This also helps to guard against heart disease.
- Decreased body fat.
- Decreased risk of certain types of cancer (e.g. colon and breast cancer).
- Reduced time off work by around 30 per cent.
- Increased life expectancy.
- Improved mental health.

The respiratory system

Your respiratory system consists of your lungs and air tubes, and its main function is to take in air and 'process' it. It works alongside your cardiovascular system. The two systems, therefore, are sometimes known collectively as your cardio-respiratory system.

The breathing section of the respiratory system is a complex arrangement of airways, each section of which has a particular function (see Figure 4.10). Your mouth and nose take in air. This air passes down your pharynx, past your epiglottis (a flap that acts like a trapdoor to prevent air from entering your stomach and food entering your lungs).

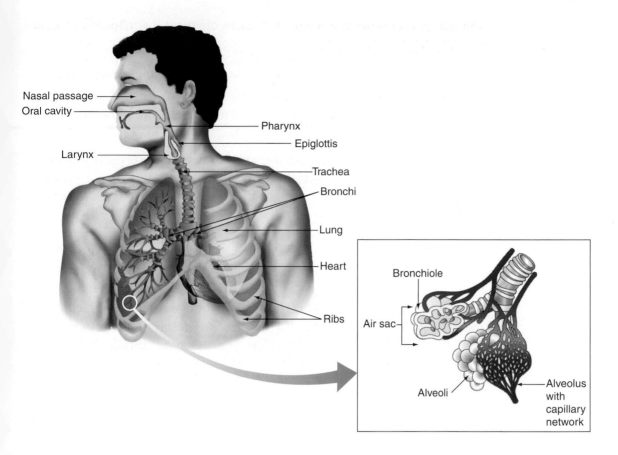

Figure 4.10 *The respiratory system*

The air then flows past your larynx (or voice box) and passes into your trachea, which is a tube 12 cm long surrounded by rings of cartilage The air now flows along each bronchus (one to each lung) and the narrower bronchioles into the air sacs. Each air sac is made up of pouches called alveoli (each one is an alveolus).

Your lungs have a large surface area (almost 85 m^2), which is made up of the surfaces of the alveoli. The walls of each alveolus are very thin (two layers of cells) so that oxygen can pass very easily between the alveolus and the capillary running next to it.

Air passes from your lungs into your bloodstream by a process known as diffusion. As oxygen enters your bloodstream in your lungs, carbon dioxide passes out of your blood to be exhaled in your breath. Blood is then transported around your body by your circulatory system. When the blood arrives at the individual cells, oxygen leaves the blood to be replaced by carbon dioxide. The cells use this oxygen to break down foods, etc., and to create energy to use, for example, during aerobic exercise.

GLOSSARY

Haemoglobin: the molecules in your blood cells that transport oxygen round your body.

This process is known as respiration, which comprises the following processes:

● Breathing – air moves in and out of your lungs.
● Oxygen from the air moves from the lungs into the blood stream, while carbon dioxide moves the other way.
● The oxygen is then carried in blood to the cells of the body.
● When cells need oxygen they take it out of the blood.
● The oxygen is then used by the cells to release energy – a process known as 'cellular respiration'.

ACTIVITY

Explain the structure and function of the cardiovascular system and the respiratory system.

How do you breathe?

You breathe by a combination of movement of your thorax (your chest) and your diaphragm (the muscle that separates your thorax from your abdomen – i.e. your belly) (see Figure 4.11). Occasionally, breathing involves moving your abdomen (see below). As your diaphragm contracts, the muscles between your ribs (the intercostal muscles) pull your rib cage up and out, and thus air is sucked into your lungs (inspiration).

When you breathe out (expiration), your diaphragm relaxes, doming up as it does so, and your rib cage moves down and in.

Although breathing usually uses both your intercostal muscles and your diaphragm muscle, the amount each muscle is used depends on your demand for air. For example:

● Thoracic breathing uses the intercostal muscles – your chest can be seen to rise and fall.
● Abdominal breathing uses your diaphragm – your abdomen moves in and out.
● Quiet breathing is mainly abdominal, with most of the work being done by your diaphragm muscle.

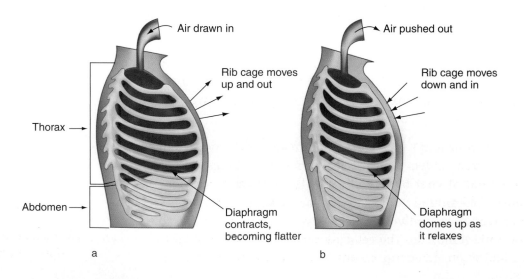

Figure 4.11 *Breathing: (a) Inspiration; (b) expiration*

DID YOU KNOW?

- The surface area of your lungs is about the same size as a tennis court.
- The normal respiration rate at rest for adults is 15–20 breaths per minute.
- You only exchange about one third of the oxygen you breathe in – so that about 13 per cent of the air you breathe out is oxygen. Because of this, if you were locked in a completely sealed room, you would die of carbon dioxide poisoning before you would die of oxygen deprivation.
- It is the increased level of carbon dioxide in your lungs that makes you breathe out, not the lower level of oxygen.
- Male athletes have about 4 per cent more lung capacity than non-athletes, and female athletes have 7 per cent more.

4.4 Investigate and illustrate the short-term and long-term effects of exercise on body systems

This section covers
- Anaerobic energy systems
- Aerobic energy system
- Other sources of energy
- The short-term effects of exercise on your body
- The long-term effects of exercise on your body

Your body needs a constant supply of energy during exercise, and this is obtained from the food you eat. Energy is your capacity or ability to work and is measured in joules or calories. In your body, energy is provided by a compound called ATP. Your body makes this compound from the food you eat (i.e. carbohydrates, fats and proteins).

GLOSSARY

ATP: adenosine triphosphate.

ATP is made up of one adenosine molecule and three phosphate groups. When this breaks down through a chemical reaction then energy is released within the cells, but each cell contains only a fixed amount of ATP. ATP, therefore, must be continually reformed so that the body has a constant supply of energy. This reformation can happen either aerobically or anaerobically, depending on how quickly you need the energy.

Figure 4.12
The release of energy from ATP

....
GLOSSARY
....

Calorie: the amount of energy needed to raise the temperature of 1 gram of water by 1° centigrade. A kilocalorie (Kcal) is 1,000 calories. When we talk about food calories, we actually mean kilocalories.

One Kcal = 4.2 kilo-joules: the joule is the standard scientific unit of energy.

There are three methods of ATP production. Via:

1 The phosphocreatine (ATP/PC) system (sometimes called the alactic system).
2 The lactic acid system (anaerobic glycolysis).
3 Aerobic respiration within the cell.

The ATP/PC and lactic acid systems are anaerobic, whilst aerobic respiration requires oxygen. It is important to realise that all three systems usually function at the same time but that one system will dominate according to the activity you are doing.

Anaerobic energy systems

The phosphocreatine or alactic system

Phosphocreatine (PC) is a high-energy compound found in your muscles. When an enzyme also present in the muscles breaks this substance down to a phosphate and creatine, energy is released. This energy is, in turn, used to reform ATP.

This sequence of reactions occurs in an instant, and there is enough PC in your body to provide it with about 10 seconds worth of energy. The process produces no waste products and is the only way of producing fast, explosive energy such as that needed for sprinting or jumping (see Figure 4.13).

Anaerobic glycolysis (lactic acid system)

The second method of anaerobic energy production is anaerobic glycolysis. The carbohydrates your body consumes as part of your diet are broken down by the digestive system into glucose. This is

Figure 4.13 *Jumping requires the fast, explosive energy produced by PC*

transported by the bloodstream to your muscles and liver where it is stored as glycogen.

When needed, glycogen is broken down into glucose. This glucose is, in turn, broken down by another enzyme and, in the process, energy is released, which is used to reform ATP. A by-product of this energy-releasing mechanism is lactic acid (hence the alternative name for this system of producing energy). For each molecule of ATP produced by the phosphocreatine system, two are produced by the breakdown of glucose in anaerobic glycolysis.

This system provides energy for up to about 50 seconds and so comes into play in such events as the 400-metre sprint.

Aerobic energy system

The aerobic system uses oxygen to break down glucose and release energy. This is done in several stages within the mitochondria of the cells and each of these creates ATP.

This system is much more efficient than the anaerobic systems and also longer-lasting. In theory the aerobic system can produce energy indefinitely as long as oxygen and glucose (from food) is available to it. This is the system mainly used by endurance athletes such as marathon runners and long-distance cyclists.

GLOSSARY

Mitochondria: small structures within a cell where ATP is produced through aerobic respiration.

ACTIVITY

Identify three sporting activities where the alactic system of energy production would play a major role and three where anaerobic glycolysis would be important.

GLOSSARY

Molecule: a group of atoms joined together chemically.

Aerobic glycolysis

Aerobic glycolysis is the process whereby glucose is broken down to produce two molecules of ATP, which can be used as energy for muscular contraction. This process takes place in the mitochondria of the muscle cells and can only happen in the presence of oxygen.

ACTIVITY

Think of three sports that mainly involve the use of aerobic respiration to provide the athletes with the energy they need.

Other sources of energy

Fats and proteins can also be used by the body as fuels, but this tends to happen only when reserves of glycogen (stored glucose) are low. Fat is stored in the form of triglycerides, and when these substances are broken down a great deal of energy is released (about twice as much as is released from glycogen). You need, however, about 15 per cent more oxygen to break down triglycerides compared to glycogen, so glycogen is always used first.

Protein is only used as a fuel when the body has no stores of either glycogen or triglycerides (i.e. when you are starving or exhausted), and so is used as a last resort. One protein molecule yields about the same amount of energy as one glycogen molecule.

DID YOU KNOW?

- In a lifetime, the average US resident eats more than 50 tonnes of food and drinks more than 60,000 litres of liquid.
- Every time you lick a stamp, you're consuming one tenth of a calorie.
- Women burn fat more slowly than men, by a rate of about 50 calories a day.

The short-term effects of exercise on your body

To provide the extra oxygen needed for aerobic respiration, your cardiovascular system has to work harder to:

- take in more oxygen;
- transport the extra oxygen around your body; and
- take waste products, such as lactic acid and carbon dioxide, away from your muscles.

Your body does this by increasing your heart rate, respiration rate and cardiac output.

Heart rate

You learnt earlier in this unit that your maximum heart rate (MHR) is calculated using the formula: MHR = 220 minus your age. When you are exercising, your body uses aerobic respiration until your MHR reaches 80 per cent of its maximum, after which your body relies on anaerobic respiration. This point is called your aerobic threshold.

Respiration rate

To supply your body with extra oxygen, your lungs expand and thus take in more air. Your breathing rate (the speed at which you breathe in and out) also increases, enabling you to take in around five times more oxygen than normal (and expel five times more carbon dioxide).

Cardiac output

Your cardiac output is your heart rate multiplied by your stroke volume. During exercise, stroke volume can increase by up to 50 per cent. As your heart rate increases, therefore, your cardiac output increases accordingly.

> **GLOSSARY**
>
> **Aerobic threshold:** the point above which your body has to use anaerobic respiration to provide you with sufficient energy for the activity you are engaged in.

> **GLOSSARY**
>
> **Stroke volume:** the amount of blood expelled by your heart each time it beats.

> **DID YOU KNOW?**
>
> - During heavy exercise, the volume of air exchanged by your lungs is about 110 litres per minute, and your heart pumps around 17.5 litres of blood per minute.
> - A quarter-pounder burger meal gives you enough energy to walk for 5 hours or run a marathon.

The long–term effects of exercise on your body

People who exercise regularly have several advantages over those who do not in the long-term. Some of these are:

- Lower resting heart rate.
- Greater stroke volume.
- Lower levels of body fat.
- Increased aerobic capacity.
- Increased muscular endurance and strength.

If you continue to exercise throughout your life, your bodily systems will be able more easily to resist the effects of ageing. Compared with people of the same age, older people who exercise regularly are:

- less likely to develop osteoporosis;
- thinner;
- half as likely to have heart diseases such as angina or heart attack;
- one third as likely to have diabetes;
- less likely to develop lung disorders such as asthma or bronchitis;
- less likely to have cancer;
- likely to live longer; and
- less likely to develop Alzheimer's disease.

If you take exercise throughout your life, you not only stay fitter and healthier but also live longer.

4.5 Describe a range of psychological factors that affect a performer before and during sporting activity, and outline how those factors may influence performance

This section covers
- Personality
- Confidence
- Concentration
- Motivation
- Arousal, anxiety and stress
- Aggression

So far in this unit we have looked at the physical aspects of performance and how factors such as fitness, etc., contribute to sport. Another important aspect of sports performance is, however, the psychological fitness of the athlete. Some coaches believe that psychological fitness is the most important factor in winning or losing, and sports psychology has now become a major tool used by both coaches and athletes to improve performance.

The main psychological factors influencing performance are shown in Figure 4.14. In this section we will look at each of these factors in turn.

Personality

There are four basic personality types, and individuals have characteristics (known as *traits*) from each type which combine to form that individual's unique personality:

1 *Extrovert*: An extrovert is someone who is outgoing, sociable and expressive. Extroverts enjoy crowds and attention and may often speak without thinking about others. Extroverts can be opinionated and may appear arrogant or rude. Extroverts outnumber introverts 3 to 1 in the general population.

2 *Introvert*: Introverts, however, focus on themselves and live in an inner world of ideas – they would rather listen than talk. They often

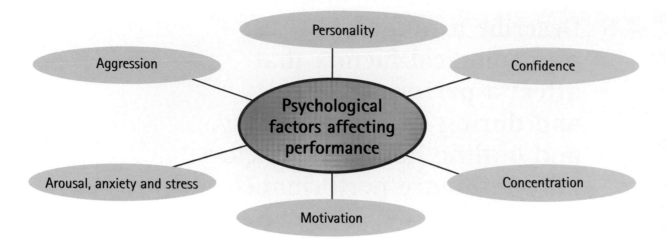

Figure 4.14 *The psychological factors that influence performance*

appear shy and need private time to recharge. Introverts can suffer from low self-esteem and may feel underestimated.

3 *Stable*: People with stable personalities tend, as the name suggests, to prefer order in both their work and daily lives. They are 'creatures of habit' and will feel more comfortable with a structured programme for work and play.

4 *Unstable*: Unstable personalities tend to be more unpredictable and plan ahead poorly. They can be unfocused in both their work and daily lives and often feel stifled by routine.

It is not possible to categorise athletes (as opposed to non-athletes) according to personality profiles, but all athletes will show some or all of the traits listed in Figure 4.15.

In general, team players also tend to be more extroverted than individual athletes, and extroversion tends to increase with increased participation

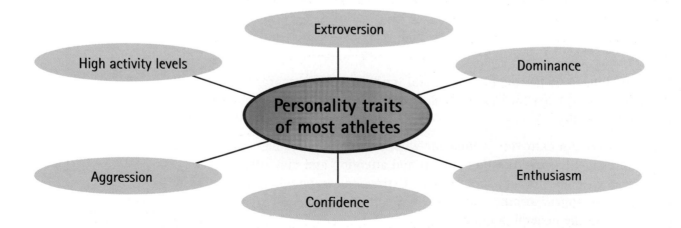

Figure 4.15 *The personality traits shown by most athletes*

in sports. It has been said that 'An athlete is more: independent, objective, intelligent, socially outgoing, extroverted and less anxious than a non–athlete' (Cox, 1994).

Confidence

'To become a champion you must first look and act like a champion!' (Muhammad Ali). Perhaps one of the greatest attributes a competitor can have is confidence in his or her own abilities. Studies have shown that confident people are more optimistic and that they outperform pessimistic people. More importantly, people can learn to be optimistic through a variety of techniques, one of which is self-talk.

Self–talk

Confident people reinforce their confidence after a good performance by saying such things as:

- I am that good.
- That's like me.
- I can do this consistently.

After a poor performance they would say:

- That's a one-off.
- I had a bad day.
- My opponent got lucky.

Concentration

Successful athletes have high levels of concentration, sometimes to the point of obsession. They are very task-oriented and will often be able to shut out other stimuli, such as crowd noise and so on, in order to concentrate on their own performance (they have a positive focus). Studies on runners have shown that running speed can be increased by as much as 4 per cent following psychological 'focus' training, where runners are trained to concentrate on their running action and how their bodies feel during the activity.

Motivation

Motivation is often called the 'will to win' and is an important aspect of sports performance. Motivation is often said to work on the basis of rewards and punishments (sometimes known as the carrot and the stick). Rewards and punishments for athletes are shown in Table 4.2.

REWARDS	PUNISHMENTS
Recognition from their coach, team-mates, the general public, their families, etc.	Criticism from their coach, team-mates, the general public, their families, etc.
Success – the number of competitions or medals won, financial success, fame	Removal from the team
Self-esteem – athletes often seem to achieve a high self-esteem only through competitive success, and they may feel unfulfilled if they do not meet or exceed their goals	Failure – competitions lost, contracts from sponsors cancelled, etc.
	A loss of self-esteem

Table 4.2 *The rewards and punishments for athletes*

This is not a complete list. There are many more pressures – both positive (motivators) and negative (de-motivators) – on all athletes, and these can include family pressures and pressures from fellow athletes, the effects of competitions, physical health and the effects of injuries, to name but a few.

Parents are often not aware of the pressures they put on their children to perform well

Arousal, anxiety and stress

Athletic performance is influenced by the performer's state of mind and whether or not he or she is ready to perform to his or her best. Arousal is your response to the stress you are under, anxiety is the degree of confidence you have in your ability to perform well, and stress is the demands of the situation you are in. All three are linked. For example, your are entering a competition for the first time. Stress is caused by the fact that you are in an unknown situation. This means you will be anxious about your performance but will also be 'psyched up' (aroused) to perform to your best.

There are three main theories that try to explain the relationship between arousal and athletic performance.

The inverted-U hypothesis

The American psychologist, Oxendine (1988), has said that it is important for an athlete to mange his or her levels of anxiety and arousal so that optimum performance is achieved. Increased arousal will lead to increased performance but only up to a point: if arousal continues beyond that point, performance will suffer. The relationship between arousal and performance, when plotted on a graph, looks like an inverted U (or a bell) (see Figure 4.16).

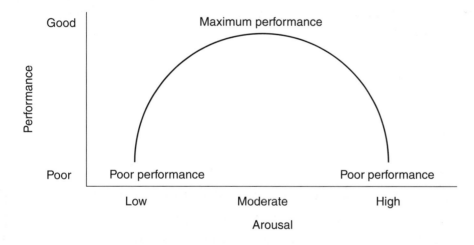

Figure 4.16
The inverted-U hypothesis

Catastrophe theory

Developed by Hardy and Fazey (1988), two British sports psychologists, catastrophe theory also suggests that stress and anxiety will affect performance. Each individual, however, will respond in a unique way to competitive anxiety. This unique response will be reflected in the individual's performance, and consequently may be difficult to predict.

Optimum arousal theory

Yuri Hanin's optimum arousal theory (1983) says that athletes have a zone of optimal functioning (ZOF) and that, if their level of anxiety/arousal falls within their ZOF, their performance will be at its peak. It is the sports psychologist's job to maintain athletes in their ZOF during a competition.

Aggression

Aggression has been defined as the deliberate intention to hurt someone. It has been argued that aggression is either a personality trait, a learned habit or a biological process, but what is agreed is that a certain level of aggression is required to be successful in all sports. Some psychologists say that sport is a safety valve for your natural aggressive instincts, whilst others say aggression is the result of frustration: people act aggressively (over-competitively) to achieve goals that may seem beyond their reach.

Some factors that increase levels of aggression in competitors are as follows:

- Losing.
- Playing/competing away from home.
- The type of sport.
- Current values and norms within both the sport and society.
- The game's importance to the individual.

As with arousal, what is clear is that too much aggression can lead to a decline in performance or even a withdrawal from the activity (e.g. being sent off in football), as the competitor is more focused on other competitors than the event itself.

TEST YOUR KNOWLEDGE

1 What are the functions of the skeleton?

2 Name the three types of muscle found in the body

3 What is the difference between the anaerobic and aerobic energy systems?

4 What are the short-term adaptations to exercise?

5 Give three long-term adaptations to exercise

6 Give three personality traits shown by successful athletes.

Social Issues in Sport

Introduction

You saw in the previous unit that athletes are under a great deal of pressure to perform to the best of their abilities. Sometimes these pressures can result in athletes taking short cuts to improve their performance. They can also result in violence, both on and off the field of play, among both the players and the spectators. Pressures in society can also affect an athlete. For example, women are often discouraged from taking part in sports because sports are viewed as somehow un-feminine. Disabled people also often feel sport is not for them, again because society does not encourage them to take part.

Some sporting events, such as the Olympic Games, attract worldwide attention. This attention does not pass unnoticed, and such events are widely reported – for good or bad – on TV and in newspapers. Politicians have not been slow to realise that the eyes of the world are turned to such major sporting events and have used them to promote their own views and beliefs. During this unit you will debate and discuss the issues listed below inorder to develop your own opinions and beliefs which you will then present in your portfolio.

How you will be assessed

For this unit you will produce a portfolio of work that shows you have met all the assessment objectives for the unit. Your portfolio could contain posters and newsletters you have created to encourage greater involvement in sports by minority groups, evidence of research you have conducted to see how local and national centres have adapted their facilities to cater for disabled people, videos or audio tapes of presentations you have given and proof of research you have undertaken into contemporary issues (drugs, violence, politics, etc.) that affect sports in an adverse way.

In this unit you will learn how to:

① Investigate the common effects and misuse of performance-enhancing drugs within sport, providing at least two examples of each

② Identify three reasons why women typically participate less in sport than men

③ Explain the reasons for violence within sport amongst players and spectators within the UK

④ Examine two effects that mass media has on sport

⑤ Profile three major sports activities or sporting events that are or have been influenced by politics

⑥ Summarise three issues associated with accessibility of sport for people with a disability

5.1 Investigate the common effects and misuse of performance-enhancing drugs within sport, providing at least two examples of each

This section covers
- Stimulants
- Narcotics
- Anabolic steroids
- Diuretics
- Peptide and glycoprotein hormones
- Beta-blockers
- Blood doping

Performance-enhancing drugs have been used in sport for as long as competitive sport has been played (see Table 5.1). The first recorded use of drugs by a sportsman is from the writings of Galen, a trainer of gladiators in 300 BC. In the modern era, the first report of athletes attempting to use drugs to improve their performance was in the Amsterdam Canal Race of 1865. In the latter half of the last century, the prevalence of drugs really became apparent and, in 1955, 20 per cent of cyclists on the Tour de France where found to be using drugs.

DATE	INCIDENT
1886	The first recorded death from drugs when a cyclist, Linton, died from an overdose of trimethyl
1904	The first near-death in the modern Olympics. A marathon runner, Thomas Hicks, was using a mixture of brandy and strychnine, which nearly killed him. At this time the most widely used drug was a cocktail of alcohol and strychnine. Heroin, caffeine and cocaine were also widely used until heroin and cocaine became available only on prescription
1930s	Amphetamines were first produced. They quickly overtook strychnine in popularity
1950s	The Soviet team used male hormones to increase their power and strength. The Americans developed steroids in response
1952	One of the first major doping cases involving amphetamines occurred at the Winter Olympics. Several speed skaters became ill and needed medical attention
1960	At the Olympics, Danish cyclist, Kurt Jensen, collapsed and died from an amphetamine overdose
1963	Pressure started to mount on the International Olympic Committee (IOC) to control drug use. The Council of Europe set up a committee on drugs but couldn't decide on a definition of doping
1964	There was a noticeable increase in the muscular appearance of the athletes at the Olympics, and drug use was suspected
1967	The IOC took action after the death of Tommy Simpson (due to the illegal taking of amphetamines) in the Tour de France
1968	The IOC decided on a definition of doping and developed a list of banned substances. Testing began at the Olympic Games
1988	At the Seoul Olympics, Ben Johnson tested positive for a banned anabolic steroid, was stripped of his gold medal and was suspended for two years
1990	The Australian Sports Drug Agency was established by the Australian Sports Drug Agency Act 1990
1998	The Festina team were forced to withdraw from the Tour de France when customs police discovered 234 doses of the blood-boosting agent EPO and other banned substances in a car belonging to the team's masseur
1999	The World Anti-Doping Agency (WADA) was established on 10 November. Its mission is to promote and co-ordinate the fight against doping in sport internationally

Table 5.1 *Drugs in sport: a timeline*

DATE	INCIDENT
2002	At the Salt Lake Olympics, three star cross-country skiers tested positive for a drug called darbepoetin that helps patients recover from chemotherapy by producing red blood cells
2003	The Copenhagen declaration was signed. All major sporting federations and 73 governments approved a resolution accepting the World Anti-Doping Code as the basis for the fight against doping
2004	The BALCO laboratories were investigated by a US grand jury as they had been accused of supplying the steroid THG to sprinters, including Dwain Chambers of the UK

Table 5.1 Continued

When it comes to government-approved doping, the former East Germany must surely lead the field. Following the disintegration of East Germany in 1989, it was discovered that a state-sponsored plan had ordered the systematic doping of East German athletes during the 1970s and 1980s. In a worldwide context it appears that this distribution of drugs has not stopped.

DID YOU KNOW?

- The rate of positive drugs tests in sport fell from 4.25 per cent in 1989 to 1.05 per cent in 2003.
- Until 1967, it was not illegal for Olympic athletes to use drugs to enhance their performance during a competition.
- The average cup of coffee contains more than 1,000 different chemical components.
- Some 40 members of the Chinese Olympic team were disqualified from entering the Sydney Olympics in 2000, and 14 athletes were sent home following positive drug tests.

The issue of drug abuse in the Olympic Games has grown enormously since the first drug-related death of a competitor in the 1960 games. The IOC's anti-doping campaign is based upon three principles:

1 The protection of the athletes' health.
2 Respect for medical and sports ethics.
3 Ensuring an equal chance for everyone during the games.

The IOC's definition of drug abuse includes the deliberate or inadvertent use of substances that enhance performance. The IOC's code requires all competitors to abide by its requirements, including testing for banned substances.

The IOC Medical Commission oversees the collection of urine samples from athletes. The commission also ensures that samples are securely sealed and numbered before being sent to an accredited laboratory for testing. Since 1994, their testing procedures have been expanded to include blood as well as urine samples. A list of both banned and allowed substances is published and updated regularly, and this has now grown to around 150 substances. Any athlete taking these is liable to disqualification if found guilty.

There are several different classes of drugs banned in sport, and some of these are outlined below.

Stimulants

Stimulants are substances that excite the central nervous system: they make you feel more alert and more in charge of the situation. Some stimulants occur naturally in the body, such as adrenaline, which heightens your body's ability to cope in times of stress by increasing your heart and respiratory rates, thus making more energy available to your body.

The most commonly used stimulants in sport, however, do not usually occur naturally in the body: amphetamines, cocaine, ephedrine and caffeine. Athletes use these stimulants to attain increased alertness, to reduce tiredness and to increase their competitiveness and aggression. They can also help athletes exercise more strenuously and to become less sensitive to pain.

The effects of stimulants

Stimulants can cause problems with the body's ability to regulate its temperature, which means the body may become overheated. They can also stop the heart and other vital organs from working properly. The other side-effects of using stimulants are shown in Figure 5.1.

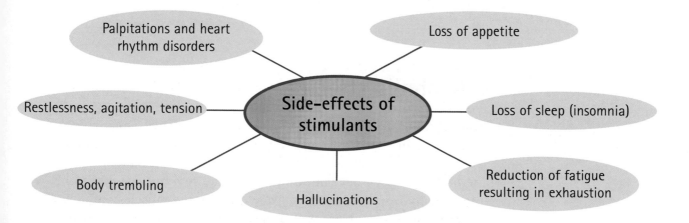

Figure 5.1 *The side-effects of using stimulants*

Narcotics

The narcotic drugs that are banned from use in sport also affect the central nervous system, but these drugs reduce feelings of pain. Examples of such drugs include heroin, morphine and hydrocodeine. They mask the sensation of pain so that athletes are able to train harder and for longer and ignore injury. They may also produce the sensations of euphoria (feeling 'high') and invincibility ('no one can beat me'). Like stimulants, however, there are side-effects to using narcotics, and these are summarised in Figure 5.2.

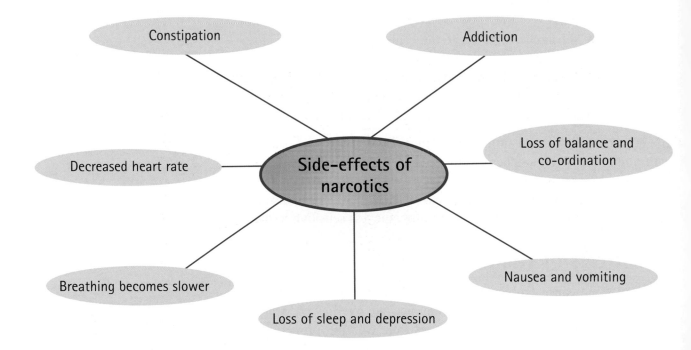

Figure 5.2 *The side-effects of using narcotics*

Anabolic steroids

Anabolic steroids are the most common performance-enhancing drugs used in sport. The word 'anabolic' refers to muscle building and 'steroids' to a class of drugs. Over 100 different anabolic steroids have been developed, but they require a prescription to be used legally in most countries. They develop the muscles and delay fatigue, which means users of these drugs are stronger and are able to train harder (Figure 5.3 lists some of the side-effects of using anabolic steroids).

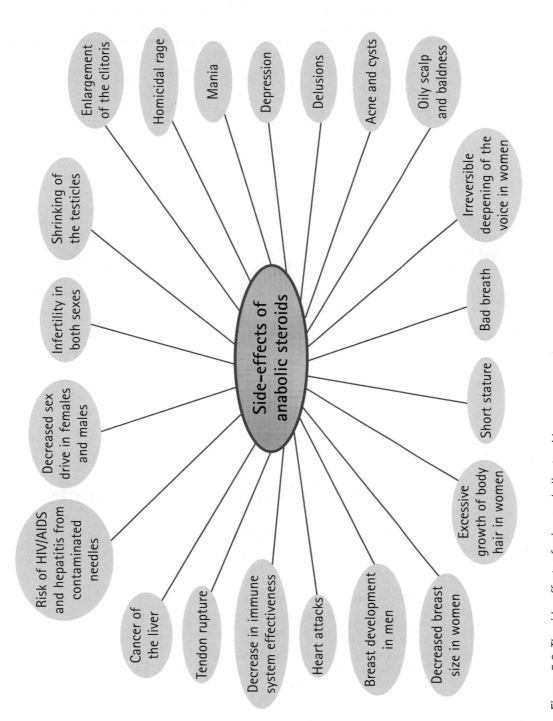

Figure 5.3 *The side–effects of using anabolic steroids*

Diuretics

Diuretics are drugs that increase the amount of urine the body produces. They generally act directly on the kidneys. Athletes use diuretics for two main reasons. To:

1 achieve rapid weight loss in sports where weight categories are involved. Such sports include horse racing, boxing, weightlifting, rowing and judo; and

2 dilute the concentration of other drugs in the urine. This means that the detection of other illegal drugs may be more difficult.

Figure 5.4 lists the harmful side-effects of diuretics.

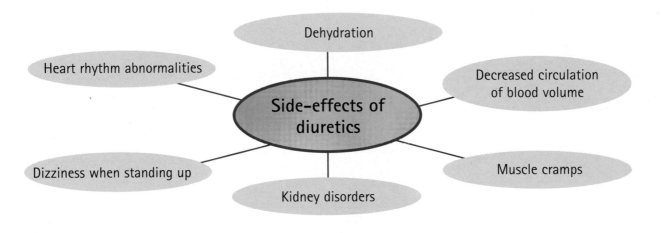

Figure 5.4 *The side-effects of using diuretics*

Peptide and glycoprotein hormones

Peptide hormones include a number of substances that promote the production of other hormones. Examples include HCG, HGH, ACTH and – the most well-known – EPO:

- *HCG (human chorionic gonadotropin)*: The effects of this drug are similar to those of anabolic steroids. Like anabolic steroids, HCG increases the levels of testosterone (the male hormone) in the body. It is used to disguise other illegal drugs the athlete may have taken. It is also thought to increase muscle size and strength.

- *HGH (human growth hormone)*: Athletes use this to help build muscle size and increase strength. It occurs naturally in your body, promoting growth until you reach puberty.

- *ACTH (adrenocorticotropic hormone)*: This is used to repair damaged tissue and muscles.

- *EPO (erythropoietin)*: This hormone increases the amount of red blood cells in the blood. It is used to achieve better levels of endurance.

Figure 5.5 summarises the side-effects of peptide and glycoprotein hormones.

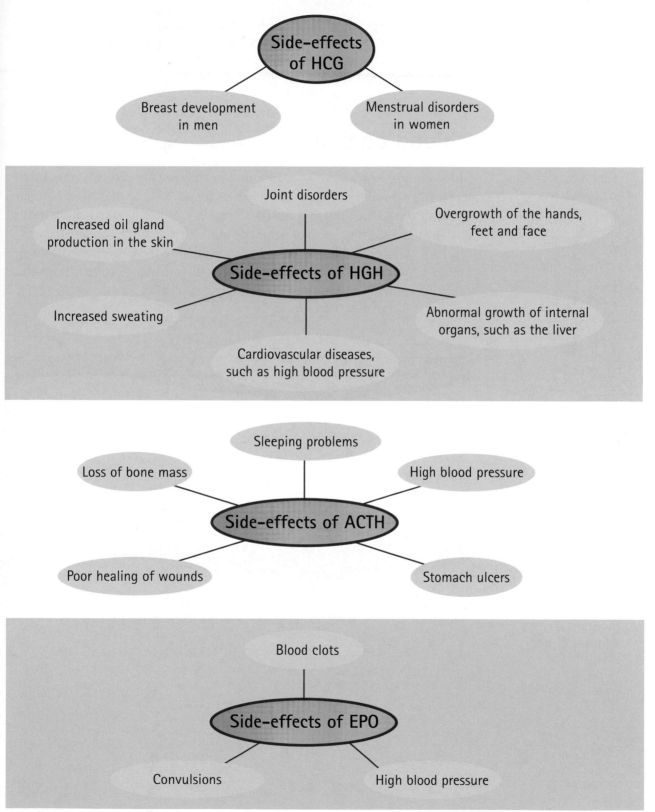

Figure 5.5 *The side-effects of peptide and glycoprotein hormones*

Beta-blockers

Beta-blockers are used medically in the treatment of such conditions as hypertension (raised blood pressure) and anxiety. Because they reduce the shaking and palpitations associated with anxiety, they are sometimes used in sports that need fine muscle co-ordination (i.e. target shooting).

Blood doping

Blood doping is a way of speeding up the transport of oxygen round the body. It works by increasing the athlete's blood volume and haemoglobin concentration. The athlete withdraws from his or her bloodstream a unit of red blood cells. This is stored until the athlete's haemoglobin levels have returned to normal. The stored red blood cells are then re-injected into the athlete's bloodstream. This results in a significant improvement in aerobic capacity and endurance, rather like the effect of EPO.

ACTIVITY

In groups, discuss the advantages and disadvantages of performance-enhancing drugs for athletes. Consider the long and short-term effects of the drugs and whether you think athletes should be allowed to take drugs to improve their performance or not. Give the reasons for your opinion.

ACTIVITY

Produce a report that demonstrates your understanding of the effects of the misuse of drugs in sport and exercise, and how these effects may differ according to gender.

5.2 Identify three reasons why women typically participate less in sport than men

This section covers

- Social effects on female participation in sport
- Title IX
- Social trends
- Women's sports and the media
- Other barriers to participation

Generally speaking, women and girls tend to participate less in sports than men and boys (39 per cent of women and girls participate in sport compared to 54 per cent of men and boys). Researchers have suggested there are four main reasons for this:

1 Virtually from the age they are able to walk, boys are encouraged to explore the environment and to be active, whereas girls are more restricted in what they are encouraged to do.

2 Girls prefer different sports from boys and participate in far fewer numbers, even in their favourite sports.

3 Historically, men's athletic programmes have received substantially more money than women's programmes.

4 What is seen as appropriate behaviour for men and women in life generally may not be appropriate behaviour for sport – to be a successful female athlete, it is necessary to possess the same traits, characteristics and behaviours as male athletes: 'Men who display typical female or feminine behaviours (e.g. nurturing) and women who display typical male or masculine behaviours (e.g. aggression) may be punished with psychological isolation, economic hardship and social ostracism for violating culturally appropriate gender norms' (Unger and Crawford, 1992).

Social effects on female participation in sport

We saw above that most boys become involved in sport whilst most girls do not. This is may not be the result of biological differences between the sexes but, rather, subtle social learning. Sport is often

DID YOU KNOW?

- Girls aged 7–11 years are less than half as likely to take part in physical education and sport as boys.
- By the age of 18 years, 40 per cent of girls have dropped out of sport and physical recreation.
- Only 8 per cent of British Olympic team coaches at the Sydney Games in 2000 were women, compared with the Atlanta Games in 1996 when 11 per cent of coaches were female.
- Only one of the 25 Olympic team managers in Sydney 2000 was a woman.
- Some 40 per cent of the British Olympic team at the 2000 Olympic Games were women. These athletes went on to win 42 per cent of the medals.

considered a masculine activity, and success in sport leads to enhanced male status (athleticism = virility, machismo, male heterosexuality). In addition, as children, boys are given toy trucks, guns and tractors, whilst girls are given dolls, toy kitchens and such dressing-up clothes as nurses' uniforms. Boys and girls come to accept these toys as normal, and this could go on to affect their attitudes to sports.

By the time children reach school age they have decided for themselves that active sports are masculine and not feminine. This view continues throughout school, with boys' play tending to be outdoors, complex and in large groups, whereas girls' play tends to be indoors, small group, repetitive, turn-taking and less challenging. Boys therefore learn how to set goals, to be independent, to settle disputes and to abide by compromise; girls learn to co-operate and to avoid competition.

This view that sport is essentially male has led to female athletes being considered as somehow abnormal: women who play team sports use skills that are thought to be masculine. This had brought about the stereotypical idea of the 'lesbian athlete' (i.e. women who play masculine sports are not real women and so must be lesbians).

The potential risks of vigorous exercise have also been exaggerated, and this may limit women's participation in sport. In fact, it has been shown that women are more durable than men (from a physiological standpoint), and one of the benefits of physical activity is health improvement (see Figure 5.6).

Women athletes also generally earn less money from competitions and sponsorship than their male counterparts. For example, in 2000, the women's Wimbledon champion, Venus Williams, won $666,500, whereas Pete Sampras, the male champion, won $740,125.

In an effort to decrease the gap in participation in the USA, a law called Title IX was passed in 1972.

Figure 5.6 *Women are more physiologically durable than men*

Title IX

Title IX says that 'no person in the United States of America shall, on the basis of sex be excluded from participation in, denied the benefits of, or be subject to discrimination under any program receiving federal assistance'. Title IX was initially quite successful. Participation rates in women's athletics increased significantly in the first 10 years after it was passed, but numbers have remained relatively stable since. Not only that but, before Title IX became law, 90 per cent of female teams had women coaches; this figure has since dropped to 44 per cent (perhaps the opposite effect from what the law intended).

Social trends

Even before the introduction of such measures as Title IX, participation by women in sport had been steadily increasing throughout the twentieth century. This is perhaps best shown in the history of women's participation in the Olympic Games (see Table 5.2 overleaf).

DATE	EVENT
1896	The first female competitor in the Olympics was a Greek woman who ran the marathon (alongside the men)
1900	The first female Gold medallist: Charlotte Cooper from Great Britain, who won Gold in the tennis singles (see Figure 5.7)
1932	The first female Olympic star. Mildred 'Babe' Dickinson of the USA won Gold medals in the hurdles and javelin, and a Silver in the high jump
1948	Female athletics really came to prominence in the Wembley Olympics of 1948. Fanny Blankers-Koen won four Gold medals on the track. This was a remarkable feat made even more remarkable since she was 30 years old and a mother of two children. Besides her Olympic triumph, she had a 20-year athletic career in which she set 20 world records. Fanny is regarded as one of the greatest athletes of either sex of the twentieth century
1992	Despite these pioneers, however, at the Barcelona Olympics in 1992 there were still 34 countries that sent no female athletes to the games

Table 5.2 *The history of women's participation in the Olympic Games*

Figure 5.7

Charlotte Cooper: Britain's first Olympic gold medallist in 1900

Women have been denied equal access to Olympic sport for four main reasons:

1 *Tradition*: Some sports have never involved women, and these traditions are very difficult to overcome. For example, women have never taken part in steeplechases.

2 *Institutional*: Some sporting institutions and organisations do not permit women to take part (e.g. women are not allowed to box professionally).

3 *Cultural*: Some religions do not allow women the same freedom as men to compete in sport.

4 *Domestic*: Some countries have customs that prevent women from being free to compete in sport (women should stay at home to look after their husbands and children).

A good example of the last two constraints is that of the Algerian runner, Hassiba Boulmerka. Since Algeria is a Muslim country, women are discouraged from participating in sport, especially in public, and therefore Boulmerka had to live and train in Europe for most of her athletic career. Even when she became Algeria's first-ever Gold medallist in 1992, she was criticised by some Algerians for behaving in an unseemly manner and revealing too much of her body, and by others for following her career rather than being a wife and mother.

ACTIVITY

Ask ten people the following questions and see how many right answers they get:

1 What did Sally Gunnel win in 1992?
2 Who is the England Women's Football Team coach?
3 Which team won the Women's FA Cup in 2004?
4 Who won the first Olympic women's modern pentathlon Gold medal?
5 What sport is Laura Davies famous for?

Women's sports and the media

Two other issues that affect the participation rates of women in sport are the way women's sport is portrayed in the media and the amount of coverage women's sport is given. Some studies have shown that, on average, only 15 per cent of media coverage in the USA is devoted to women's sports.

Media coverage can be split into:

1 the broadcast media (television and radio); and
2 the print media (newspapers, magazines, etc.).

Broadcast media

At the 2000 Olympic Games in Sydney, the games received almost 219 hours of media coverage from the main TV broadcaster. Of these hours, only 29 per cent (just over 63 hours) were concerned with women's events. This is despite the fact that 44 per cent of the events were women's events!

It is, however, not just the amount of coverage women's events receive that is telling of differences between the genders: the language used during commentaries differs markedly. For example, when female athletes are being discussed, commentators note their physical appearance, style of dress and their lives as a heterosexual wife, mother or girlfriend. When male athletes are discussed, on the other hand, it is their power, strength, endurance, struggles and strategies in competition that receive the attention. Errors in performance are also reported differently. When a woman misses, commentators tend to use such phrases as 'She missed' or 'she missed the shot'. But when a man misses, they say 'too strong', 'unbridled power' or 'Smith is not giving up'.

Print media

In a study of newspaper and sports magazine coverage in Europe during 2002, Laura Capranica found that 61 per cent of all sports articles and 64 per cent of photographs related to male athletes or teams. In another study in the USA in 2004, Bailey found that these images were mainly of 'acceptable' female sports, such as gymnastics, swimming, tennis and diving, with very few images of football or basketball, despite the fact that the USA was ranked second (in 2004) in women' s world football by FIFA.

This lack of coverage means the public has little awareness of women's achievements in sport. For example, in 2003, a survey by the Women's Sports Foundation found that around 60 per cent of the people surveyed could not name any British female world champions or their sport, and 66 per cent could not name three female British sports stars.

Other barriers to participation

As well as the factors listed above, there are other barriers to women who wish to participate in sports, at whatever level:

- *Funding*: In 2000, the UK sports market (i.e. the money generated from such things as advertising and sponsorship) was worth some £13 billion. However, about £600 million of this was generated by just seven Premiership football clubs (nearly 5 per cent of the total). In the same year, government grants intended to promote greater participation in sport equalled £600 million, none of which was specifically earmarked for women's sport. Figures for the amount of money spent on sponsoring women's sport are difficult to establish, but it has been estimated that it is about 15 per cent of that spent on men's sport.

- *Lack of childcare facilities*: Although childcare facilities are becoming more common, the average cost of nursery care is about £134 per week. This represents a significant extra cost to female athletes.

- *Lack of role models*: As you saw above, 66 per cent of people cannot name three British female athletes, and only 8 per cent of coaches are female. This means that girls in sport have fewer role models than men.

> **GLOSSARY**
>
> **Role model:** someone you look up to; a person who has qualities and abilities you admire and that you try to copy.

ACTIVITY

Look at several newspapers to find out how much coverage they give to women's sport. Note down:

1 The amount of text they devote to women's sport (with a ruler, measure the length of the columns that report women's sport).

2 The number of photographs of women athletes.

3 The size of these photographs.

Compare these to the amount of space given to male sports.

5.3 Explain the reasons for violence within sport amongst players and spectators within the UK

This section covers
- Theories of aggression
- History of sports violence
- Other forms of sports violence

GLOSSARY

Aggression: behaviour aimed at harming or injuring a person who does not want to be harmed or injured.

Violence: harming or intimidating someone illegally.

'Winning isn't everything, it's the only thing' – Vince Lombardi, US football coach. Aggression is usually considered to be a desirable quality in an athlete, as most people think that it helps athletes to win (i.e. to beat their opponents). When aggression leads to violence either on or off the field of play, however, players, coaches, commentators and spectators condemn it. In this section we will look at the various theories people have put forward for violence in sport.

Theories of aggression

Instinct theory

This theory suggests that aggression is natural: it occurs in all animals, including humans. It also suggests that we get rid of our aggression in such activities as competitive sports or games. However, research has shown that aggression does not occur to the same degree in all cultures, and that aggression is at its highest in times of war.

Frustration–aggression theory

This theory suggests that aggression is a natural response to frustration. When we are frustrated because we cannot achieve our goals, we become aggressive. However, frustration does not always lead to aggression, and aggression is not always caused by frustration.

Social learning theory

This theory suggests that we learn to be aggressive by watching others and by observing others' reactions to our behaviour. A great deal of research seems to support this view since aggression appears to be at its highest after people have witnessed aggression or have received positive reactions to their own aggressive behaviour.

So how do these theories relate to sport?

As you can see from Tables 5.3 and 5.4, sports that have high levels of aggression on the field of play tend to attract spectators who demonstrate the highest levels of anti-social behaviour, such as verbal or racial abuse. You can also see that, in the five-year period up to 1992, parents' behaviour became more aggressive, especially towards officials and opposing players.

These figures would seem to reinforce the social learning theory of aggression, as spectators could be said to be reacting to violence on the field, and children are learning from their parents how to be aggressive.

SPORT	FOUL LANGUAGE		RACIAL/ETHNIC ABUSE	
	OCCURRENCE	NET INCREASE/ DECREASE	OCCURRENCE	NET INCREASE/ DECREASE
Australian Rules	75.2	+26.7	38.6	+5.4
Baseball	42.9	−6.7	23.1	+2.4
Basketball	34.8	+16.3	14.9	+7.8
Cricket	32.9	+21.2	15.3	−8.7
Netball	32.1	+8.7	10.3	+4.1
Rugby League	70.0	+23.1	35.5	−7.7
Rugby Union	42.3	+23.1	19.2	+12.5
Soccer	80.8	+35.4	49.0	−12.5
Softball	15.0	+27.7	n/a	n/a
Tennis	10.8	+12.9	5.7	−4.7

Source: O'Hara (1992)

Table 5.3 *Spectator misbehaviour by sport (per cent)*

BEHAVIOUR	OCCURRENCE	NET CHANGE OVER FIVE YEARS
Foul language by parents	17.0	+8.4
Verbal abuse of officials	31.4	+15.6
Physical abuse of officials	1.5	−6.7
Reticent children pushed into playing	18.9	+0.5
Parents 'coaching' from sidelines	60.0	+16.5
Criticism of opposition by parents	42.8	+16.1
Inciting children to unsporting behaviour	19.1	+9.8

Source: O'Hara (1992)

Table 5.4 *Children's sport: observed behaviour (per cent)*

ACTIVITY

1. Look out for accounts in the media of violence, both on and off the field of play. Which sports seem to have most violent incidents? Which sports have the most incidents of crowd violence?
2. Search the Internet or textbooks to find out whether crowd violence in football is increasing or decreasing.

History of sports violence

All sorts of people – sports commentators, journalists and academics – have put forward reasons for violence in sports, but there appears to be no one single cause for violence both on and off the field. One thing that is certain, however, is that violence is not a modern phenomenon. Violence in sport began in ancient times, and there is a report of a chariot race in ancient Rome where 30,000 people were killed due to crowd violence.

In 1602, Sir Richard Carew spoke of players 'retyring home as from a pitched battaile, with bloody pates, bones broken and out of joynt, and such bruises as serve to shorten their daies'. An unknown author in the early nineteenth century similarly wrote that 'many kicks would be given and taken, so that on the following day the competitors would be unable to walk, and sometimes a kick on the shins would lead the two men concerned to abandon the game until they had decided who was the better pugilist [boxer].'

However, the gradual emergence of the middle class in the nineteenth century led to changing attitudes towards sport. For example, attempts were made to make football respectable enough for 'gentlemen' to take part in. To achieve this, it had to get rid of much of the roughness characteristic of the old form of the game but without killing off the element of risk and danger completely.

The first written rules for football were produced at Rugby School in 1845. The intention in these rules of making the game more respectable can be seen in the following: 'no hacking with the heel or above the knee is fair' and 'no player may wear projecting nails or iron plates on the soles or heels of his shoes or boots.' Then in 1847 at Eton, the leading public school in England, there was a near total prohibition on the use of hands. This led to the rugby–soccer split, an event created, it seems, by Eton–Rugby rivalry.

During the 1850s, the popularity of soccer and rugby increased, leading to a demand for standardised rules. The spread of football to Cambridge was particularly significant because its version of the Eton no-handling game formed the basis of the 'laws' of the Football Association, which was founded in 1863.

These changes were reflected in other sports. In boxing, for example, weight classes were introduced, and the Queensberry rules outlawed punches 'below the belt'. There was also a change in taste away from the more brutal sports (such as bare-knuckle fighting) towards ball games and athletics. This trend has continued to the present day, with changes still being made to the laws of certain sports (for example, the tackle from behind in football). Some commentators have argued that sport is less violent now than it has ever been.

As on-field violence has declined, however, there has been a reported rise in off-field violence by athletes: 21 per cent of current US National Football League (NFL) athletes have been charged with domestic violence (Watson, 2003). Some people think this is because there has been greater reporting recently of such incidents, but others say this violence is the result of accepting or even promoting on-field violence, which often goes unpunished. For example, between 1945 and 1995, 1,500 boxers died, with no one facing legal charges for their deaths. In a great many sports, some forms of violence are seen as acceptable, such as fights on the field or teams recruiting players to provide them with some 'steel' or 'bite'. Owners and coaches do not stop this but often promote it in the interests of winning.

Off the field, crowd violence is a particular problem, and football hooliganism is one of the biggest problems facing the world's most popular sport (see Figure 5.8 overleaf). So why does this violence happen? Some people, such as Professor Eric Dunning of Leicester University, argue that soccer offers a context for some forms of, largely, male violence to occur. This is because soccer involves intense emotional excitement: the idea of an enemy and a defence of territory. For people who find it hard to control themselves, this can easily lead to a hatred of the opposing team. Also, because football is a low-scoring game with little physical contact (unlike American football or rugby), it is argued that the slow build-up of emotion in the fans can lead to an explosion of violence.

Figure 5.8

Football hooliganism is one of the biggest problems facing the world's most popular sport

Another cause of violence may be the media, in particular the popular press. Newspapers may encourage hooligans by placing them in the limelight, such as publishing league tables of hooligan notoriety. They have also been accused of inciting hooliganism by promoting xenophobia. For instance, prior to England's semi-final clash with Germany in Euro 96, the *Daily Mirror* ran a headline of 'Achtung Surrender' whilst the *Sun* went with 'Let's Blitz Fritz'.

DID YOU KNOW?

- Between June 1996 and October 1999 there were three football-related murders in England, five in Italy and 39 in Argentina.
- Football was banned from London by King Edward II in 1314 because it was so violent.
- Before boxing was regulated, a round lasted until one of the boxers was knocked down and the match could not continue.

Other forms of sports violence

Racism

During the 1970s and 1980s, racism was a problem in UK football, with Afro-Caribbean players in particular being targeted for abuse. Recent campaigns, such as 'Kick Racism out of Football', have helped to reduce this problem. Perhaps the greatest change has come about because of the numbers of Afro-Caribbean players now in the game (in 2004 approximately 22 per cent of all Premiership players were of Afro-Caribbean descent).

Gamesmanship

Gamesmanship can be defined as the use of ploys that are contrary to the spirit of a game in order to gain an unfair advantage. This can include shirt pulling, shoving, taunting and even the goalkeeper bringing up his knee when rushing out and jumping up to catch the ball. Such actions often provoke a violent reaction in the opposing players (which may be the intention), who then usually try to turn the situation to their advantage.

Professionalism

Professionalism usually means being properly prepared for a sport, but it can also be used to describe actions that border on gamesmanship, such as taking as long as possible over a free kick or tennis serve. Again, professionalism is sometimes used in an attempt to provoke an illegal or violent action from the opponent.

5.4 Examine two effects that mass media has on sport

This section covers
- Effects of television coverage
- Stereotypes
- Other effects of mass media coverage

Over the past few decades there has been an explosion of sports reporting in the media. This has been the result of new broadcasting services, such as Channel 4, Channel 5, BskyB and the Racing Channel on TV, as well as radio channels such as Radio 5 Live and Talksport. In addition, some Premiership football teams have their own TV and radio stations, and this rise in media involvement has had some profound effects on the way sport is run in the UK.

Effects of television coverage

Television is probably the most important of the mass media in the UK, and many sports and their sponsors consider widespread television coverage as essential to their continued popularity. One good example of is the 2003 Rugby League Test Series between Great Britain and Australia: a total of 1,791,000 people watched the series. This television coverage was worth £129,244 to the series' sponsors, and 14 per cent of the viewing population watched the matches, thus increasing their awareness of the sponsor and their products.

This pales in comparison to a football tournament, however, with Euro 2004 having a worldwide audience of 93 million and sponsors paying up to £20 million each to have their products associated with the tournament. The 2004 Olympics also attracted a huge TV audience, with coverage of the closing ceremony providing the BBC with its highest ratings for the day. The average audience was 6.3 million (29.4 per cent of the TV audience), whilst the peak was 8.1 million (37.4 per cent of the TV audience).

The benefits, however, are not all one way and, in 1999, Rupert Murdoch, the part owner of Britain's largest satellite broadcaster (BSkyB) stated that 'Sport overpowers film and everything else

CASE STUDY

Football and TV

The increased popularity of English football was also a result of TV developments during the 1990s. Satellite and cable TV brought new companies into the industry to rival the established channels (the BBC and Independent Television), resulting in larger contracts for the right to televise football. Thus, the TV rights to show 10 games cost £2.6 million in 1983 (£260,000 per game), compared with £130 million for 60 games in 1997–98 (£2,160,000 per game).

1 How many times more expensive was it to show a football match in 1997–98 than 1983?
2 Do you think these rising costs to televise football matches are a good thing? For example, if the major matches go to BskyB and other satellite channels, how are people who do not subscribe to these channels going to be able to watch them?
3 Can you think of any other sports where the TV rights to broadcast matches have soared in recent years?

in the entertainment genre . . . Football, of all sports, is number one' (Szymanski and Kuypers, 1999).

Sports programming delivered large numbers of viewers to the TV channels, which, in turn, permitted the selling of prime-time advertising slots. But TV companies were not the only winners. Clubs benefited from TV in two ways: first, substantial revenues flowed from new TV contracts; and, secondly, the greater number of games aired at prime viewing times fuelled the interest of fans.

Amongst nine Premiership clubs, their income from TV coverage grew from 21 per cent of total revenues in 1996–97 to 26 per cent in 1997–98. Such income is obviously very important for the top clubs. For example, those teams that qualified for European competitions received additional money from the televised coverage of those games and, in the 1996–97 season, Arsenal earned around £5.7 million from TV but, in the next season (1997–98), this went up to £10.5 million.

Stereotypes

Media coverage of sports may also have some negative effects, however, and some studies have shown that sports reporting and broadcasting often help to reinforce stereotypes.

GLOSSARY

A stereotype: a widely held impression that is often untrue and based on prejudice.

To stereotype: to treat or classify someone or something according to a commonly believed stereotype.

Stereotypes can cause problems because they tend to:

- reduce a wide range of differences in people to simplistic generalisations;
- turn misguided assumptions about particular groups of people into 'realities';
- be used to justify the position of those in power; and
- maintain social prejudice and inequality.

Some studies have found that commentaries on sport reinforce the idea of 'violent masculinity'. By praising athletes who continue to play whilst injured, and by using the language of conflict and war to describe action, it is said that sports commentaries stereotype violence and aggression as exciting and rewarding.

Another common stereotype is that all women football or rugby players are lesbians, since rugby and football are not generally seen as women's sports. As you saw earlier in this unit, women are less likely to participate in sport compared with men, and many people believe this is a result of stereotyping. Some forms of sports reporting could be also be classified as sexist: they overemphasise the gender of the players (usually women) in an attempt to attract more spectators.

Racial stereotypes are also common in sports. For example, a study has confirmed that many people actually do believe that 'White men can't jump'. This stereotype implies that black basketball players are naturally superior in athletic ability than white players. White players, in contrast, are falsely perceived as smarter and harder working than blacks. Such stereotypes set up misleading expectations that distort the perceptions of fans, coaches and sportswriters. The resulting misperceptions, in turn, help to perpetuate the stereotypes.

ACTIVITY

1 Look at the two images shown in Figure 5.9. Could these be considered to be sexist?

2 Using sports coverage on the TV, in newspapers and on the radio, etc., identify three stereotypes in sport related either to race or gender.

3 In groups, discuss why you think these stereotypes have come into being and whether you think they are true or not.

Figure 5.9 *Are these two images sexist?*

Other effects of mass media coverage

The production of educational videos

There has been a growth in educational videos in all sports over the past few years, and these are often endorsed by sports stars. A few examples are:

- *England Skills Uncovered 2003*
- *Play Like a Soccer Legend*
- *Bob Woolmer Cricket Coaching Set.*

All these videos use celebrity players and/or coaches to get their point across, which yet again increases these celebrities' profiles and income.

Take-up of new skills/sports

Research has shown that people who watch or follow a particular sport keenly are more likely to participate in that sport as well. In an average daily newspaper, 14 per cent of the content is devoted to sports coverage, and 20 per cent of daytime weekend TV is sports orientated. If the research is correct, this means that any sport that receives a great deal of coverage in the mass media is almost bound to receive a boost in participation rates.

Creation of media stars

Mass-media reporting of sports also helps to create media stars, such as David Beckham. However, not all media stars are as widely known as David Beckham. Tennis player Anna Kournikova, for example, was the second highest-earning female tennis player in the world during 2002, despite never having won a tournament! That year she earned US$11 million although only US$700,000 of that came from prize money.

DID YOU KNOW?

- In 1998, Tiger Woods collected $25 million in endorsement fees.
- David Beckham's yearly income of £10.53 million makes him the highest-paid footballer in the world, even though his basic wage is less than that of team-mates Zinedine Zidane and Ronaldo.
- Kelly Holmes could earn £25 million from her double Olympic triumph in Athens in 2004.

5.5 Profile three major sports activities or sporting events that are or have been influenced by politics

This section covers

● The modern Olympics

● The Commonwealth Games

● Sport and South Africa

● The Football World Cup

Although politics in sport is often considered a modern phenomenon, some authors believe that sport had a political purpose as far back as Roman times when *panem et circenses* (bread and circus games) were used to keep the Roman public quiet. However, Roman citizens often expressed their disapproval of 'bad' emperors by booing the teams these emperors backed. The crowd sometimes addressed itself to the emperor on more important issues. Under the emperors Tiberius, Gaius and Nero, for example, there are reports of crowds at games complaining about levels of taxation.

In this section you will look at political influences on sport in the modern era. The areas that we are going to look at are:

● the modern Olympics;

● the Commonwealth Games;

● sport and South Africa; and

● the Football World Cup.

The modern Olympics

One of the main objectives stated in the Olympic Charter is 'to oppose any political abuse of sport and athletes', but for many years the Olympic Games have been influenced by politics. The modern Olympics have been cancelled three times (1916, 1940 and 1944) because of the two world wars, although the reverse of this happened in Ancient Greece – wars were suspended during the time of the games.

The other major disruption to the games in the twentieth century was the use of boycotts: boycotts affected the 1956, 1976, 1980 and 1984 games in particular.

> **GLOSSARY**
>
> **Boycott:** a country's or a group of people's refusal to compete in an event, usually for political reasons.

Olympic boycotts

The 1956 Suez crisis prompted the withdrawal of Egypt, Iraq and Lebanon from the games of that year. Spain and Switzerland also boycotted these games, but as a result of their objection to the soviet invasion of Hungary, which occurred in the same year. In response the IOC President, Avery Brundage, made the following comment: 'by their decisions these countries show that they are unaware of one of our most important principles, namely that sport is completely free of politics.'

The mass boycotts of the 1970s and 1980s were the result of two things:

1   New Zealand's insistence on maintaining sporting links with South Africa (unlike many other countries); and

2   the invasion of Afghanistan by the Soviet Union just before the Moscow games of 1980.

There was much opposition to Britain's decision to compete at the 1980 Moscow games. The withdrawal of the US team from these games (they were directed to do so by the US government) subsequently led to the withdrawal in retaliation of Russia and other Soviet bloc countries from the 1984 Los Angeles games.

Propaganda in the Olympics

The first use of political propaganda in the Olympics was at the Berlin games of 1936, which are sometimes called the 'Nazi Olympics'. Problems occurred even before the games took place, due to Germany's treatment of its Jewish communities. This contradicted the terms of the Olympic Charter, which states that no group should be discriminated against.

Hitler was determined to turn the Olympics into a display of the German nation's strength and of the superiority of his 'Aryan' race. However, Hitler failed in his attempt to use the games as a stage for a demonstration of racial superiority because of the extraordinary performances of Jesse Owens, a black American who won four Gold medals (see Figure 5.10).

Other political uses of the Olympics

The games of 1916 were cancelled due to the First World War, and the IOC did not invite Austria, Bulgaria, Germany, Hungary and Turkey to the 1920 games because of their role in this war. Similarly, the games of 1940 were cancelled because of the Second World War, and invitations to Germany and Japan to the 1948 games were withdrawn.

The IOC were firm in their decision to exclude South Africa from the games because of the South African government's policy of apartheid (see 'Sport and South Africa' below for more about apartheid), and so South Africa was excluded from the 1964 games, not to return until 1992.

Figure 5.10
*Jesse Owens during
the 1936 Olympics*

In 1968, East Germany participated for the first time at the games
as a separate nation. These games are also remembered for the American
'Black Power' salute given by the athletes Tommy Smith and John Carlos
(see Figure 5.11). This was both a political and a cultural gesture in
support of the American Civil Rights Movement. The 1972 Olympic Games
in Munich saw the horror of terrorism brought to an Olympiad, when
eight Arab terrorists killed eleven Israeli athletes.

Figure 5.11
*The 'Black Power' salute
at the 1968 Olympics*

The Commonwealth Games

The Commonwealth Games are held every four years midway between the Olympic Games. All the competing nations come from the British Commonwealth. This is a multi-sport competition, which always includes swimming and athletics. The host nations choose the other eight sports that are to be contested. The 50 Commonwealth member countries are divided into 67 separate nations for competition at the games.

The first Commonwealth Games were held in 1930 in Hamilton, Ontario, Canada. Bobby Robinson, a major influence within athletics in Canada at the time, finally brought into being an event that had been talked about amongst Commonwealth nations for over 30 years. Eleven countries with a total of 400 athletes participated in the first Commonwealth Games. Some C$30,000 was provided by the City of Hamilton to these nations to help cover travelling costs. Since then, the games have been conducted every four years, except for the years 1942 and 1946 (because of the Second World War).

From 1930 to 1950, the games were known as the British Empire Games, and then (until 1962) the British Empire and Commonwealth Games. From 1966 to 1974 they took on the title of the British Commonwealth Games and, from 1978 onwards, they have been known as simply the Commonwealth Games.

Politics have affected the Commonwealth Games almost from their birth, with the second games (which were originally scheduled for Johannesburg, South Africa) being hosted by London. This change of venue was an attempt to avoid a political crisis over South Africa's apartheid policy (see below).

The Cardiff Games of 1958 were to be South Africa's last until its post-apartheid return to the games in 1994. There had been a number of objections at the Cardiff games that South Africa had chosen its team on the basis of race and colour rather than ability. South Africa subsequently withdrew from the Commonwealth in 1961.

Even though South Africa had withdrawn from the Commonwealth, it continued to be a problem for the Commonwealth Games organisers. The 1986 games (the second to be staged at Edinburgh) were to become known as the 'Boycott Games' because 32 Commonwealth nations, mainly from Africa, decided that they could not attend because of their opposition to apartheid in sport.

Sport and South Africa

The term 'apartheid' was coined in the 1930s, and it was used as a political slogan for the South African National Party in the early 1940s. Apartheid, however, goes back to the beginnings of white settlement in South Africa in the 1650s, when it became the custom for white and black people to live their lives as separate from one another as possible.

After the Nationalists came to power in 1948, this social custom of apartheid became law. Apartheid resulted in a separation of jobs, transport, schools, housing and other facilities for different ethnic groups.

This policy of apartheid was also applied to sport: non-whites were not allowed to play for their country, and players of different races were not allowed to play on the same team at any level.

In 1971, the Springboks' rugby tour caused some of the most violent demonstrations witnessed in Britain and Ireland for many decades. The protests centred on the issue of apartheid, and the protest march to the Landsdowne Road stadium was described as 'the largest public assembly this century'. It was the last time the Springboks were to come to Britain until 1995. In the same year as this ill-fated tour, the International Olympic Committee (IOC) suspended South Africa from the Olympic Games for its refusal to accept inter-racial sport, a ban that was to last for over twenty years.

Three years earlier, shortly after the 'Black Power' affair, the England cricket tour to South Africa was called off because of the host nation's refusal to accept the presence of Basil d'Oliviera in the tourist's party. D'Oliviera had been born in South Africa, but his colour prevented him from playing there, so he moved to England where he gained his residence qualification. The England selectors had originally chosen another cricketer, Tom Cartwright, to play, but injury to Cartwright meant that d'Oliviera was picked to replace him.

Whilst apartheid was not a new political issue (see 'The Commonwealth Games' above), it was not until 1977 that the countries of the Commonwealth took united action against the South Africans. Following a much-publicised meeting of sports ministers at Gleneagles, in Scotland, they produced the Commonwealth Statement on Apartheid in Sport, more commonly known as the Gleneagles Agreement (there had been a less decisive meeting in Singapore in 1971, and it had taken six years to get the representatives around the table again). Although the agreement did prove effective in officially excluding South Africa from competitions such as the Commonwealth Games, the vague nature of its wording left the door open for individual nations to pursue their own political line on such issues as racial discrimination.

The election of Margaret Thatcher's Conservative government in 1979 resulted in tensions over South Africa, given traditional Tory support for the white government in that country. It came as no surprise, then, that the Sports Council sent a fact-finding mission to the republic to investigate progress made in multi-racial sport. There were suspicions, however, that the group was shepherded about to visit one or two model sports integration programmes, although their reports claimed that they had witnessed 'significant advances' in terms of racial integration in sport. Their impressions were certainly favourable, for the following year the council pressed for South Africa to be readmitted to the international sporting scene.

GLOSSARY

Apartheid: an Afrikaans word meaning 'separation' or, literally, 'apartness'. It has come to mean any legally sanctioned system of racial segregation, such as existed in South Africa between 1948 and 1990. The first recorded use of the word is in 1917, during a speech by Jan Smuts, who became Prime Minister of South Africa in 1919.

Asians: people primarily from India who were brought to South Africa to work on sugar plantations.

Coloureds: people of mixed race (often Europeans and Africans) and pure black Africans.

Whites: European settlers.

ACTIVITY

Look up the controversy surrounding the inclusion of Basil d'Oliviera in the England touring cricket team of 1968. Would that happen now?

Since then, South African politics has been turned upside down, and black South Africans have been given the rights they had been fighting for three quarters of a century. Nelson Mandela's release from prison on Robben Island and his subsequent election as president did a great deal for sport in South Africa.

The Football World Cup

Football and politics have always been closely linked, ever since the second World Cup of 1934, which was hosted by Italy, a country then ruled by the fascist dictator Benito Mussolini. Rather like the later Berlin Olympics, Mussolini used the World Cup in an attempt to show the superiority of the fascist political system and, when Italy retained the cup in 1938, the propaganda value of this success was enormous. In the 1934 World Cup, Austria were runners-up and Germany came third, and this was again used by the Nazis to 'prove' Aryan superiority.

CASE STUDY

The 1966 World Cup

Perhaps the greatest political threat to the World Cup finals came in 1966 (the only time the World Cup has been held in England). This World Cup became known as the 'North Korean crisis'. FIFA allocated just one place in the finals for Africa, Asia and Oceania, and all the countries in these groups, except for the Democratic People's Republic of Korea (DPRK) and Australia, saw this as too restrictive. Qualification for the one available place, however, went ahead, and it was settled by a two-match play-off, staged in Phnom-Penh in November 1965. North Korea won both matches, 6–1 and 3–1, respectively.

The North Koreans' qualification was immediately problematic to the British government, which did not recognise the DPRK as a country in its own right. If the North Korean team were to come the UK, this might imply that the government did, in fact, recognise the DPRK, particularly if the ceremonies at matches involved flags and national anthems. The team's presence might also offend British Korean War veterans (although this was only a minor consideration as there were no problems relating to West Germany's presence). More importantly, there was a genuine fear that if the UK made any exceptions for the DPRK, this could be taken as a sign by other unrecognised countries, most particularly the German Democratic Republic (East Germany), that they should be recognised too. The admission of the North Koreans would also damage British relations with South Korea.

CASE STUDY

The 1966 World Cup (Cont.)

The solutions eventually arrived at included the minimal use of any national symbols, restrictions on the formal presentation of the teams to the government and to royalty and the insistence that the team play under the name of 'North Korea' rather than their preferred (and FIFA recognised) title of DPRK.

These issues were dealt with tactfully and diplomatically. The North Koreans came; the potential crisis was not only averted but also kept out of the press; and the government and sport proved that, despite their different views, they could work together. Whilst most people's attitudes towards the 'troublesome North Koreans' were not very favourable, they were kept quiet in the interests of diplomacy. (The Koreans went on to be one of the stars of the tournament, losing to Portugal in the quarter finals.)

1 **Do you think the British government's decision to allow the DPRK team to visit the UK was right?**
2 **Should the interests of sport be given more importance than political considerations?**

Political interference in the World Cup is not confined to the teams on the pitch, however. In 2000, Germany was elected to host the 2006 World Cup by 12 votes to 11 over rival South Africa. The president of the Oceania Football Confederation (OFC), Charlie Dempsey of New Zealand, abstained from the final ballot because he feared a vote for Germany or South Africa would be detrimental to soccer in the 11 Oceania nations, and also because a vote either way would have made enemies for the OFC in FIFA. He hoped his no-vote would ensure the OFC would make no enemies and so stay friends with all concerned: 'It had also been made clear to me by influential European interests that if I cast my vote in favour of South Africa, there would be adverse effects for OFC and FIFA.' This led to allegations of corruption amongst FIFA members, particularly from South African President Thabo Mbeki, who said that the voting procedure 'has got elements of dishonesty about it'.

5.6 Summarise three issues associated with accessibility of sport for people with a disability

This section covers
- History of the Paralympic Games
- Other barriers to participation
- Adaptation of sports and/or equipment

There are several issues that face people with disabilities who wish to play sport and, in this section, we will look at some of the most common. Attitudes to disability changed during the twentieth century, but the major change only took place after the Second World War. Before the war, people with disabilities (especially mental disabilities) were often kept out of sight in special institutions because they were regarded as being something of an embarrassment.

However, the earliest sports for people with physical disabilities date back to the First World War when sport was used as a form of treatment for blind and amputee servicemen. Medicine at that time was not very advanced, though, and the life expectancy of people with major physical disabilities (such as spinal injuries) was very short. As the numbers of servicemen who took part in such sports began to wane, therefore, interest in sport as a treatment for the physically disabled similarly began to wane.

During the Second World War, the idea of sport as an aid to treatment and rehabilitation of war casualties was revived. However, it was not until 1944, when Sir Ludwig Guttman, a specialist in spinal injuries, was appointed medical director of Stoke Mandeville Hospital that the idea of sports for the physically disabled took hold. Guttman was determined that spinally injured soldiers should not only have a longer life expectancy but that they should also function as full, contributing members of society. To meet these high ideals, Guttman introduced sport into his rehabilitation programme, primarily to train the body but also to revive among the injured the spirit of accomplishment and self-worth. This led to disabled sports events becoming more acceptable to society as a whole and, ultimately, to the establishment of the Paralympic Games.

History of the Paralympic Games

The first games for athletes with a disability were held at Stoke Mandeville Hospital, on the same day as the opening ceremony of the 1948 Olympic Games in London. It was at these Stoke Mandeville games that the first competition for wheelchair athletes was organised. Four years later, athletes from the Netherlands joined the games and, thus, the international movement, now known as the Paralympic movement, was born.

Olympic-style games for disabled athletes were organised for the first time in Rome in 1960, immediately after the Olympic Games. These are considered the first Paralympic Games. About 400 athletes from 23 countries competed in eight sports. Since then, the Paralympic Games have been held every four years, in the same year as the Olympic Games. At the Toronto games in 1976, different types of disabled people competed together for the first time in international sport competitions. In the same year, the first Paralympic Winter Games took place in Sweden.

The 1988 Seoul Paralympic Summer Games marked another significant change, as both the Olympic and Paralympic Games were held at the same venues. Since then, the Paralympic Games have always taken place at the same venues as the Olympic Games. The Paralympic Games have evolved into a major media event, with the BBC providing daily coverage of the games for the first time in 2004.

Disabled athletes still face barriers to participation, however, and the following case study is an example of some of these barriers.

CASE STUDY

Making sports accessible: how far should we go? PGA Inc. Tour v. Martin

----

Casey Martin was diagnosed at birth as suffering from an inherited disorder. Over time, this disorder led to pain and muscle wasting in his right leg. In spite of this, he became an excellent golfer, but his disability made it hard for him to walk around the golf course. When Martin was at college, the National Collegiate Athletics Association (NCAA) allowed him to use a cart during competitions so that he could easily get round the course.

When Martin became a professional golfer, however, things changed. He asked the

Professional Golfers Association (PGA) Tour to let him use a cart in competitions, but his request was denied. Being able to walk the course is part of the game, the PGA argued, and letting Martin use a cart would give him an unfair advantage over other golfers who had to cope with the fatigue caused by walking.

In 1997 Martin sued the PGA Tour for violating the Americans with Disabilities Act, arguing that a cart is a 'reasonable modification'. The case eventually reached the Supreme Court

Making sports accessible: how far should we go? PGA Inc. Tour v. Martin (Cont.)

----

which, in May 2001, ruled in Martin's favour. The court agreed with Martin's lawyers, who argued that letting Martin use a cart would not 'fundamentally alter' the nature of golf or give him an unfair advantage over other players.

1   Do you agree with the Supreme Court's decision to let Casey Martin play using a golf cart?
2   How far should sporting organisations go in accommodating the disabled? Would allowing a disabled bicycle racer a head start in bike races be fair, or would it 'fundamentally alter' the nature of a bike race?
3   Should all organisations or public places be forced to make accommodations for the disabled? Does this unduly affect small businesses? Who should pay for the improvements?
4   Have you or anyone you know experienced discrimination because of a disability?

Other barriers to participation

As we have seen, accessibility is a major physical barrier to participation for disabled athletes, but there are other, more subtle reasons that people with disabilities are prevented from participating in sport.

Perceptual

People with disabilities are often seen as deserving of pity or as second-class citizens, and disability once was considered to be a medical problem. People who see disability this way believe that the person is the problem and that he or she cannot make any decisions concerning his or her life. Thus the disabled community are seen as needing a cure and, until there is a cure, disabled people can never be equal to non-disabled people.

This old way of viewing disability also contains many stereotypes about disability. These stereotypes are usually untrue and very painful to those whom they involve. People with disabilities are considered incapable of doing things they want to do. They start to see themselves in a lesser light and become more passive as they attempt to lead what others call a 'normal' life.

The new perception of disability is much more accepting of disability. Disability rights are being fought for every day. Equality, an end to discrimination, accessibility and reasonable adaptations for people with disabilities are all key issues that are being lobbied for by disability groups.

Attitudinal

Although the 2004 Paralympics Olympics were held in Athens, Greek TV did not cover the event (neither did the USA). Paralympian Tanni Grey-Thompson (see Figure 5.12) also described how she was prodded in the street during a pre-games visit in 1997 as Athenians were not used to seeing people in wheelchairs.

Figure 5.12
Tanni Grey-Thompson

Greek society has, until recently, tended to institutionalise people with disabilities. A recent European survey showed that people in Greece, Germany and France are ill at ease in the presence of people with disabilities. People in Denmark, the UK, Sweden and the Netherlands, on the other hand, seem to have no real problem with people with disabilities. When asked, 'How much and in which context do you feel at ease with someone in a wheelchair?' most Europeans replied that did feel at ease with people in wheelchairs, the average positive response rate being 84 per cent. The UK had the best score (94 per cent), followed by Denmark and Sweden. The Netherlands, however, like Greece and Germany, had a lower score.

Financial

If we compare the sponsorship of the Olympics with that of the Paralympics, the difference is staggering. Figures from Sydney in 2000 show that the final total sponsorship revenue achieved for the Paralympics was $45.9 million (Australian) compared to $600 million (Australian) for the Olympics themselves. In 2004, corporate sponsors provided around €436.7 million for the Athens Olympics. At the time of writing no figures were available for the Paralympics, but if we estimate that the same proportion was raised as in Sydney, then only €33.6 million was raised in sponsorship for Athens 2004.

Again, however, attitudes appear to be changing, as can be seen from this statement by Scot Smythe, Visa International Vice-President for Sponsorship: 'We see disability sport as a business opportunity and not a cause and it is a worthwhile investment.'

DID YOU KNOW?

- The British Paralympic team had to pay for their own team kit in 2004; the Olympic team got theirs free.
- The GB Winter Paralympic team got £1,500 of government funding compared with the £4 million spent on their able-bodied counterparts.
- The GB women's wheelchair basketball team spent £30,000 of their own money to qualify for the Paralympics, as they had no funding.

Adaptation of sports and/or equipment

One other issue regarding disabled sport is that of adaptations – either of rules or equipment. Some examples arc as follows:

- *Blind football*: The ball contains a bell, and certain modifications are made to the rules, such as no goals can be scored from a header.
- *Blind cricket*: A size-three football is used to help partially sighted players to see it, and this is filled with ball bearings so that totally blind players can hear it.
- *Wheelchair rugby*: To give everyone an opportunity to compete on equal terms, a player classification system is used. Each person is given a class according to arm and hand muscle function and strength. If individuals have some leg or trunk movement, this is also taken into accounted. Classes range from 0.5 to 3.5 in 0.5 increments, with the maximum points total for the four team members on court at any one time set at 8.

ACTIVITY

Find three other sports that have been adapted for use by people with disabilities. Make a note of four changes that have been made to the rules to take into account disabilities.

For many people with mobility impairments, equipment is the most important adaptation. Specially designed wheelchairs, hand cycles and skis are some of the more common pieces of adapted equipment. Smaller pieces of equipment can also help, such as a glove to grip a tennis racquet or a strap to improve balance, and many adaptations can be 'home-made' from low-cost materials. Environmental modifications, such as the use of special surfaces on a sports field, can make a sport more accessible for people with disabilities.

ACTIVITY

Describe three pieces of modified equipment used by disabled competitors. Compare these with normal sports equipment in terms of price. Do you think any variations in price between normal and modified equipment are justified?

TEST YOUR KNOWLEDGE

1. Outline the issues related to drug abuse in sport.

2. Name three classes of drugs banned in sport.

3. In which year was Title IX passed as law?

4. Name two sports that have a high level of aggression and anti-social behaviour amongst spectators?

5. Why was South Africa banned from taking part in the Olympic Games?

6. Where were the first official Paralympic Games held?

Sports Skills

Introduction

By studying this unit you will develop knowledge, understanding and practical skills in a range of sporting activities, including those that are games-based, athletic-based and gymnastic-based. As this is a practical unit it is an ideal opportunity for you to develop your own sports skills and to acquire new ones. You could perhaps also try sports that you have always wanted to try or that you have not considered before.

As a result of the work you do for this unit, you will also develop and evaluate your practical skills, improve your sporting performance and improve or develop your abilities to referee a range of sporting activities.

How you will be assessed

For this unit you will produce a portfolio of work that shows you have met all the assessment objectives for the unit. This could contain certificates that show you have achieved proficiency awards for the sports you have chosen (e.g. National Governing Body Awards). If this is not possible, it could include diaries, log books, records of sessions, videos and witness statements, etc., that demonstrate you have met the assessment objectives.

To meet the assessment objectives for this unit, you must show that you can use the coaching skills you have developed to improve your own performance, rather than just organise and deliver a coaching session. You must also demonstrate that you have identified areas where you could develop your skills further. You must do this for three different sports. The tasks below, therefore, should be undertaken for each sport you have chosen.

In this unit you will learn how to:

① Select and describe one sport from each of the three areas of sporting discipline

② Demonstrate knowledge of skills, techniques, tactics and strategies in the three selected sports

③ Demonstrate improvements in own individual playing ability and team skills in the three selected sports

④ Demonstrate improvements in ability to referee/umpire in the three selected sports

⑤ Evaluate own performance and progress in developing the skills required for the three selected sports

⑥ Produce a plan to further develop sports skills in the three selected sports

6.1 Select and describe one sport from each of the three areas of sporting discipline

This section covers
- Games-based sports
- Athletic-based sports
- Gymnastic-based sports

Sports can generally be divided into three main areas:

- games;
- athletics; and
- gymnastics.

Games-based sports

Games-based sports are often team sports, such as football, cricket, rugby, hockey, etc. They include such elements as tactics, team selection and co-operation between team members. Their characteristics include the following:

- *A defined field of play.* For example, football pitches all over the world have the same dimensions even if the stadiums they are in are different sizes. Not only that but the ball is the same size and weight, the goals are the same size and each team has the same number of players.

- *Timed play* – i.e. the fixed duration of the game (the time, the number of overs, etc.). If you play cricket in England or India, you play in one-day, four-day or five-day 50-over or 20-over matches.

- *Supervision by officials* (referees) who interpret the rules of the game. The number of officials is again set as a standard (e.g. one referee and two assistants in football and rugby, two umpires in cricket, and a referee and three judges in boxing and so on).

Some individual sports (such as tennis – see Figure 6.1) can also be defined as games-based sports because they meet the above criteria. Tennis is played on a court, with clear dimensions; the net is of a regulation height; and the size and weight of the balls used are regulated, as is the size of the rackets used in a match. It is also controlled by an umpire, assisted by line judges and a net-caught judge. The duration of the game is variable but limited by the number of sets played and the number of games per set, as well as by the use of tie-breakers, etc.

Figure 6.1 *Tennis may be defined as a games-based sport*

In this unit you are going to look at rugby as a games-based sport, and you will consider training throughout a competitive year (including pre-season), as well as looking at some sample drills which can be used to develop both fitness and skills. The unit also contains case studies so that you can see the relevance of these drills to players and how they affect the game as a whole.

Rugby meets the definition of a games-based sport since:

- the rugby pitch has to conform to certain size standard and so it has a defined field of play. Once the ball leaves the pitch it is out of bounds and has to be returned by a line-out or drop-kick before play can continue;

- each rugby match is 80 minutes long, which is split into two halves of 40 minutes; and
- each match is supervised by a referee who is assisted by touch judges and a video referee so that they can make decisions based on the rules of the game.

Athletic-based sports

Athletic-based sports tend to be individual sports, such as track and field athletics (see Figure 6.2). Athletic-based sports are often against the clock, with the fastest athlete over a set distance being the winner. Alternatively, the athlete achieving the greatest distance may be the winner. Athletic-based sports include:

- jumping (including the triple jump, the long jump and the high jump);
- running and walking; and
- throwing (the discus, hammer and shot-put).

Figure 6.2 *Long-jumping is an athletic-based sport*

For this part of the unit you will look at a competitive athlete's training programme. This is a cross-country runner who is preparing for an autumn competition, and you will take him through a 12-week pre-competition programme to improve his performance.

Cross-country running meets the criteria of an athletic-based sport because:

- it is usually an individual sport. The only exception to this is a relay race, but even here the runners race in individual legs rather than together with their team-mates;
- the race is always over a set distance; and
- the winner is the runner who completes the course in the fastest time and reaches the finish line before the other runners.

Gymnastic-based sports

These sports tend to be aesthetically pleasing (see Figure 6.3), and they include such things as aerobics, acrobatics, gymnastics (artistic and rhythmic) and trampolining. They are judged against a standard by a panel of judges with marks awarded for technical skill and artistic merit. These sports are highly technical in nature and tend to be performed individually.

Figure 6.3 *Gymnastic-based sports are aesthetically pleasing*

A good example of gymnastic sports is trampolining, and in this part of the unit you are going to look at a basic trampolining programme for a novice trampolinist.

Trampolining meets the requirements of a gymnastic-based sport because it is:

- judged by a panel of experts according to whether a series of movements meets certain aesthetic standards; and
- technically demanding, with each performer having to complete a series of manoeuvres in the correct manner.

Trampolining is performed individually. The only team event is synchronised tramoplining, where two trampolinists perform simultaneously for the judges.

6.2 Demonstrate knowledge of skills, techniques, tactics and strategies in the three selected sports

This section covers
- Characteristics of a skill
- Ways of classifying skills
- Techniques
- Tactics and strategies

For this assessment objective you will need to know how to recognise and define a skill, how to recognise and teach appropriate techniques to improve performers' skill levels and tactics, and how to devise strategies so that they are successful.

Characteristics of a skill

It is important to realise that a skill is a learned behaviour, and that performance of a skill has to improve over time so that it becomes more consistent in terms of:

- accuracy;
- efficiency; and
- adaptability.

This means that learning is:

- not a 'one-off' lucky effort/performance;
- relatively permanent (this means that the consistency of the skill is increased, not that the skill is 100 per cent perfect); and
- due to past experience and/or practice.

Some ways to check whether an athlete has learnt a skill are as follows:

- *Observe*: Is his or her performance consistent?
- *Measure/test*: Is the performance improving (faster times for runners, more accurate passes, etc.)?
- *Evaluate*: What features of the performance are strong or weak?

Three common ways of evaluating a skill are as follows:

- Practice observation (i.e. watching performers perform).
- Retention tests (can the athlete (or athletes) repeat the skill week after week?).
- Transfer tests (can the athlete (or athletes) transfer the skill to a game situation?).

Rugby

Two skills used by virtually every rugby player are the tackle (see Figure 6.4) and the pass. If we look at these two quite separate skills, we can see that they have some characteristics in common:

- Both need a decision about where the tackle or pass is best used.
- The players needs to be aware of the other players on the field – not only their team-mates but also the opposition.
- Both need to be performed correctly the first time.

Figure 6.4
Rugby players must know how to use and avoid the tackle

A good coach should be aware of these common characteristics and should use drills that will help with both skills, before practising the skills on their own.

One simple drill to help with awareness is to practise a movement. The players run from one goal to the other, switching positions all the time. At random intervals the coach shouts 'Stop!' and then asks a player to say where one or more of the other players are. For example, at the command stop, the coach may ask number 8 where number 14 is. Number 8 must then give number 14's position without turning around to look.

Cross-country running

An essential element of any runner's performance is the sprint which, for cross-country runners, is usually used at the end of a race. At this point the runner is tired and so needs good technique in order to perform well. One drill often used is called 'heel flicks' (Figure 6.5).

Figure 6.5
Cross-country runners use a drill called the 'heel flick'

The usual method of doing this drill is for the athlete to flick the heel high behind the body, attempting to make it come into contact with the buttocks. During this movement the knees are deliberately kept low. This drill is best done if the heel is flicked up behind quickly, at the same time as the knee is pulled forward. The body must be kept upright and not bent slightly forward in the middle. The arms must also be used in a correct sprinting manner. The emphasis should be on speed of movement rather than running speed.

Trampolining

Before the novice trampolinist can begin to work on the trampoline, he or she must work the positions on the floor as statues. Where possible, the coach should try to pull the athlete's legs apart and push at different body parts to help the gymnast understand the tightness of each skill. One example of a statue is the 'front drop' (Figure 6.6).

Figure 6.6 *The front drop*

In order to practise the front drop, the gymnast lies in a prone position, flat from his or her knees to his or her chest. The knees are bent at 90 degrees, with the feet aiming up to the ceiling. The elbows are down on the floor, with hands on the floor, slightly in front. The neck is straight, with the face looking towards the floor. The head is in the military chin position (i.e. tucked in without the neck being bent forward).

ACTIVITY

Working in pairs, select two skills from each of the sports listed above. Use a demonstration or a video to analyse each skill. Do these different sports have any features in common?

Ways of classifying skills

Skills can be classified into these four pairs of independent parameters, summarised in Table 6.1. Any given skill can be categorised within all few parameters simultaneously.

SKILL CLASSIFICATION	EXAMPLE
Self-paced The performer determines the nature of the skill him– or herself	Pistol shooting
Externally sourced The nature of the skill is determined by an external source	The start of a 100-metre race
Fine motor skills Small muscle groups that are used to produce delicate movements	Darts
Gross motor skills The major muscle groups are used	Putting the shot
Open The environment affects the skill	Passing the ball in a rugby match
Closed The environment has no effect	A trampolining routine
Discrete The skill has a clear beginning and end	A serve in tennis
Continuous There is no clear beginning or end	Cycling

Table 6.1 *Ways to classify skills*

ACTIVITY

Look at the skills involved in the three sports considered in this unit. Using a table similar to Table 6.2, classify them according to the list given above. Remember not every sport will contain examples of all types of skill.

SKILL	TYPE OF SKILL	REASONS
Pass	Open	Opponents can intercept the pass
Penalty kick	Self-paced	You decide when to kick after the referee has blown the whistle
Line-out catch	Externally paced	You have to jump when the ball is thrown in by another player

Table 6.2 *Classifying specific skills*

Techniques

Each sport has its own specific set of techniques, which will improve performance. These range from differing handgrips in tennis to which side of the boot is used during a rugby place-kick.

Rugby

To improve change of direction, cut-backs of 15 minutes can be practised in groups of three:

1 Number 1 drop-kicks the ball 3–5 metres out and sprints after it.
2 Number 2 passes the ball back to number 1 and sprints to the end of the line.
3 Number 2 repeats the kicking and passing to number 3 and so on.

The players should execute a quick turn to alternate sides, passing immediately they have picked up the ball. This can be repeated several times and then performed with obstacles (for example, cones). By dodging mock tackles from their team-mates, the players will learn how to evade real tackles.

Cross-country running

Technical training for the cross-country runner needs careful planning, as each session must progress safely from the last whilst developing the athlete's running skills. An example training schedule for nine weeks before a competition would be as follows:

- *Monday*: Warm up, jog a mile, stretch then run 45 minutes, with 5 minutes at good effort and 9 minutes relaxed. Do this four times, then stretch and jog a mile for the cool-down.
- *Tuesday*: 40 minutes easy stretch after run.
- *Wednesday*: Warm up, jog 1 mile, stretch, 20-minute tempo run, run at 30 seconds per mile slower than current 5-kilometre pace, jog 1–2 miles, cool down, stretch.
- *Thursday*: Stretch, 40-minute easy run, stretch, cool down.

- *Friday*: Stretch, 1–2-mile warm-up, hill workout, six to eight 130–180-metre hill, run up hard, jog down 1–2 mile, cool-down stretch.
- *Saturday*: 30-minute run.
- *Sunday*: 55-minute run at a relaxed pace.

This workout enables the runner to develop a sense of pace and to work out running speeds for use in competitions. It also enables him or her to understand how to change pace during a run which, again, may well be needed in competitions.

Trampolining

In the early stages of learning to bounce, all jumps on the trampoline are done with arms in various positions. The first position is straight up, with the shoulders covering the ears. The second position is straight forward. The third position is out to the side and, finally, with the arms straight down. In all these positions, the arms are straight and remain straight. They do not bend when the body feels the G-force as the feet touch. The body is very tight and the focus is on a tight body during the bounce. This is very important for increasing strength and for forming the body ready for more advanced skills.

The gymnast must keep the hips flat in all jumps, and the body straight and flat. When the arms are up, this is the take-off, beginning and ending positions. This is sometimes called the number 1 position: hips flat, hands in the same direction as the armpits and the fingers joined together. It is important to form the body from day one.

ACTIVITY

In groups, choose a technique in one sport, such as bowling in cricket or throwing the discus. Look at a number of players/performers and discuss the differences in the techniques used. Produce a poster to highlight these differences.

Repeat this exercise for a skill in one of the three sports considered in this unit. Make notes of the performers' technique, as in the example given in Table 6.3. Now video yourself doing the same skill and analyse yourself in the same way.

Both players analysed in Table 6.3 are successful kickers and have scored a high number of points for their teams, although they have completely different approaches to the same skill. This shows that it is important to have an individual approach to the teaching of skills and techniques, particularly at the elite level.

COMPONENT OF SKILL	JONNY WILKINSON (ENGLAND)	ELTON FLATLEY (AUSTRALIA)
Position of ball	Vertical	Pointing at posts with the ball at a shallow angle to the ground
Movement to kicking position	Five steps backwards and to the right	Three steps back followed by two to the left
Body position before the kick	Arms held in front with elbows bent and hands together	Arms hanging down beside body
Action before the kick	Looks at the ball, then at the posts, then at a point high in the stands, back to the posts and then back to the ball	Looks once at the posts
Kicks with	Left foot	Right foot
Approach to the ball	Four steps	Two steps back and slightly left, then four to the ball
Follow-through	Long and across to the right	Long and left

Table 6.3 *Analysing an individual player's techniques*

Tactics and strategies

The dictionary definition of tactics is 'short-term actions taken to solve specific problems or accomplish specific goals'. By contrast, a strategy is a long-term action taken to solve specific problems or to accomplish specific goals.

If we look at these terms in a sporting context, we can then say that, as a coach, you will use tactics to win a game, but you will adopt a strategy to win the league. In terms of developing a performer's skills, tactics are used during a single training session whereas a strategy is used over an number of sessions to improve performance and skills.

A good way to look at the difference between tactics and strategy may be to contrast a football team's performance in the FA cup and the football league. A cup match is a one-off game and so each area of the game and even each player can be considered in greater depth by the coach or manager. Motivation levels may well be higher than normal for a team from a lower division and but lower for a team from a higher division. One tactic that has been used successfully by many lower-league teams is to rush the play and not allow their opponents to have time on the ball. This tactic can only be used in one-off games as the physical and motivational demands are too great to be sustained throughout a season.

The factors that need to be considered when deciding tactics are as follows:

- The game position – are you winning or losing?
- What are your opponents' strengths and weaknesses?
- Are you in possession or not (i.e. are you attacking or defending)?

By contrast, a season-long strategy may involve developing a strong defence, holding the ball in midfield and defending a lead. This means that a system is developed where each player has a role that varies very little from game to game, and the primary aim is not to concede goals in order to provide a platform for the team's strikers.

The factors in determining a strategy may include the following:

- What personnel do you have available (i.e. if players are injured during the season, do you have enough strength in your squad to cope without them)?
- What system of play are you going to use?
- What role is each player going to have within the team?

CASE STUDY

Tactical decisions in cricket

In a cricket match, the captain will have to make several tactical decisions, such as the following:

- If I win the toss, do I bat or bowl?
- Do I play with a spinner or not?
- How many recognised batsmen do I have/does the other team have?

- When will I declare?
- Do I use an attacking or defensive field?
- Which bowlers do I use first?

Think of other questions a cricket captain may ask before play, and how the captain's tactics may change during the course of a five-day test match.

Rugby

Goal:
To pass the ball from a line-out across the field to a winger.

Skills needed:
- Lifting of the catcher.
- Catch the ball safely and cleanly.

- Turn and pass the ball to another player.
- The second player catches and passes the ball in 25 metres to a winger.

Techniques:
- Develop catching skills (both hands behind the ball, hand–eye co-ordination).
- Develop awareness (decide which way to pass the ball, determine the position of team-mates).
- Develop accurate passing skills.

Tactics and strategy:
- Session 1: practise lifting and catching at different positions in the line-out.
- Session 2: practise throwing the ball between players to develop passing skills.
- Session 3: practise passing to both sides of the body.
- Session 4: add skills from sessions 1–3 together.
- Session 5: practise the skills in a game scenario.

Cross-country running

Goal:
To vary the running pace during a race.

Skills needed:
- Develop an awareness of race pace and how to judge running speed.
- Increase the pace smoothly without breaking into a sprint.
- Sustain the new pace for a significant period before slowing down.

Techniques:
- Develop running rhythm at average race pace.
- Develop the ability to change rhythm as required.
- Develop a sense of timing.

Tactics and strategy:
- Session 1: practise running at race pace (i.e. a pace comparable to competitors of same standard and age, etc.).
- Session 2: smaller runs at more than race pace to determine what increased pace is realistically achievable and comfortable.
- Session 3: compare running rhythm to a stopwatch to develop an accurate sense of timing.
- Session 4: Fartlek session (Figure 6.7 overleaf) running at race pace and various faster paces as determined by the coach.
- Session 5: Fartlek session running at race pace and various faster paces as determined by the athlete over the race distance.

Figure 6.7
Fartlek training improves aerobic fitness

Trampolining

Goal:
To change from one position to another (e.g. pike position to splits on the trampoline).

Skills needed:
- The ability to hold the pike position.
- The ability to hold the splits position.
- The ability to change body position between the two during a trampolining sequence.

Techniques:
- Develop the pike position.
- Develop the splits position.
- Develop spatial awareness during flight.

Tactics and strategy:
- Session 1: practise positions separately on a gym mat.
- Session 2: practise each position separately on the trampoline.
- Session 3: practise the linking position on a gym mat.
- Session 4: practise the linking position on the trampoline.
- Session 5: insert into previously developed complete sequence.

6.3 Demonstrate improvements in own individual playing ability and team skills in the three selected sports

This section covers

- Strategies
- Analysing and evaluating an athlete's performance
- Performance analysis

Strategies

This assessment objective is best met through a practical course of study. For example, you may wish to follow a Governing Body coaching programme or gain a Community Sports Leaders Award. However, there are common features all effective coaches use in order to improve performance, no matter what their sport is. These include the following:

- *Good time management*: Effective coaches start and finish on time. Not only that, but their sessions are structured so that each activity has enough time allocated to it to so that all participants can perform it properly.
- *Clear plan*: Each session should be structured and have clear aims and objectives.
- *Progressive instruction (build on last session)*: Each session should follow from the last so that skills are developed progressively.
- *Set SMART goals*: Goals should be specific, measurable, attainable, realistic and time-limited.
- *Maintain on-task behaviour*: Effective coaches make sure that everyone has something to do throughout the session (i.e. no one is standing idle).

A few other strategies that will aid your coaching are shown in Figure 6.8 overleaf.

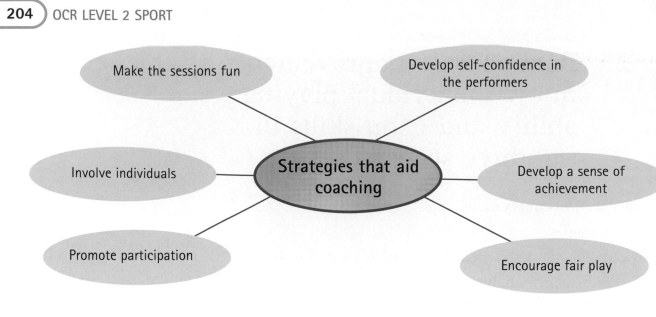

Figure 6.8 *Strategies that aid coaching*

Analysing and evaluating an athlete's performance

As part of this unit you will also have to analyse and evaluate an athlete's performance and, in order to do this, you need not only to observe a performance but also to know what to look for:

- What are the good points?
- What are the faults?
- What are the results like? Do the skills need refining due to failed performance?
- Ways to improve skills – devise practices.
- Are the players fit?
- Fitness testing – suggest how fitness tests may be used to assess fitness levels.

Rugby

Analyse the passing skills in rugby:

- Does the player catch the ball cleanly?
- Does the player release the ball promptly?
- Is the pass accurate?
- Can the player accurately complete a pass repeatedly?
- Can the player pass accurately during a match scenario (e.g. whilst sprinting)?

Cross-country running

Analyse the running skills in cross-country running:

- Is the runner running at a constant speed?
- Does the runner plant his or her foot correctly?
- Is he or she on balance?
- Can the player complete the race distance easily?
- Can the player complete the race distance in an appropriate time?

Trampolining

Analyse the trampolining skills:

- Does the performer maintain adequate height in order to complete the gymnastic movements?
- Does the performer land accurately and symmetrically on the trampoline?
- Can the performer hold his or her body position during flight?
- Can he or she change between body positions smoothly and accurately during flight?
- Can he or she complete the sequence in the time allowed for the competition?

Performance analysis

Once you have analysed someone's performance, what do you do with the information? It is important to present the information in a format that is easy to understand and that makes sense to both you and the performer. You could present it as a graph (see Figure 6.9 for different styles of graphs) or as a table. Table 6.4 overleaf is an example of a tally chart for two football players.

Self-evaluation is also a major part of any performer's or athlete's development, and there are several ways of doing this. Later in this unit you will study an example of a runner's training diary, which is one way of evaluating your long-term progress in a sport. Another way is to complete a checklist of your achievements against your goals, along with the reasons why you have/have not achieved certain goals and which new goals you are going to set yourself.

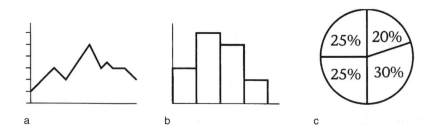

a   b   c

Figure 6.9
Different types of graphs:
(a) line graph; (b) bar graph;
(c) pie chart

SKILL	PLAYER 1	PLAYER 2	COMMENTS (PLAYER 1)	COMMENTS (PLAYER 2)
Shots on target	4	2	Often off balance	Provides for other players
Successful passes	12	22	Good short-ball passes	Regularly beats two or three players with long passes
Passes missed	9	6	Rushes the release of the ball	Occasionally dwells on the ball
Assists for strikers	7	15	Tends to go for goal rather than pass	Pivotal team player
Interceptions made	6	20	Not a strong part of the game	Good defensive qualities

Table 6.4 *A tally chart for two football players*

One way to do this is to create a training log which you complete after every training session and game. Table 6.5 is an example of a training log for a novice volleyball player, and it gives the goals for each session. Each session is built on the previous session and goals are set for the next session according to what has been previously achieved (or not).

Figure 6.10 is an example of a simple competition analysis for a tennis player.

GOALS	TECHNICAL	TACTICAL	FITNESS	MENTAL
Overall goals	Achieve the basic skills of volleyball	Build up to 3 vs. 3 teamwork	Maintain fitness levels	Develop goal-setting habits
Session 1	Posture Ball-flight Volley pass	1 vs. 1 (establish) base	Warm-up and cool-down	
Session 2	Volley-pass Contact point Body weight	1 vs. 1 (attack) Long, short cross-court plays	Warm-up and cool-down	Introduce goal setting

Table 6.5 *A training log for a novice volleyball player*

Date: 12/05/2005	Time: 6.30	Venue: *away*	Event: *league*
Competitor: *Sam Jones*		Opponent: *Ben Rhydding*	
Goal/s set: *Reduce double faults to four a set and reduce the return errors to one per game*		Goal/s achieved: *Double faults set 1—2, 2—0, 3—3 Return errors reduced*	
Comments: *Service is much better with improved confidence. The tennis is improved*			

Figure 6.10 *A simple competition analysis for a tennis player*

6.4 Demonstrate improvements in ability to referee/umpire in the three selected sports

This section covers

- Rugby
- Cross-country running
- Trampolining

In order to fulfil this assessment objective, you will need to understand the rules and regulations of the individual games as well as show that you can take control of the game. Since you are dealing with three different sports and/or three different age groups, you also need to be able to adapt the rules to different groups of performers. Refereeing or umpiring a game or activity is the best way to meet this objective.

The three sports have different methods of refereeing in terms of what to look for (punishments for rule-breakers, etc.), but to referee effectively in all three you must do the following:

- Make a personal commitment to keep abreast of refereeing principles.
- Be fully aware of the context of the game you are refereeing (e.g. age group, numbers, etc.).
- Be fully aware of laws of the game or activity and any variations which may apply to the players because of their age or any special needs.
- Ensure that the spirit of the game is not lost by too much whistle.
- Remember that the players are there for *fun*. You can make a positive contribution to their enjoyment.

- Help clubs and schools ensure that decisions are being applied fairly.
- When refereeing young players, constructive coaching can be as useful as good refereeing.

It is of course vital to know the rules of the game, and few examples of rules with regard to the three sports are given below.

Rugby

The appointment of a referee:
'There shall be a referee for every match. He shall be appointed by or under the authority of the Union or, in case no such authorised referee has been appointed, a referee may be mutually agreed upon between the teams or, failing such agreement, he shall be appointed by the home team.'

A change of referee:
'If the referee is unable to officiate for the whole period of a match a replacement shall be appointed either in such manner as may be directed by the Union or, in the absence of such direction, by the referee or, if he is unable to do so, by the home team.'

Responsibilities of the referee:
'The referee shall keep the time and the score, and he must in every match apply fairly the laws of the game without any variation or omission, except only when the Union has authorised the application of an experimental law approved by the council.'

Cross-country running

Judging or officiating athletics-based sports is rather different from that of either games-based or gymnastics-based sports. The main points are that competitors start and finish the course in the right place and at the right time, and that they complete the course fully (i.e. do not take shortcuts). Other factors that need to be considered are as follows:

Clothing, shoes and licence numbers:
- *Clothing*: 'In all events competitors must wear clothing which is clean, designed and worn so as not to be objectionable. The clothing must be made of a material which is non-transparent even if wet. The competitors must not wear clothing which could impede the view of the judges.'
- *Shoes*: 'Competitors may compete in bare feet or with footwear on one or both feet, except in all walking events where shoes must be worn throughout.'
- *Licence numbers*: 'No person resident in the UK may participate in a meeting subject to the regulations of UK Athletics or any of its

affiliated associations, unless on the date of the meeting concerned he is the holder of a licence which granted him permission to participate.'

- *Numbers*: 'Every competitor must be provided with two numbers which, during the competition, must be worn visibly on the chest and back.'

Assistance to athletes:

- 'Any athlete giving or receiving assistance from within the competition area during an event shall be cautioned by the referee and warned that for any repetition, he will be disqualified from that event.'

- 'No competitor is allowed to receive assistance or refreshments from any person during the progress of the race other than the water point. No persons, not officially instructed by the manager of the meeting, are allowed to give refreshments to athletes.'

Trampolining

The following are some of the rules for trampolining:

- Both men and women compete independently in individual events in trampolining.

- In the qualifying round, competitors complete both compulsory and optional routines, whilst the final consists of just an optional routine.

- The compulsory routine contains a prescribed set of skills, which must be performed in a set order, whilst the optional routines must contain ten recognised skills.

- These skills are submitted on cards to the judges, but can be performed in any order.

- Each of the ten skills in an optional routine should be different (i.e. the skills should not be repeated in the same routine).

- Routines should end with the trampolinists in an upright position with both feet on the trampoline bed.

- They must remain upright for at least 3 seconds at the end of the routine, with points deducted for instability.

- For all skills apart from straddle jumps, the legs should be kept together with the toes pointed.

- Only one attempt at each routine is allowed, unless the routine is interrupted by outside interference.

- There is no time limit on routines.

Remember, these are examples of rules/laws only, not an exhaustive list of the laws for each sport.

Look at Table 6.6, which identifies the roles and responsibilities of referees/umpires in the three sports outlined in this unit.

1 List three things that *all* umpires or referees have to do.
2 List three diffferences between a running official, a rugby referee and a trampolining judge.
3 Why do you think they have these similarities and differences?

ROLE/RESPONSIBILITY	RUGBY REFEREE	RUNNING OFFICIAL	TRAMPOLINING JUDGE
To keep game time	Yes	Yes	No
To record the score	Yes	No	Yes
To call fouls	Yes	No	Yes
To discipline players	Yes	Yes (if member of disciplinary panel)	N/A
To maintain a certain fitness level	Yes	No	No
To record bookings and cautions	Yes	N/A	N/A
To apply the game rules	Yes	Yes	Yes
To check the players' uniforms and dress	Yes	Yes	Yes
To carry a whistle	Yes	No	No
To carry other special equipment	Stopwatch	Stopwatch (if timekeeping)	Pen, scorebook
To wear a set uniform	Yes	Smart dress generally worn	No

Table 6.6 *The roles and responsibilities of referees/umpires*

6.5 Evaluate own performance and progress in developing the skills required for the three selected sports

This section covers
- Rugby
- Cross-country running
- Trampolining

This assessment objective is all about *you*: about how well you have either learnt a new skill or improved a skill you already have. This means that you will have to analyse the techniques that you are using in your sports, just like you did in Assessment Objective 3.

Rugby

You will need to perform a match analysis so that you can see which team members did what during the game. Some ways to do this are as follows:

- Keep a log (or take a video) of what you did during the game (for example, how many tackles and passes you made and how many reached their man).
- How many times did you catch the ball cleanly?
- How often did you manage to avoid tackles?
- How many metres did you carry the ball?
- Did you score any points? If so, did you score more points than in the last game?

All these pointers will tell you whether your performance has improved or not and, if not, why not.

Cross-country running

At first glance, it is easy to see improvements in performance in timed events such as cross-country running, but you can go through the same process as for rugby above:

- Time several practice runs over the same course and distance to see if your time has improved.

- Set targets for improvement. Remember to keep them fairly small and achievable on a weekly basis.
- Video your running action on a track or level piece of ground to see if your stride length is equal on both sides, if you are running on balance, etc.
- Do some timed sprint drills so that you can check improvement of running speed.

Trampolining

Trampolining is rather a subjective sport but, again, analysis of performance follows the same routine as the other two sports. Here video is really essential in order to view improvement in performance:

CASE STUDY

A rugby player's training diary

The following is an example of an elite rugby player's training diary and is included to show you how to achieve maximum levels of fitness prior to a tournament:

Week 1: *Gym*: back, deadlifts. *Fitness test*: 10-minute bleep test, six 60-metre shuttle sprints. *Gym*: Olympics lifts (clean and jerk), upper body. *Interval run*: 11 minutes of 30 seconds at 75 per cent, 30-second jog. *Gym session*: legs. *Team training*: Tuesday, Thursday.

Week 2: *Gym*: bench press, shoulders. *Interval run*: 12 minutes of 30 seconds at 80 per cent, 30-second jog. *Gym*: deadlift, back, arms. *Anaerobic lactate-stacking runs*: two sets of five 1-minute sprints at 80 per cent followed by 30-second rest. *Gym*: bench press, shoulders. *Team training*: Tuesday, Thursday.

Week 3: *Gym*: legs, back. *Lactate-stacking run*: 12 30-second sprints, 15-second jog in between. *Another lactate-stacking session*: 15 repeats of 30-second sprints alternated with 15-second jog. *Team training*: Tuesday, Thursday.

Week 4: *Run*: 30-minute aerobic run. *Gym*: strength tests in bench press, power clean, clean and press. *Anaerobic track work*: sprints (between 3 and 5 seconds) over 30 metres, 2–3 sets of 6 repeats, 400-metre time-trial to finish. *Gym*: leg strength test. *Gym*: back and deadlifts. *Speed-endurance test*: on the track. *Team training*: Tuesday, Thursday.

Week 5: *Run*: aerobic 1:1, 10 sets of 1 minute at 80 per cent, 1-minute jog. *Gym*: bench press, shoulders. *Gym*: back, pull-up test. *Functional anaerobic gym work*: repeated speed 4–8 seconds, 2–3 sets of 10–15 repeats with punchbag, clap press-ups, squat thrusts. *Anaerobic track work*: phosphagen sprints (3–5 seconds) over 40 metres and 30 metres, 150 metres time-trial, stair sprints, plyometrics. *Gym*: legs, Olympic lifts, core exercises. *Speed test*: on the track. *Team training*: Tuesday, Thursday.

Week 6: *Gym*: power cleans, clean and presses. *Team training*: Tuesday, Thursday. Rest and carbo-load.

- Is your body shape better than before?
- Can you complete more and more complex manoeuvres?
- Is your landing better (i.e. more stable with feet together)?
- Can you perform a competent routine?

One of the most difficult things you will have to do for this unit is to compare someone's performance against his or her potential. This means that you will have to decide what an athlete's potential is and how realistic it is to expect him or her to achieve it within the time frame of this unit.

Finally, you must identify any barriers to an individual athlete's performance. Some of these barriers are shown in Figure 6.11.

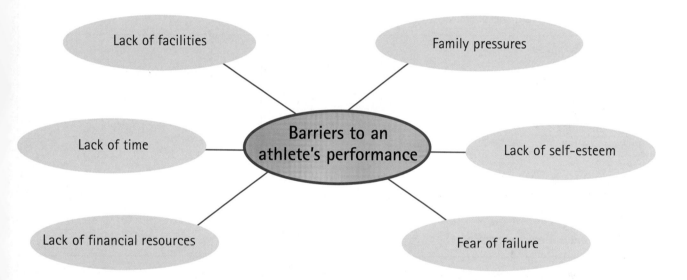

Figure 6.11 *Barriers to an individual athlete's performance*

ACTIVITY

Try to list some other barriers to performance that athletes may encounter during their careers. How can you, as a coach, help them to overcome these barriers?

Look at a video of an elite performer or team and apply the above analysis points to the performance. Then compare that video with one taken of yourself or someone you have coached, and compare them.

A further way of analysing a training programme is to ask the performers what they thought of it. This can be done through a questionnaire, such as the one shown in Figure 6.12 overleaf.

	Yes	No	Comments
Did the programme Help you develop physically? Develop your skills? Teach you strategies? Increase your desire to play? Allow you to have fun? Improve your self-confidence? Distribute awards fairly? Provide proper and safe equipment? Show concern for injured players? Provide good injury care? Have appropriate and fair team rules? Require too much from the players?			
Were the coaches Organised? Good teachers? Fair? Good role models? Approachable? Flexible? Good at giving the praise you deserved? Honest? Reasonable in their demands? Concerned about each player?			
Please provide detailed comments on any of the above			
Please suggest ways the programme could be improved			

Figure 6.12 *Training programme questionnaire*

6.6 Produce a plan to further develop sports skills in the three selected sports

This section covers
- Rugby
- Cross-country running
- Trampolining
- SWOT analysis

All coaches should undergo a process known as continuing professional development (CPD). CPD is the way coaches maintain their professional standards by updating their knowledge and by being trained by other, more experienced coaches and by such people as sport psychologists.

Successful coaches also look for additional coaching opportunities within their own sport or even in other sports. A good example of this is Sir Clive Woodward (see Figure 6.13) who, although he was head coach of the England rugby team, used techniques from other sports (such as American football) to produce a World–Cup–winning side.

Figure 6.13 *Coaches (such as Sir Clive Woodward) make use of techniques from other sports*

To develop your coaching skills, it is also a good idea to read or view resources other than textbooks or coaching manuals. One way of doing this (and for getting further training) is through a body such as Sports Coach UK, who are the training division of Sport England. They provide workshops for coaches nationwide and these can be found by accessing *www.heinemann.co.uk/hotlinks* (express code 9406P). Other resources are coaching journals, such as *Peak Performance*, *The British Journal of Teaching Physical Education* and others.

Absolutely the best way to develop your sports and coaching skills, however, is to increase your participation. Ideally, as you progress, the level of competition, etc., will increase until you and your performer's potential are realised.

In all three sports this would mean progressing through the various levels of competition.

Rugby

Start training/playing recreationally at your school, college or club. Enter intra-club competitions with a team you have put together yourself or as an individual. If possible, train with and join the club team (perhaps beginning with the third or fourth team) and progress through the ranks. Eventually aim to play or compete at county level or even above.

Cross-country running

Look to improve your personal best times with the aim of being able to compete within the club and against other runners in your age group. As your times improve, you can enter open competitions or run in fun runs. Eventually you may be able to compete at county or regional level.

CASE STUDY

A running journal

The following is an extract from a real running journal from someone who has recently begun running with the aim of competing in a 5-kilometre race over the next summer:

Week One: I owe a lot to my running partner. If it wasn't for her I would have been stuck on a treadmill all winter. Instead she was there, night after night, in the cold, dark, winter weather

CASE STUDY

A running journal (Cont.)

----

ready to run with me. Did I mention the rain and wind? My running partner returned from vacation last Sunday, and I'm thankful to have her back. Our usual run seemed twice as long while she was gone. There are many reasons why I like to run with my partner; the motivation of hearing her breath and stride as we ascend a hill, the nights our run ends before our conversation, her encouragement that carries me through a tough run, and the sharing of challenges and accomplishments. As we ran last week in the sunlit evenings, we both felt rewarded by the sun's rays. Our short-term goal is to continue our regular nightly runs varying the intensity, and we will add a longer run over the weekends.

Week Two: I was not able to run as much as I intended to this week. There are just those days when a combination of things come together and prevent the possibility of a run. I was fortunate enough to get in one $3\frac{1}{2}$-mile run and over the weekend my husband, running partner and I did an early morning 45-minute run. I did my first speed workout at the local high school track. I timed a mile for the first time since I started running. My time was 7 minutes 48 seconds. I know I am not a fast runner, but I was pleased by my time. When I was in high school (10 years ago) I found it a challenge to run a mile under 8 minutes (a requirement to make the volleyball team). After the mile my husband and I did 6 sets of 200-metre sprints followed by 200-metre walk/jog and

then ran home. It was fun to add the different workouts to my normal routine. I plan on continuing this. Plus now I have a mile time to improve on!

Week Three: It seems the monotony of our winter running has truly been broken. My muscles know it and they tell me all about it. It feels good to push myself a little harder. It was good week. My training partner and I ran $3\frac{1}{2}$ miles Thursday and Friday. Saturday was a day off. Sunday my husband and I did a long run. My plan was to run 45 minutes, however, my husband had the watch and we ran 54 minutes. I am happy that I am capable of this, but I was more tired afterward than I was last week. He agreed to keep next week's long run to 50 min and be at 60 min in 3 weeks. I took Monday off. Tuesday my partner and I ran to the track and ran timed miles. She ran a 7:40 while I was at the same pace as last week. Wednesday my husband and I ran to the track and did four 400s at slightly faster than best mile time pace. I will be gearing my training toward the Happy Valley 10K I've decided to do in four weeks.

1 Why does the author like running with her training partner?
2 What is the author's short-term goal?
3 Give two reasons why the author enjoyed Week 2.
4 What has the author decided to do at the end of Week 3?

Trampolining

As your performance improves, you should be able to compete within the club and against other trampolinists in your age group. You can then enter inter-club or even open competitions. Eventually you may be able to compete at county or regional level.

Of course, not everyone can compete at a high level (that's what makes elite athletes elite), but good competition is available at all levels in every sport. Often sport is more enjoyable for players at a club level because it as much a social event as anything else.

SWOT analysis

A good way to begin any programme of study is with what is known as a SWOT analysis. SWOT stands for Strengths, Weaknesses, Opportunities and Threats:

- *Strengths*: What are you good at? What skills do you have?
- *Weaknesses*: What do you do less well? What skills do you need to improve?
- *Opportunities*: How often can you train? Do you have access to good coaches/performers?
- *Threats*: What will stop you from developing?

Figure 6.14 is an example of a SWOT analysis for a runner.

Strengths Age General health Non-smoker	Weaknesses I have never run before, generally unfit (poor cardio-vascular capacity) No running partner
Opportunities I can run daily when I return from work I could run to and from work	Threats Work demands Family demands Illness (cold, flu, etc.) Lack of motivation

Figure 6.14 *A SWOT analysis for a runner*

After you have drawn up your SWOT analysis, you can then create an action plan in order to address your weaknesses and threats. Figure 6.15 continues with the example of the runner.

Weakness/Threat	Plan
Never run before	*Begin with small runs (10 minutes) and progress weekly by 10-15 per cent for the first six weeks and then ireview*
No running partner	*Join a local running club*
Work demands	*Timetable long runs for the weekends, run to and from work three times a week*
Family demands	*Schedule family events so that the running plan can be timetabled around them*
Illness	*Wear appropriate clothing for protection; plan nutrition and fluid intake*
Lack of motivation	*Set weekly goals and celebrate their achievement whilst maintaining long- term goal*

Figure 6.15 *An action plan for a runner*

ACTIVITY

With your tutor's help, select three sports which you are going to study to develop your own performance, your refereeing/judging skills and your coaching skills.

Before you start your training, draw up a list of your strengths and weaknesses in each sport as well as your aims for each sport. Your coaching plan will then be based on these aims, strengths and weaknesses.

TEST YOUR KNOWLEDGE

1. What are the short-term goals for a novice rugby player?
2. What would these goals be based upon?
3. Coaches talk about SMART goals. What does SMART stand for?
4. Give two ways that coaches help to improve performance.

Lifestyle and Fitness

Introduction

Most people are aware of the campaigns that are currently being aired about lifestyles: they are all aimed at persuading people to make changes to their lifestyles so that they lead happy, healthy and fulfilling lives.

Exercise is one component of a healthy lifestyle. By studying this unit you will develop knowledge and understanding of the role exercise plays in developing and maintaining a healthy lifestyle, in relation to both physical and psychological health. You will also look at the different factors that make up your overall lifestyle and what you can do to promote healthy lifestyles for yourself, your family and friends.

How you will be assessed

For this unit you will produce a portfolio of work that shows you have met all the assessment objectives for the unit. Your portfolio could contain posters and leaflets you have created to encourage people to adopt a more healthy lifestyle, case studies of people who have changed their lives in order to become more healthy and questionnaires you have devised and used to evaluate someone's lifestyle.

In this unit you will learn how to:

① Identify the elements considered to form a healthy lifestyle and describe their benefits

② Describe the benefits of exercise in the maintenance of health and psychological well-being

③ Evaluate the relationship between lifestyle choices and maintenance of physical and mental health

④ Design and carry out a healthy lifestyle evaluation on a friend/family member and make recommendations based upon the results

7.1 Identify the elements considered to form a healthy lifestyle and describe their benefits

This section covers
- Diet and nutrition
- A balanced diet
- Diet and weight control
- Exercise and physical activity
- Stress
- Smoking
- Effects of alcohol
- Disease prevention

Many elements combine to create your lifestyle. In this section we shall look at some of the most important in relation to promoting and maintaining health.

Diet and nutrition

ACTIVITY

'You are what you eat'. In groups, discuss this old saying. Do you agree with it?

There are three types of food from which you get your energy.

Carbohydrates (CHO)

Carbohydrates include all forms of sugar, as well as other substances such as starch that can be brokens down into sugar. It comes in different forms (e.g. bread, pasta and rice – see Figure 7.1). No matter in which form CHO enters your body, it is always converted to glucose because, as

Figure 7.1 *Carbohydrate comes in many different forms. In these examples, the carbohydrate is mainly in the form of starch*

you learnt in Unit 4, your body can only use glucose for energy. It is recommended that at least 39 per cent of CHO should come from starch and unrefined sugars such as those found in fruit, and no more than 11 per cent should come from refined sugar (the sort that is added to confectionery, soft drinks, biscuits, etc.).

Proteins

You body needs proteins to build and repair your muscles, heart, kidneys and liver, etc. Proteins are made up of chains of hundreds or even thousands of amino acids, and 20 different amino acids are needed to maintain your body in health. These 20 amino acids are divided into 8 essential and 12 non-essential amino acids:

- The essential amino acids need to be eaten on a daily basis, as the body cannot make them.
- The non-essential amino acids can be made by the body.

Amino acids are obtained by your body from animal protein or from vegetables (see Figure 7.2). Animal protein contains all the essential amino acids but only some vegetables have the full complement. Thus you may sometimes need to combine vegetable foods to get all 8 (e.g. beans on toast).

Figure 7.2 *Typical sources of protein*

Fats

Technically, fats are called lipids, and most are divided into two groups:

1 Saturated fats, which mainly come from animal sources. These fats tend to be solid at room temperature (e.g. butter, lard, cream).

2 Unsaturated fats, which mainly come from plant sources. These fats tend to be liquid at room temperature (e.g. sunflower oil, olive oil).

Fats are important because they:

- protect the internal organs;
- help to regulate body temperature;
- insulate nerve cells;
- store fat-soluble vitamins;
- store energy – each pound of fat is worth 3,500 calories;
- help the growth, development and repair of body tissues; and
- help in the storage and production of female reproductive hormones (oestrogen).

A balanced diet

It is often said that a healthy diet is a balanced diet, but what do we mean by a 'balanced diet'? Foods can be divided into five main groups:

1 Bread, cereal, rice and pasta.

2 Fruit and vegetables.

3 Milk and dairy foods.

4 Meat, fish, beans, eggs and nuts.

5 Foods containing mainly fat and sugar.

To have a balanced diet, you should eat a variety of foods from the first four groups each day, as this ensures you have the wide range of nutrients your body needs to remain healthy and to function properly. You should also vary your diet so that you do not become bored, as boredom with food often leads to unhealthy eating habits. Foods in the fifth group are not essential to a healthy diet (because enough fats are normally obtained from groups 1–4) but make food more appetising.

Remember it is not necessary to achieve a balance at every meal, or even every day, but the balance should be achieved over a week or two. One of the easiest ways to achieve a balanced diet is to use something called the 'food guide pyramid' (see Figure 7.3). This gives you guidelines as to how much of each foodstuff you should eat each day. It also shows you at a glance the foods that make up a good diet.

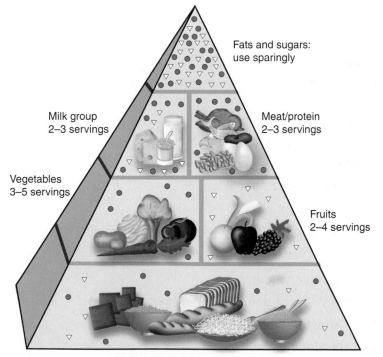

Fats and sugars: use sparingly

Milk group 2–3 servings

Meat/protein 2–3 servings

Vegetables 3–5 servings

Fruits 2–4 servings

Bread and grains 6–11 servings

Figure 7.3
The food guide pyramid

The pyramid shows you that you need to eat a variety of foods from all five groups, and how much food from each group you should eat to stay healthy. Its pyramid shape explains which foods you should eat more or less of: the foods at the pyramid's base should form the bulk of your diet. As you go up the pyramid, the amounts of the different foods you need get smaller.

To follow the pyramid guidelines, use these portion sizes.

Bread, cereal, rice and pasta group

Six to eleven servings per day. One serving equals:

- One slice of bread.
- 100 millilitres of cooked rice or pasta.
- 100 millilitres of cooked cereal.
- 25 grams of cold cereal.

Vegetable group

Three to five servings each day. One serving equals:

- 230 millilitres of raw leafy vegetables.
- 100 millilitres of other raw vegetables or cooked vegetables.
- 175 millilitres of vegetable juice.

Fruit group

Two to four servings each day. One serving equals:

- One medium-sized apple, banana or orange.
- 100 millilitres of cooked or canned fruit.
- 175 millilitres of fruit juice (such as orange juice, grapefruit juice or cranberry juice), but you're better off with real fruit than you are with juice!

Milk, yoghurt and cheese group

Two to three servings each day. One serving equals:

- 230 millilitres of milk.
- 230 millilitres of yoghurt.
- 25 grams of cheese.

Meat, poultry, fish, dry beans, eggs and nuts group

Two to three servings each day. One serving equals 55–85 grams of cooked lean meat, poultry or fish – that's a little smaller than the size of a pack of cards.

Twenty-five grams of meat is also equal to:

- One egg.
- 100 millilitres of cooked dry beans.
- 15 millilitres of peanut butter.

Fats, oils and sweets group

The food guide pyramid suggests that, when it comes to fatty, oily or sugary foods, people should use them sparingly. In other words, eat only a little bit and don't eat them very often. Figure 7.4 suggests some guidelines for a healthy diet.

- Enjoy your food
- Eat a variety of foods
- Eat the right amount to be a healthy weight
- Eat plenty of foods rich in starch and fibre
- Don't eat too much fat
- Don't eat sugary foods too often
- Look after vitamins and minerals in the food you eat
- If you drink alcohol, keep within sensible limits
- Think carbohydrate first!

Figure 7.4 *Guidelines for a healthy diet*

ACTIVITY

Keep a food diary for one week. Look at the food you have eaten to see whether, over the week, you have eaten a balanced diet (i.e. a diet that has all the five food types in it and in the proportions recommended in the food guide pyramid). Could you improve your diet and, if so, how?

DAY / MEAL	MONDAY	TUESDAY	WEDNESDAY
Breakfast			
Lunch			
Dinner			
Snacks			

Diet and weight control

The amount of energy in your diet is important to your health. Everyone needs a certain amount of energy each day so that his or her body can function – that is to say, so that you can breathe, maintain your body temperature, maintain your brain function and everything else that your body needs to do simply to stay alive.

These basic bodily functions are known as the basal metabolic rate (BMR), and BMR varies from person to person because it depends on your size (weight) and activity level. BMR is measured in kilocalories (usually called calories), and one kilocalorie (Kcal) is the energy needed to heat a kilogram of water by one degree centigrade. However, the international standard for energy measurement is the kilojoule, which equals 4.2 kilocalories.

To calculate your BMR in Kcal, take your body weight in kilograms and multiply by this by 25. So, for example, a person who weighs 70 kg has a BMR (or daily energy need) of 1,750 Kcal. Remember, though, that BMR is only the energy needed to maintain life and that you will need more energy the more active you are.

To work out your daily energy requirements you need to take account of your BMR and your activity levels, as shown in Table 7.1.

Calories come from food, and each foodstuff has different amounts of energy per gram. Carbohydrates and proteins provide four calories per gram whilst fat provides nine calories per gram. Therefore fat contains over twice as many calories per gram than either protein or carbohydrates. For this reason it is recommended that 55 per cent of your daily diet should be carbohydrates, 15 per cent proteins and 30 per cent fats. In fact, in the UK, 40 per cent of our diet is carbohydrates, 20 per cent protein and 40 per cent fat. If we then compare two individuals, one eating the

LIFESTYLE	ENERGY REQUIREMENTS
Sedentary (less than 30 minutes exercise three times weekly)	BMR + 20%
Moderately active (30 minutes exercise three times weekly)	BMR + 50%
Very active (30 minutes exercise or more daily)	BMR + 100%

Table 7.1 *Lifestyles and energy requirements*

recommended diet (A) and one the UK's actual diet (B), you can see, for each kilogram of food, individual B is eating 500 more calories than A.

ACTIVITY

Look at your food diary and calculate what percentage of your calories you are getting from carbohydrate, protein and fat. How do these compare with the recommended percentages?

If someone eats more calories than he or she uses, he or she will gain weight in the form of fat, and this can have serious health implications. As you saw in Unit 2, obesity is defined as a BMI of above 30, and obese individuals have a higher risk of:

- respiratory problems, such as severe shortness of breath;
- breathing interruptions during sleep (sleep apnoea);
- irregular menstruation;
- gallbladder disease (gallstones);
- diabetes;
- high blood pressure; and
- osteoarthritis (of the knees, hips and spine).

The social and psychological effects of obesity include:

- limited choice of clothing;
- limited physical activities (many obese people feel embarrassed in public places);
- employment discrimination;
- open ridicule in public;
- low self-esteem;
- loneliness and depression; and
- despair and frustration.

DID YOU KNOW?

- Some 19 per cent of males and 21 per cent of females are obese.
- A hundred extra Kcal a day will mean a net gain of 4.5 kg of fat in a year.
- A large beefburger contains 23 grams of fat, but a pint of milk only 6 grams.

Exercise and physical activity

A person's health can be improved by appropriate physical activity. Some of the benefits of exercise are shown in Figure 7.5.

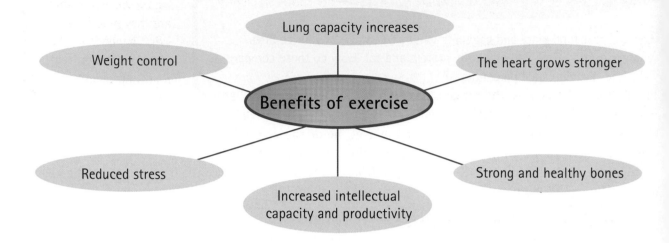

Figure 7.5 *The benefits of exercise*

Experts say that just 30 minutes of activity three to four days per week will help you stay healthy. This exercise will also make you feel better, improve your health and help you perform at your best every day. One of the reasons people don't exercise is that they often find it hard to find the time or money to go to a gym or sports club, but this should not really be a barrier to healthy exercise.

Figure 7.6 suggests a few ways to exercise without using expensive gyms or equipment.

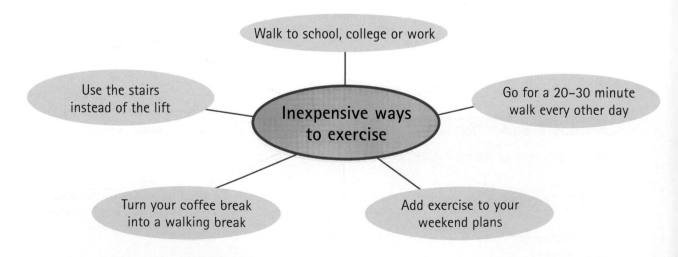

Figure 7.6 *Inexpensive ways to exercise*

Types of exercise

Exercise can be divided into four main types:

1 Cardiovascular exercises. These include activities such as aerobics, running, cycling, swimming and so on. Cardiovascular exercise helps to strengthen the heart and lungs and make then work more efficiently.

2 Strength exercises.

3 Muscular endurance exercises.

4 Flexibility exercises.

Flexibility is defined as 'the range of movement possible at a joint' and is developed by activities such as yoga. Some benefits of increased flexibility are:

● improved posture;

● improved sports performance;

● improved functional capacity (i.e. your ability to carry out the activities of your ordinary daily life);

● it may reduce the risk of injury; and

● stress management.

ACTIVITY

In small groups, discuss the value of the guidelines given in Figure 7.6. For example, are they practical? What benefits would someone obtain from following them?

Stress

Stress is simply your body's response to any demand made on it, and some stress is necessary for you to function correctly. It can become a problem, however, when it causes nervous tension or anxiety. If stress is allowed to develop it can also cause exhaustion, illness, heart attacks and other adverse conditions. Figure 7.7 suggests some ways you can recognise negative stress.

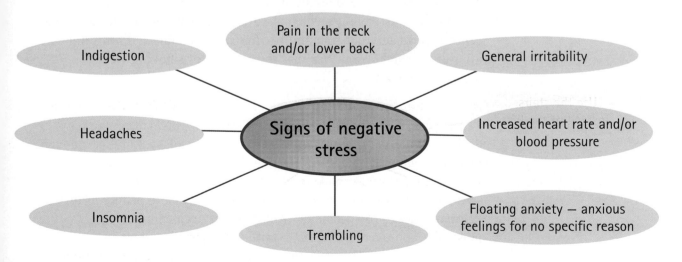

Figure 7.7 *Ways to recognise negative stress*

There are ways to deal with this negative stress. The following are a few tips on how to maintain a healthier lifestyle and to cope with the stress of everyday living:

- Plan to include a minimum of 20 minutes' aerobic exercise at least three or four days a week.
- Eat well balanced meals – more whole grains, nuts, fruits and vegetables.
- Reduce your caffeine intake as this may aggravate anxiety, insomnia, nervousness and trembling.
- Avoid alcohol and drugs which may lead to headaches, may decrease your ability to cope and may make you depressed.
- Get at least seven hours' sleep each night.
- Spend time each day with at least one relaxation technique – daydreaming, prayer, yoga or meditation.
- Go for a walk.

DID YOU KNOW?

- Stress costs industry £5 billion pounds each year.
- More than half million workers have time off due to stress.
- Six million working days are lost each year due to stress-related illness.

Smoking

Tobacco was introduced to Europe from America at the end of the fifteenth century. The smoking habit soon spread all over Europe and was regarded as having medicinal value. It was not until the twentieth century, however, that smoking became a mass habit and not until after the Second World War that the dangers of smoking were firmly established.

At present about 12 million adults in the UK smoke cigarettes (Figure 7.8): 27 per cent of men and 25 per cent of women. This percentage has declined since 1974, however, when 51 per cent of men and 41 per cent of women smoked cigarettes. Despite this decline in smoking every year, around 114,000 smokers in the UK die as a result of their habit. This means that smoking kills around five times more people in the UK than road traffic accidents (3,439), other accidents (8,579), poisoning and overdose (3,157), murder and manslaughter (513), suicide (4,066) and HIV infection (234) put together (22,833 in total, 2002 figures). In addition to this about 30 per cent of all cancers can be related to smoking.

Figure 7.8 *About 12 million adults in the UK smoke cigarettes*

Tobacco smoke contains over 4,000 chemical compounds, which are present either as gases or as tiny particles. These include the following:

- *Nicotine*: This is what is addictive. It stimulates the central nervous system, increasing the heartbeat rate and blood pressure. In large quantities nicotine is extremely poisonous.

- *Tar*: Brown and treacly in appearance, tar consists of tiny particles and is formed when tobacco smoke condenses. Tar is deposited in the lungs and respiratory system and gradually absorbed. It is a mixture of many different chemicals, including formaldehyde, arsenic, cyanide, benzopyrene, benzene, toluene and acrolein.

- *Carbon monoxide*: This binds to haemoglobin in the bloodstream more easily than oxygen does, thus making the blood carry less oxygen round the body.

Passive smoking is the act of breathing someone else's cigarette smoke, and studies have shown that the rates for certain illnesses among passive smokers (i.e. people who live with smokers) are higher than for those who do not live with smokers (a 20 per cent increase in lung cancer, a 30 per cent increase in heart disease and a 40–60 per cent increase in asthma). The good news is that giving up smoking has almost immediate benefits (see Table 7.2).

TIME SINCE QUITTING	BENEFICIAL EFFECTS
20 minutes	Blood pressure and pulse rate return to normal
8 hours	Nicotine and carbon monoxide levels in blood reduce by half, oxygen levels return to normal
24 hours	Carbon monoxide will be eliminated from the body. Lungs start to clear out mucus and other smoking debris
48 hours	There is no nicotine left in the body. Ability to taste and smell is greatly improved
72 hours	Breathing becomes easier. Bronchial tubes begin to relax and energy levels increase
2–12 weeks	Circulation improves
3–9 months	Coughs, wheezing and breathing problems improve as lung function is increased by up to 10 per cent
1 year	Risk of a heart attack falls to about half that of a smoker
10 years	Risk of lung cancer falls to half that of a smoker
15 years	Risk of heart attack falls to the same as someone who has never smoked

Table 7.2 *The benefits of giving up smoking*

DID YOU KNOW?

- More than 80 per cent of smokers take up the habit as teenagers.
- In the UK, about 450 children start smoking every day.
- About one fifth of Britain's 15-year-olds (18 per cent of boys and 26 per cent of girls) are regular smokers – despite the fact that it is illegal to sell cigarettes to children under the age of 16.
- Tobacco is the only legally available consumer product that kills people when it is used entirely as intended.
- The UK government earned £8,055 million in revenue from tobacco duty (excluding VAT) in the financial year 2002–3.
- The government currently spends around £30 million on anti-smoking education campaigns. A further £41 million is spent on measures to help people stop smoking.
- Smokers are likely to die on average six and a half years earlier than non-smokers.

Effects of alcohol

Alcohol is the most widely used drug in the world, and it has been reported that, for most people, the moderate consumption of alcohol may improve health and prolong life. The major benefit of moderate alcohol consumption is a reduction in heart attacks (the most common killer) and strokes. Most people enjoy drinking and find it a sociable and relaxing thing to do. Sensible drinking leads to no harm and is compatible with a healthy lifestyle. But there are times when drinking too much – or drinking anything at all – can cause problems.

Some of the negative effects of drinking are impaired judgement and a loss of balance and co-ordination. Prolonged alcohol abuse causes many life-threatening conditions, including heart disease, stroke and cancers of the liver, breast, mouth and throat, as well as cirrhosis of the liver.

In recent years there has been an increase in what is called 'binge drinking' – excessive drinking followed by a period of not drinking at all, and this pattern is repeated at regular intervals (see Figure 7.9). Binge drinking is particularly harmful because it causes:

- a surge in blood pressure;
- stroke (in an otherwise healthy individual);
- heart attacks; and
- an increase in accidental injury.

> ### GLOSSARY
>
> **Stroke:** blood is prevented from getting to the brain, which results in dizziness, headaches, a loss of co-ordination, etc. Strokes can be mild, lasting just a few minutes, to severe, causing death.

Figure 7.9
Binge drinking

GLOSSARY

GLOSSARY

A unit of alcohol: half a pint of beer, lager or cider; a small (125 ml) glass of wine; or a 25 ml pub measure of spirits.

Safe limits for alcohol consumption are up to three units per day for men and two units per day for women. These units will change, however, according to the strength of the drink. The measures given in the glossary relate to 'normal' strength drinks (3.5 per cent alcohol beer, 9 per cent wine and 40 per cent spirits), but some drinks (such as 'super strength' lagers) will contain more alcohol.

DID YOU KNOW?

- Alcohol features in almost a third of all UK divorce petitions, which means that the drinking habits of one or both partners have contributed to the breakup.
- Some 10 per cent of all road traffic accidents involving injury result from driving with excess alcohol.
- Nine people die every week on UK roads in drink-related accidents – half of them innocent victims.
- Alcohol is believed to feature as a reason behind 25 per cent of school exclusions in the UK.
- Some £200 million is spent each year on alcohol advertising.
- Alcohol-related absenteeism and poor work performance cost British industry more than £2 billion a year.

GLOSSARY

Autism: a brain disorder that begins in early childhood and persists throughout adulthood. It affects three crucial areas of development: communication, social interaction and creative or imaginative play. This means autistic people are often difficult to understand and to deal with.

Disease prevention

As we have seen in this unit, there are many steps that can be taken to help to promote good health. These include controlling weight, not smoking, sensible drinking and taking regular exercise. There are, however, other steps which can be taken to promote good health. Some examples are given below.

Immunisation/vaccination

In the UK the standard immunisation procedure for babies is the MMR 'triple vaccine' (see Figure 7.10). MMR stands for measles, mumps and rubella, and these are three potentially fatal diseases which were virtually wiped out in the UK during the twentieth century. Unfortunately, over the past few years, there has been a loss of confidence in this vaccination as some people feel that it has caused a rise in autism in children, and this has led in some areas of the country to a rise in the number of cases of measles, mumps and rubella.

Self-examination

In the case of diseases such as breast cancer and testicular cancer, one method of prevention or early detection is regular self-examination.

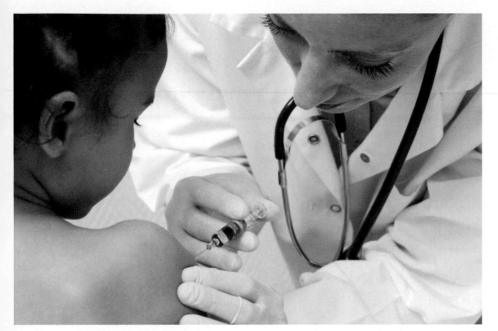

Figure 7.10
Immunisation

Many health experts suggest that women examine their breasts and men their testicles monthly so as to detect any abnormalities (such as lumps, tenderness or hardening of the tissues) as these may be early signs of cancer. For older women a mammogram (an X-ray of the breasts) is recommended every three years after the age of 40. Women should also have a smear test, which detects cervical cancer, every three years after they become sexually active.

DID YOU KNOW?

- Breast cancer death rates fell by 21.3 per cent in women aged 55–69 between 1990 and 1998. Some 30 per cent of this fall was attributed to screening.

- Four million women benefit from cervical screening each year, and the cervical cancer death rate has been falling by 7 per cent a year.

- Although it is rare, testicular cancer is the most common cancer in men aged 15–44, with around 2,000 cases diagnosed each year in the UK.

- Testicular cancer incidence rates in Great Britain have more than doubled since the mid-1970s.

- As yet there is no screening programme for male cancers in the UK.

7.2 Describe the benefits of exercise in the maintenance of health and psychological well-being

This section covers
- Obesity
- Osteoporosis
- Heart attacks
- Cholesterol levels
- Blood pressure
- Stroke
- Cancer
- Diabetes
- Stress

As you saw in the preceding section, exercise is good for you because it has the following effects on your body.

It helps to prevent obesity

Exercising helps people reduce their weight, maintain weight loss and can help fight obesity (see Figure 7.11). Studies suggest that overweight but fit people have half the death rate of overweight but unfit people, and that people who have trained for a long time develop more efficient mechanisms for burning fat and are thus able to stay leaner. Not only that, but exercise improves psychological well-being and replaces sedentary habits that usually lead to snacking. Exercise may even act as a mild appetite suppressant. People who exercise are more likely to stay on a diet plan.

It helps to prevent osteoporosis

Regular exercise contributes to the prevention of osteoporosis by helping people achieve their peak bone mass as adults and then to maintain their bone health as they age. Many studies have

Figure 7.11 *Exercise can help to fight obesity*

shown that people who exercise have stronger bones than those who did not.

It reduces the risk of heart attack

People who do not exercise are almost twice as likely to suffer heart attacks as people who exercise regularly. Mental stress is as important a trigger for heart disease as physical stress, and it has been shown that, in people with heart disease, stress presents a higher risk for serious cardiac events, such as heart attacks, and even death. In one study, middle-aged women who were hostile, self-conscious in public and who suppressed their anger had an increased risk of developing heart disease. Regular moderate aerobic exercise, such as brisk walking, lowers the heart rate and reduces stress in both men and women.

It lowers cholesterol levels

Cholesterol is a fatty substance which is often present in high levels in people with heart disease. It is transported in two forms in the blood: LDL, which tends to damage blood vessels, and HDL, which repairs

GLOSSARY

LDL: abbreviation for low-density lipoprotein.

HDL: abbreviation for high-density lipoprotein.

blood vessels. A study of overweight adults showed beneficial changes in cholesterol levels, including lower LDL levels (the so-called bad cholesterol), when people performed low amounts of moderate or high-intensity exercise (e.g. walking or jogging 12 miles a week). With more intense exercise, HDL (the so-called good cholesterol) levels are increased.

It lowers blood pressure

Regular exercise helps keep arteries elastic, even in older people, and this in turn ensures good blood flow and normal blood pressure. People who do not exercise have a 35 per cent greater risk of developing hypertension than athletes.

It reduces the risk of stroke

According to one major study, men cut their risk of stroke in half if their exercise programme is roughly equivalent to about an hour of brisk daily walking, five days a week. In the same study, exercise that was combined with a recreation activity (e.g. football or dancing) was more protective against strokes than exercise routines that consisted simply of walking or climbing. A study of women also found substantial protection against strokes as a result of brisk walking or striding (rather than casual walking).

It helps to reduce the risk of some cancers

A number of studies have shown that regular, moderate, exercise may reduce the risk of colon cancer and, in fact, any cancer related to obesity. A number of studies have also suggested that regular exercise, particularly if it is vigorous, reduces the risks of breast cancer in women and prostate cancer in men.

Several studies are currently measuring the effect of exercise on patients who have been diagnosed with cancer. Even though these people are in the early stages of cancer, the studies already suggest that exercise has a positive physical, mental and emotional effect. It seems exercise can improve physical strength, the body's ability to function normally and a person's determination to battle the negative side-effects of chemotherapy, including nausea and fatigue.

It reduces the risk of diabetes and helps diabetics to manage their condition more easily

A 58 per cent lower risk for Type 2 diabetes has been reported in adults who performed moderate exercise for as little as 2.5 hours a week. Other studies suggest that the risk is also reduced in overweight people, even if they don't lose weight.

Regular, moderate aerobic exercise improves the body's ability to use insulin efficiently, thus reducing the need for people with diabetes to take medication that contains insulin. People with diabetes are also at risk of heart disease, so the heart-protective effects of aerobic exercise are very important for this group of people. Moderate exercise, in fact, protects the heart in people with Type 2 diabetes, even if they have no risk factors for heart disease other than diabetes itself. Strength training, which increases the muscles and reduces fat, may be particularly helpful for people with diabetes, but evidence is needed to confirm this. One study reported that yoga helped patients with Type 2 diabetes to reduce their need for oral medications containing insulin.

DID YOU KNOW?

- The World Health Organisation estimates that more than 2.5 million people die each year from weight-related illnesses, a figure that is expected to grow to 5 million by 2020.
- Exercise can add years to your sex life. A study has shown that men over the age of 50 who exercise regularly have a 30 per cent lower risk of impotence than men of the same age who do not exercise.
- Everyday physical activity, such as taking the stairs instead of the lift, gardening and walking, is as effective as structured gym workouts in improving fitness.

It reduces stress

Tensing and releasing your muscles during exercise uses up surplus energy and is relaxing. Intense and prolonged aerobic exercise also produces natural chemicals in your body called endorphins, which produce feelings of euphoria (a 'high') and relaxation. What is more, these chemicals are free, legal and don't have the side-effects of drugs and alcohol!

Exercise is a good distraction from your worries and anxieties, and it can even let your brain digest information and solve problems.

GLOSSARY

Diabetes: diabetes covers a range of disorders, but the most widespread of these is diabetes mellitus. People with this disorder have increased levels of glucose in their blood and urine. This can lead to excessive thirst as the glucose in the blood causes sufferers to urinate more than normal. It is because the body is unable to make insulin that such high levels of glucose are in the blood. Insulin is a hormone that regulates the amount of glucose in the blood. There are two types of diabetes mellitus: Type 1 is often present from a very early age, whereas Type 2 is acquired later in life. It has been reported that Type 2 diabetes mellitus often develops in people who are obese.

Exercise improves people's self-image and appearance, and it controls people's weight. The social contact people have with others during exercise can be pleasant, and it provides relief from worries. People who exercise regularly appear to have lower levels of depression than those who do not.

Studies have also shown that if you exercise regularly you will not only live longer (on average about six years) but you will also remain independent for longer. A study has shown that men and women who exercise regularly were three times more likely to remain independent in old age, as well as being two to three times healthier.

7.3 Evaluate the relationship between lifestyle choices and maintenance of physical and mental health

This section covers
● Occupational factors
● Social/recreational activities and their effect on health

As you have seen in this unit, factors such as diet, exercise and stress have an effect on your physical health. There are, however, several other things in life that may affect a person's physical health, such as his or her job, work patterns and so on.

Occupational factors

An individual's job will affect his or her health and fitness. For example, a condition known as 'vibration white finger' (a disorder in the hands) occurs in people who use power tools excessively or who use the wrong types of tool. This is such a problem in miners in the UK that the government has set up a compensation scheme for those affected.

More and more evidence now suggests there is a strong relationship between job strain and heart disease. There appears to be a greater level of heart disease in workers whose jobs place high psychological demands on them and in people who have little control over their jobs. Professional drivers (especially bus drivers in towns and cities) demonstrate the most evidence of an increased risk of heart disease as their jobs are demanding (rush-hour traffic, etc.), yet they have no control over the route they take, the traffic, the passengers or the timetable (Figure 7.12).

Figure 7.12
Among common occupations, urban bus drivers show the most evidence of an increased risk of heart disease

DID YOU KNOW?

- Unskilled manual workers have considerably increased risk of heart disease compared with professional workers.
- Studies have shown that New York City bridge and tunnel officers (people who work in toll booths) have higher than normal levels of heart disease due to their exposure to carbon monoxide in traffic fumes.
- In 2001–02, an estimated 1,126,000 people in Great Britain suffered from a musculoskeletal disorder which, in their opinion, was caused or made worse by their current or past work. This estimate is roughly equal to 2.6 per cent of people who have ever worked.
- A 2001–02 survey estimated that there are over half a million people in Britain who believe they are experiencing work-related stress at a level that is making them ill.

Another factor that affects people's health is shift work. Disrupted work patterns usually mean disrupted sleep patterns, and this can lead to fatigue. The effects of fatigue are summarised in Figure 7.13.

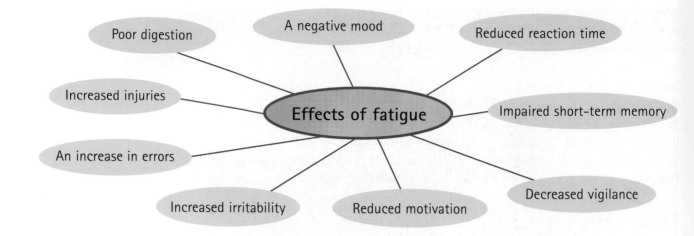

Figure 7.13 *The effects of fatigue*

The combined effect of all these is reduced work performance, increased stress levels and poor health. Research has shown that the cost to healthcare of night work is equivalent to smoking 20 cigarettes a day, and that night work increases the likelihood of coronary heart disease by 40 per cent. Also, an individual who works four night shifts a week is 40 per cent more likely to be involved in a car crash.

The Future Foundation's report (2005), *The Shape of Things to Come*, found that night workers are:

- eight times more likely to suffer from peptic ulcers (ulcers of the stomach or oesophagus);
- at a higher risk of developing chronic fatigue syndrome;
- more likely to have disrupted eating patterns, which cause nausea, indigestion, constipation and bowel irritation;
- some 50 per cent more likely to be involved in a traffic accident;
- more likely to have a marriage breakup;
- social isolated – i.e. have a reduced number of friends; and
- excluded from the community – they attend fewer social and cultural events.

DID YOU KNOW?

- Some 7 million people in the UK currently work between the hours of 6 pm and 9 am (that is, one in seven of the population).
- Some 58 per cent of those people interviewed believed that night work is destructive to family life.
- On the other hand, 67 per cent of people think that supermarkets opening 24 hours a day is a positive trend.

Social/recreational activities and their effect on health

Earlier in this unit you learnt about the effects of alcohol consumption and smoking on health. A recreational activity we have so far not discussed is the consumption of illegal drugs. Drug consumption is on the increase in the UK, and it is estimated that around 500,000 people are regular users of ecstasy and perhaps 3 million people use cannabis. Drugs can be divided into three groups, according to their effects.

Stimulants (uppers)

Stimulants include amphetamines and cocaine. They lead to an increase in energy, activity, heart rate and blood pressure.

Depressants (downers)

These include alcohol, heroin and solvents (glue). These drugs slow down a person's reactions, heart rate and breathing.

Hallucinogens

Hallucinogens include LSD, cannabis and magic mushrooms. These drugs all cause hallucinations – they make people see, hear and feel things differently.

DID YOU KNOW?

In a 2002 (Scottish Schools' Adolescent Lifestyle and Substance Use) survey:

- Some 34 per cent of 13-year-olds said they had been offered a drug; 13 per cent said they had used a drug.
- Some 65 per cent of 15-year-olds said they had been offered a drug; 37 per cent said they had used a drug.
- Cannabis was the most commonly used drug: 31 per cent of 15-year-olds said they had taken it in the last year.
- Over half of 13-year-olds said they have been drunk at least once.
- Girls and boys who smoked and drank alcohol regularly were more likely to take drugs.
- Children aged 13 and 15 years were less likely to take drugs than they were to drink alcohol and get drunk.

7.4 Design and carry out a healthy lifestyle evaluation on a friend/family member and make recommendations based upon the results

To meet this assessment objective you will have to design a questionnaire which measures whether someone has a healthy lifestyle or not. An example of a simple questionnaire is given in Figure 7.14.

ACTIVITY

If you are to question someone about sensitive areas of his or her life, there are a number of issues you should be aware of, such as confidentiality. In small groups, discuss the issue of confidentiality. A good starting point is to ask yourself how you would feel if you were to be asked personal questions about your lifestyle. How is this information to be used? Who else will read it? What other issues do you think you and your group should consider before undertaking a questionnaire? When you have finished your discussion, report your findings to your tutor. You must not carry out your survey until your tutor gives you the go-ahead.

When you undertake your questionnaire, it is important to remember that people may be rather sensitive about some of the questions you ask and may not know all the answers (for example, many people under-estimate their weight and overestimate their height!). As you no doubt decided in your discussion, all the answers you are given are confidential and must not be discussed with anyone else. You should carry out your questionnaire privately as part of a one-to-one consultation.

Your questionnaire should include questions that aim to find out the following:

- If the respondent (i.e. the person filling in the questionnaire) smokes and, if so, how much.
- Whether or not his or her diet meets recommended guidelines.
- The amount of alcohol he or she drinks.
- The respondent's medical history.
- What level of stress the person considers he or she is under.

PLEASE ANSWER ALL THE QUESTIONS.

*DELETE AS APPROPRIATE.

Do you suffer from: High/low blood pressure?	Yes/no*	If yes, please give date of diagnosis:
Diabetes?	Yes/no*	
Asthma?	Yes/no*	
Arthritis?	Yes/no*	
Fainting or dizziness?	Yes/no*	
Shortness of breath during exercise?	Yes/no*	
Do you smoke?	Yes/no*	If yes, please say how many cigarettes you smoke a day:
Do you drink?	Yes/no*	If yes, how many units do you drink each week (one unit = $\frac{1}{2}$ pint of normal-strength beer/larger or one glass of wine):
Have you had any operations in the last 5 years?	Yes/no*	Please list (with approximate dates):
Do you exercise regularly?	Yes/no*	If yes, how often and for how long each time?

Please give your height and weight:

Height =
Weight =

I confirm that all the answers given are accurate and truthful to the best of my knowledge and belief.

Name:

Signature:

Date:

Date of birth:

Figure 7.14 *Sample questionnaire*

You can include any other questions you think are relevant to the respondent's health.

After you have looked at your results you should make recommendations to the respondent as to how he or she can improve aspects of his or her lifestyle in order to improve his or her health.

Figure 7.14 is an example of a basic health questionnaire you could use as a model for your own. You could adapt this to include questions for areas you are particularly interested in. For example, you may want to include a question about sleeping patterns, how many hours per week the respondent works, and so on. You may also want to devise some questions about recent life-changing events, such as bereavements, marriage, divorce or moving house.

Once you have completed your questionnaire, you may need to ask supplementary questions so that you get a more detailed picture of, for example, the respondent's exercise and diet habits, and this may mean that you need to produce another questionnaire.

TEST YOUR KNOWLEDGE

1. What are the main food groups?
2. Give three risks to health caused by obesity.
3. Besides lung cancer name two others smoking-related illnesses.
4. How does shift work affects people's health?
5. What are the two most commonly used recreational drugs?
6. Give three beneficial effects of exercise.

Outdoor Activities

Introduction

This unit will give you an understanding of the outdoor activity sector of the sports industry. You will learn that private, public and voluntary organisations provide a wide range of activities. Each type of activity presents risks as well as benefits to those who take part in them. However, with careful planning, the risks can be minimised and the benefits (such as improving your personal effectiveness and social skills) maximised.

Actual participation in outdoor activities is preferable to complete this unit and will greatly help improve your understanding of the theory associated with this section of the book.

This unit draws on underpinning knowledge and skills developed in Units 2 and 3.

How you will be assessed

For this unit you will produce a portfolio of work that shows you have met all the assessment objectives for the unit. Your portfolio could contain a logbook of your preparation for, participation in and review of your performance in the outdoor activities you take part in, a diary, videos and witness statements, etc.

In this unit you will learn how to:

① Describe the characteristics of four outdoor adventure activities

② Profile three outdoor activity centres which provide the outdoor adventure activities described in AO1

③ Describe the benefits of participation in outdoor activities for three community groups

④ Identify possible hazards involved in participation in a range of outdoor activities and explain measures used to reduce risk

⑤ Take part in three outdoor activities and review own performance

8.1 Describe the characteristics of four outdoor adventure activities

This section covers
- Canoeing
- Hillwalking
- Orienteering
- Camping
- Skiing
- Rock climbing
- Sailing

There is an enormous range of activities that can be classified as taking place in the outdoors. However, the term 'outdoor activities' usually refers to those activities that are dependent on a natural resource. Such sports as sailing and rock climbing are therefore classified as outdoor activities because you require access to a body of water or a rock face. Football, on the other hand, is not classified as an outdoor activity because you can play this anywhere, even in the built-up areas of cities.

All outdoor activities have different requirements in terms of time, equipment, training and the preparation needed. We will now examine in detail some of the more popular outdoor activities.

Canoeing

You can canoe on many rivers and reservoirs, but there are also a number of purpose-built centres that divert water along a course specially created for canoeing. In this way the water's flow rate can be controlled to suit the beginner or the more advanced canoeist.

Depending on your ability level and transport arrangements, you will usually need at least half a day to participate in this activity. This includes preparation and practice time. You will also need the following equipment to participate in canoeing:

- A change of clothes.
- Some old trainers or wetsocks/boots.
- A thermal T-shirt.

- A helmet (supplied by the centre).
- A wetsuit (supplied by the centre).
- A canoe and paddle (supplied by the centre). There are various types of canoe suitable for differently sized people and different ability levels. Canoes are also designed to take one or more canoeists.
- A spashdeck (supplied by centre). This is a sheet of waterproof material that is fastened tightly to the body of the canoe. It repels water, thus preventing it from entering the canoe.
- A lifejacket/buoyancy aid.

To gain proficiency in canoeing requires a considerable amount of training and practice (Figure 8.1). There are many safety rules and manoeuvres that must be learnt. For example, participants must learn how to 'roll' a canoe and how to cope in an emergency. This is very important: if the canoe capsizes the canoeist must either attempt to get it the right way up again or get out of it.

Figure 8.1 *To canoe proficiently requires a considerable amount of training and practice*

Canoeing at an advanced level can be very exciting, particularly in whitewater or fast-flowing conditions. However, many hours of practice are needed before this can be attempted. Amongst other skills, you will need to be able to turn, stop and reverse the canoe by using various paddle techniques.

Hillwalking

Hillwalking is the name given to walking over difficult terrain, mainly in hilly or mountainous areas. Many areas in the UK are used for this activity, including the national parks (for example, Dartmoor, the Peak District and Snowdonia). Walking in these areas is safe as long as certain safety precautions are taken, coupled with a knowledge of how to navigate in open country.

There are several key pieces of personal equipment that are necessary to participate safely in this activity. These include the following:

- Walking boots.
- A change of clothing (trousers, T-shirt, socks).
- Extra layers of warm clothing.
- A waterproof coat and trousers.

CASE STUDY

Clothing

You must be careful to choose the appropriate clothing if you go on long treks in wild country. Whilst boots are the usual choice of the hillwalker, some multi-activity trainers are suitable for low-level walking but, for hillier ground and rougher terrain, boots provide robust protection, particularly around your ankles. When choosing socks, make sure they are made of material thick enough to soak up the sweat and that they provide some padding and protection at potential rub points.

Rucksacks come in a range of shapes and sizes. One type of rucksack is called a 'daysack'. Daysacks are relatively small and compact but big enough for you to carry spare food, drink and a change of clothing. For multi-day trips you may be expected to carry everything you will need whilst away, such as a tent, sleeping bag and cooking utensils. Therefore a much larger rucksack with additional padding and support may be required.

Coats for walking in the outdoors come in a variety of fabrics. You will need to consider carefully the conditions that you will be walking in before you buy a coat. Ideally your coat should be waterproof and windproof. Buying a coat for hillwalking can be confusing as you will find terms such as 'showerproof' and 'water resistant' on garments. Such garments may be satisfactory in light drizzle or repel some water in the event of rain, but you will certainly need a coat that is both warm and waterproof if you are walking at higher levels where the weather is unpredictable.

1 Why are boots preferable to trainers for hillwalking?
2 What kind of rucksack would you need for a multi-day walking trip?
3 What factors should you consider when purchasing a coat for hillwalking?

- A woolly hat (mainly worn in winter but at certain heights this will be needed all year round. Some form of sunhat may also be needed in summer).
- Gloves.
- A rucksack to carry spare kit.
- A drinks bottle.
- Spare food/water.
- Sunscreen.
- Survival/bivvy bag (a high-visibility plastic bag that can be used like a sleeping bag in the advent you become stranded on a mountain due to injury or adverse weather conditions).

In addition, the group as a whole will need the following items of equipment:

- maps;
- a compass; and
- a first-aid kit.

Hillwalking requires certain technical skills. You will need to learn how to read a map and how to take bearings using a compass so that you can plan your route and stick to it. This requires much practice, as you must know your precise location if you are to walk in open country safely.

You should plan your route on a route card (see Figure 8.2). The information on this card should include such things as the distance between

Destination: *Bleaklow Stones*								Date: *21/6/05*			
Party members: *M Lost, H Kelp, M Day*											
Speed: *4 km/hr*								Emergency contact number: *044 2659 098*			
From	To	Distance	Rests	Time taken (a)	Height climbed	Time taken (b)	Height lost	Direction	Time (a + b)	Description	Escape routes
Cairn, Nether Moor 147873	*Druid's Stone 134874*	*1300 m*	*0*	*19.5*	*40 m*	*14*	*0*	*278*	*33.5*	*From flat head uphill to stone on 2nd footpath*	*Lady Booth Brook to YHA*
Druid's Stone 134874	*Spot height, Hartshorn 115877*	*2400 m*	*0*	*36*	*60 m*	*6*	*30 m*	*w*	*42*	*Carry on along footpath, at upper or head up to high ground*	*Ollerbrook Clough to Vale of Edale*
Spot height, Hartshorn 115877	*Ford, Blackden Rind 115883*	*650 m*	*0*	*9.75*	*10 m*	*1*	*30 m*	*012*	*10*	*Follow bearing across plateau to footpath*	*Colaen Clough to Corinds- book Booth*

Figure 8.2 *A route card*

checkpoints and the time it should take to cover these distances. A route card is an invaluable aid: you can monitor your progress and get back on track quickly if you make a mistake.

Orienteering

Orienteering is competitive: using a map, you race between a series of checkpoints or markers. This sport requires a high level of cardiovascular fitness if you are to run between the points in the fastest time possible. You also need to be able to navigate to the next point on the map quickly and accurately.

You will need the following equipment to participate in orienteering:

- Sports clothing (T-shirt/shorts. More experienced participants prefer to wear orienteering suits made of Lycra or thin nylon).
- Running shoes (the more experienced prefer lightweight, studded orienteering shoes similar to cross-country running shoes).
- A map.
- A compass.
- A watch.
- A whistle (for emergencies. Compulsory at some events).

To get the maximum enjoyment from participation in this sport, you will need to develop your map-reading and compass skills (see Figure 8.3).

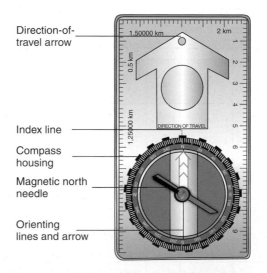

Figure 8.3
An orienteering compass

Specially drawn maps with many extra features that help the runners are often used in orienteering events. Planning is essential as you will need to know your route from one checkpoint to the next so that you don't waste time standing still whilst you decide on the best route.

Once you have mastered the basic skills, there are shortcuts to learn, such as 'running on the needle' (i.e. following the needle on the compass to run due north or south). Orienteering is both competitive and fun, but it does require good mental and physical fitness.

Camping

Camping can be an extremely rewarding social activity. With modern technologies it is possible to camp almost anywhere and in any weather conditions. A camping trip requires considerable planning to make sure that you are safe and that you get the maximum enjoyment from the activity.

The basic kit that you will need for a camping trip will include the following:

- A tent (various shapes and styles, individual or multi-person).
- A sleeping bag.
- A cooking stove and fuel.
- Cooking utensils.
- Clothing as for hillwalking.
- A bivvy bag.
- A washing kit (toothbrush, soap, flannel, etc.).

Camping should only take place in designated areas. Camping just anywhere in open country can do considerable damage to the environment. Therefore you will need to plan exactly where you are going to camp and make sure that you can reach the area in good time, particularly if you are on a walking expedition. Other safety points include checking weather conditions and checking your equipment prior to departure.

Some campsites have extensive facilities (such as social and recreational areas), whilst others may provide only basic washing facilities. Whatever campsite you visit, the main appeal of camping is to get closer to nature.

ACTIVITY

Using catalogues, brochures, the Internet, etc., produce a table that shows the various types of cooking stoves that are available, together with the different fuels.

Skiing

With the exception of some mountainous areas of Scotland, most of the UK does not have the natural resources needed to learn to ski. Therefore artificial slopes have become popular. There are two main types. Dry-slope skiing takes place outdoors using a kind of matting that generates some friction but still allows the skier to pass freely over it. Technological advances have allowed the development of indoor slopes. For example, the Snowdome at Milton Keynes (see Unit 1) has real snow which is sprayed on the slope overnight. Sessions booked on an artificial slope can be as short as one hour. You must therefore allow plenty of time to travel to your nearest slope if this is some distance away.

Unless you intend to ski regularly, it is wise to hire ski equipment rather than buy it. Whether you decide to hire or purchase, you will need the following equipment:

- Skis (these come in a range of lengths, styles, etc., depending on your ability level – see Figure 8.4).
- Bindings (these connect your ski boots to the skis).
- Ski-boots.
- A ski suit (usually one-piece for warmth and to repel water).
- Ski poles.

Downhill   Free ride skis   New   Skiboard
are for advanced   School
skiers

Figure 8.4 *You must select the correct pair of skis for your ability level*

There are some basic techniques you will need to learn before you can begin to enjoy skiing and to ski safely. Obviously, being able to turn and stop on skis are the most important considerations for the beginner. The single hardest thing in skiing is to shift your weight and balance fully on the gliding ski. Once this has been mastered, a range of turns and more advanced manoeuvres become possible. Many people use artificial slopes to learn the basics so that they can enjoy a holiday abroad on real snow.

Most skiers stay on recognised slopes, which is known in skiing as being 'on-piste'. Skiing off-piste requires greater technical ability and local knowledge because of the increased risk of avalanche.

Like most outdoor activities, there are important safety rules to follow. The FIS (International Ski Federation) has established a code of conduct for skiers:

1 Respect (do not endanger others).
2 Control (adapt the manner and speed of your skiing to your ability).
3 Choice of route (the skier in front always has priority).
4 Overtaking (leave plenty of space when overtaking someone else).
5 Entering and starting (look up and down the mountain before starting or entering).
6 Stopping (only stop at the edge of the slope or piste or where you can easily be seen).
7 Climbing (when climbing up or down always keep to the side).
8 Signs (obey all signs and markings).
9 Assistance (in case of accidents, provide help and alert the rescue service).
10 Identification (all those involved in an accident should exchange details).

As long as these rules are followed, skiing is an exciting and safe activity.

ACTIVITY

Many outdoor activities have their own jargon or words for different skills you must learn. Find out what the following terms mean for the sport of skiing:

1 The snow plough.
2 Schussing.
3 Traversing.
4 Side slipping.

Rock climbing

Climbing can be enjoyed at many levels and at many different locations. Not too long ago, most people learnt to climb on real rock but, these days, they are more likely to use an indoor climbing wall. Most large indoor climbing centres run introductory taster sessions of around 45 minutes. You will need the following equipment to participate in rock climbing, which most centres will provide:

- A helmet.
- Rope (for the beginner this will probably be provided by the centre and fixed in place).

- A harness (a sit harness spreads the weight between your waist and legs when you are hanging from a rope).
- Rock boots/shoes/slippers (you will need footwear that grips the rock. What you choose is a matter of personal preference).
- A belay device (this enables you to control the rope and stop it from slipping).

You will need many technical skills to rock climb, and some of these must be learnt at the outset for safety reasons. Most beginners start by learning how to top-rope. A top-rope is a fixed rope threaded through a strong anchor point at the top of the climb with both its ends on the ground. The climber is attached to one end of the rope and the other end is threaded through a belay device attached to a climbing partner. When he or she has reached the anchor point, the climber is lowered back to the ground by the partner or the belayer. To do this safely, the climber must first learn how to fit the harness properly and how to attach a rope to it using a knot such as a bowline knot (see Figure 8.5).

Care must be taken to thread the rope properly through the belay device. The belayer should position him or herself sideways, allowing his or her hands to move freely and to take in or pay out rope without being restricted by his or her hips. The skill of belaying requires the person to be attentive at all times and to take in slack rope as required so that, if

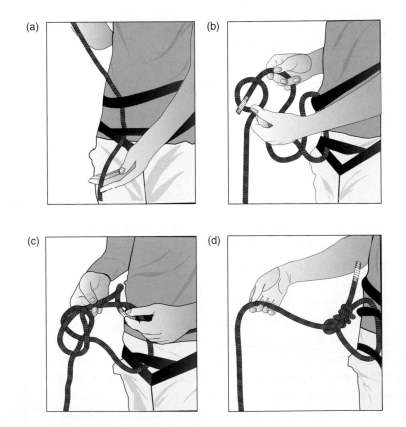

Figure 8.5 *Tying a bowline knot*

the climber slips, he or she has less distance to fall and is less likely to be injured.

Most climbers agree that the skill of climbing itself owes much to good footwork rather than relying on strong arms to support your weight. Having the patience to stop and look for suitable holds (crevices, crags, etc.) is the key. Sometimes moving sideways is the only way, eventually, to move vertically up the wall or rock face.

Once the basic techniques have been learnt, a range of indoor and outdoor climbs becomes possible.

Sailing

There are many different types of sailing on open water. Most beginners start by learning to sail on a inland body of water, such as a lake or reservoir, where the boat and rigging are supplied by the centre. However, you will need appropriate clothing, such as a waterproof top and trousers, and trainers or footwear that are comfortable if they get wet. There are many local sailing centres, so it unlikely you would have to travel a long distance to learn to sail.

You will learn the following sailing techniques and manoeuvres through instruction:

- Reaching (sailing across the wind).
- Stopping.
- Controlling speed.
- Tacking (turning the front of the boat through the wind).
- Sailing upwind.
- Sailing downwind.
- Gybing (turning the back of the boat through the wind).
- Launching and recovering the boat.

A beginner will also need an understanding of the following:

- Basic meteorology (an awareness of offshore and onshore winds, and sources of weather information).
- Emergency equipment and safety precautions.

ACTIVITY

Using your local tourist information centre, telephone directories, the Internet, etc., find three centres in your area where you can learn to sail. Compare these three centres in terms of price, availability of tuition and the time it takes to get there, etc. Put them in rank order of choice and justify your decision.

ACTIVITY

You work for your local council as a sports development officer and have been asked to suggest a programme of outdoor adventure activities for a group of college students aged 16 years and over. You need to produce a report to submit to the council that includes details of four suitable activities. For each activity you should cover the following points:

- A description of the activity itself.
- The time required.
- The equipment needed.
- The preparation that must be done.
- The basic skills required of the students.

8.2 Profile three outdoor activity centres which provide the outdoor adventure activities described in AO1

This section covers

- Private sector organisations
- Public organisations
- Voluntary sector organisations
- Skern Lodge Outdoor Activity Centre
- Okehampton YHA

The types of centre and the activities they offer vary greatly across the UK. Some are located close to towns and some are situated on the coast or in more remote locations. Broadly speaking, however, they can be categorised according to whether they are private, public or voluntary organisations.

Private sector organisations

There are private outdoor activity centres that offer a range of sports or that specialise in just one or two activities. For example, you may find a centre that specialises in scuba-diving, sailing or horse riding. Some may concentrate on providing activities for schoolchildren (see Figure 8.6) whilst others may cater for the lucrative corporate market (e.g. providing courses on team development for a company's staff).

Figure 8.6
Some centres provide courses specifically designed for children

Public organisations

Local authority centres are usually located in remote areas and they can be used for a variety of activities, such as walking, canoeing and caving. Often a local authority will purchase a centre that is in the countryside, hundreds of miles away. For example, Northamptonshire County Council owns a residential outdoor activity centre in Wales which enables children from county schools to visit the countryside and to participate in outdoor activities.

There are also nationally important outdoor centres that are run by government agencies. These include Holme Pierrepoint watersports centre in Nottinghamshire and Plas-y-Brenin mountain centre in North Wales (see Unit 1).

Voluntary sector organisations

There are many small clubs and community groups that take people out into the countryside to enable them to participate in outdoor activities. There are also larger organisations, such as Outward Bound and the

Scout Movement, that run courses in the Lake District and Scotland. The Youth Hostel Association (YHA) offers activities through its own centres which are very popular with schools and colleges.

You will need to profile three centres from the range above in order to fulfil the assessment criteria for this unit. One way to do this is to select one organisation from the private sector, one from the public sector and one from the voluntary sector.

Your profile should consider the following:

- *Location*: A map may be useful. Show access by private and public transport.
- *Activities offered*: Centres may use the facilities they have on-site to stage various activities. These may include climbing walls, high ropes, assault courses and areas that can be used for problem-solving activities or navigation exercises. They are likely to make use of the wider natural environment to enable participation in other activities. For example, they may use a local river or reservoir for canoeing and sailing. You should make a list of the activities offered by the centre and specify whether these take place at the centre or off-site.
- *Staffing*: How many staff work at the centre? What sort of qualifications do they have? How many are full time and how many part time?
- *Costs*: How much does it cost to participate in different activities? Are there any activity packages or special deals available? What discount is available for larger groups?
- *Accommodation*: Many centres will have residential accommodation on-site as courses can last a number of days and people may have travelled long distances to reach the centre. What type of rooms are available, and what is the cost of the accommodation?
- *Tuition/courses offered*: What type of instruction is available? Can they cater for all ability levels? Are there certificated courses available in any of the activities?

Let us now put this into practice by examining two outdoor centres in detail.

Profile 1: Skern Lodge Outdoor Activity Centre, Appledore, Bideford, Devon

Location

The centre is located in Appledore, a small fishing village in North Devon. It is located near to the town of Bideford which has national rail and bus links. It is easily accessible by road.

Activities offered

This centre offers many outdoor activities, and it provides training for some of these on-site. It has a number of seminar and conference rooms, and an assault course and high-rope course that can be used for personal development training. However, the centre mainly provides activities in the natural environment. These include the following:

- Hillwalking (using Dartmoor and Exmoor National Parks).
- Camping.
- Surfing (using nearby areas of the North Devon coast).
- Canoeing/kayaking (using local rivers).
- Rock climbing (using rocky outcrops/cliffs within the national parks).
- Abseiling.
- Coastal traversing.
- Orienteering.

Staffing

The centre employs a general manager and senior instructors who oversee the various courses and groups. The senior instructors tend to be more highly qualified and have a number of Governing Body Instructor Awards. There are usually about six full-time instructors with several others working on a part-time basis. The instructors are qualified in the outdoor activities they teach but may not have the same range of Governing Body Awards as the senior instructors or be qualified to the same level.

Costs

The cost depends on the activity and group size. Group discounts may be offered for larger groups. Activities which require a higher instructor to participant ratio are more expensive.

Accommodation

The centre has rooms designed for multiple-occupancy, which can accommodate school and college parties. It also has smaller rooms that house corporate customers or teachers/instructors. Some rooms are en-suite whilst others make use of communal facilities.

Tuition/courses

The centre can offer tuition in most outdoor activities. It can design packages of activities to cater for almost any group (for example, a watersports week made up of canoeing, surfing, etc., or a hillwalking weekend).

The centre also offers instructors' courses from time to time. Skern Lodge has been approved by the British Canoe Union (BCU) as a centre that offers high-quality instruction. Residential and day programmes are run throughout the year for the following courses:

● Introduction to White Water.
● BCU 1–3 Star Kayak Awards (training and assessment).
● BCU 4 Star Kayak Inland/Sea/Surf.
● Level 3 Surf Kayak Coach Training and Assessment Courses.

Profile 2: Okehampton YHA

Location

This centre is part of a network across the south west of England. It is conveniently located on the edge of Dartmoor National Park and is easily accessible by road, rail and bus. Some of the highest peaks and remotest areas of Dartmoor are within walking distance of the centre.

Activities offered

The centre can provide for most outdoor activities, but specialist activities can be arranged if required. The activities offered include:

● canoeing;
● kayaking;
● sailing;
● windsurfing;
● raft building;
● rock climbing and abseiling;
● mountain biking;
● orienteering;
● camping;
● pony trekking; and
● gorge walking.

All these activities make use of the local natural environment. For example, gorge walking is made possible by the deep streams and gorges that are carved through the Dartmoor rock.

Staffing

The centre has a number of senior and other full-time instructors. At busy times additional part-time staff are recruited. All have recognised Governing Body qualifications.

Costs

Costs vary according to the activities undertaken. The cost is usually fully inclusive and includes equipment hire and instruction.

Accommodation

The centre can accommodate large groups in dormitory-style accommodation. There are also smaller single/double rooms for instructors and the staff accompanying groups.

Tuition/courses offered

The centre runs several courses that are certificated by recognised bodies in the UK. These courses can be arranged if a group of six or more people wishes to participate. Although courses are only arranged in groups of six or more, it may be possible to find places for individuals who wish to take part in the courses. The cost depends on the number of people participating, whether hostel accommodation is required and transportation requirements.

The courses offered include the following:

- First Aid Course.
- BCU Star Awards.
- BCU Coach/Instructor Courses.
- MLTB Mountain Leaders Certificate.

ACTIVITY

Following on from the report you produced for the council about four outdoor adventure activities for a group of college students, you have now been asked to write another report that gives details of centres where the students can participate in these activities.

Your report should include descriptions of three centres (one each from the public, private and voluntary sectors) where the group can participate in the activities you described in your earlier report. You must include as much detail as possible so that a decision can be made as to which centre to choose. Your report should cover the following points:

- The location of each centre.
- The activities offered.
- The number of staff and examples of their level of qualifications.
- The costs.
- The accommodation and facilities.
- The courses and instruction offered.

8.3 Describe the benefits of participation in outdoor activities for three community groups

This section covers
- Increased confidence
- Teamwork
- Trust
- Problem-solving/decision-making skills
- Organisation skills
- Leadership
- Communication
- Motivation
- Organisations that make use of outdoor activities

Various community groups use outdoor activity centres. These include the Prince's Trust and the Scout and Guide Associations, as well as local community groups (such as charities) that help people with mental and physical disabilities. Each group will have different reasons for participating in outdoor activities. For some groups it may simply be the benefit of getting out into the open air, whilst other groups may be more interested in the transferable skills (such as teamwork and leadership) that can be developed through participation.

We will now examine in detail some of the main benefits of participating in outdoor activities.

Increased confidence

Increased confidence usually comes about as a result of overcoming a risk. Instructors often suggest that there is a risk involved in a particular activity so that, when a participant overcomes his or her fear of this risk, he or she receives a boost to his or her confidence. In reality, however, this

Increased confidence usually comes about as a result of overcoming a risk

risk is usually minimal and is controlled by the instructor, so the participants are not really in any danger.

Teamwork

Participants can learn a lot about the nature of teams and teamwork from outdoor activities. Often, groups will be set tasks by their instructor and the group's work will be reviewed after completion. The feedback received is valuable and is taken forward to the next task, with learning points that have implications for the wider world.

Trust

Many outdoor activities require you to trust other members of your group. For example, during a navigation exercise you will depend on the navigation decisions taken by your group leader. You must therefore be

CASE STUDY

Learning teamwork from an outdoor activity

A group of college students have been given the task of navigating in open country in the Peak District. In class the students do not take this seriously. They produce a route card but this is not very detailed and includes very few timings.

On the day of the walk everybody is keen and prepared. The group sets off. However, when they come to an intersection where the path splits into three other tracks they become confused. All go in the general direction they think they should be travelling in. No one takes control but, eventually, after a few minutes,

several team members wander off along one of the tracks. The rest follow. The group walks another kilometre until someone in the group gets out his map and cross-references this to the route card. He realises the mistake and takes control of the situation, taking the group back to where the tracks cross each other and then along the right path to the checkpoint where the group arrives forty minutes late.

1 What mistakes did the group make?
2 What positive learning points can be gained from their experience?

able to trust the leader to take his or her job seriously and to make the right decisions.

Problem-solving/decision-making skills

In many outdoor activities there are decisions to be made and problems to be solved. For example, if during a hillwalk a bridge has fallen into the water, the group must decide whether to cross the water now or find an alternative crossing point. The decision taken will depend on a number of factors, including the depth of the water and flow rate. Decision-making usually follows a set process, and once this process has been learnt it can be applied to other situations (see Figure 8.7).

Other decisions must be reached quickly and under pressure. For example, during a climb the weather conditions deteriorate rapidly. The climber must decide either to keep on going and make for shelter along a ledge, or to return to the ground. Finding quick solutions to different problems is an important skill in everyday life.

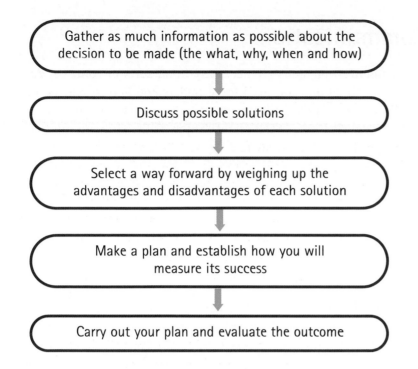

Figure 8.7 *The decision-making process*

Organisation skills

Most outdoor activities require some form of planning and organisation. For example, on a camping expedition you must decide what supplies to take with you and put together a checklist to make sure that you have taken all the necessary safety equipment. Again, you can transfer such skills to a variety of other contexts.

Leadership

Setting challenges and tests in the outdoors enables people to prove themselves as leaders or to develop leadership skills. Many companies use outdoor activities for this very reason (i.e. to develop leadership skills amongst their managers). For example, a manager may be given the task of leading a group on a navigation exercise. The instructor will analyse his or her leadership ability and not just the technical skills of navigating. The type of questions he or she would ask include: did the manager consult other members of the team? Was he or she assertive and confident in his or her communication?

ACTIVITY

Think of a well-known leader. This could be a sportsperson or a politician. What leadership skills does he or she have? Now pick an outdoor activity and state how you would develop each skill he or she possesses through participation in that activity.

Communication

Good communication skills are necessary in all sorts of contexts. At work and in social situations you need to be understood and to understand others. It is therefore no surprise to learn that many organisations use outdoor activities to develop people's communication skills. Through outdoor activities people can learn how to:

- listen clearly to instructions;
- compose messages in a way that the recipient can understand;
- think about the best way of conveying a message (verbal or written using such technology as a mobile phone);
- check that a person has received the message; and
- check that someone has put into action the content of the message.

This is made clearer through a few examples. In abseiling, the participants must listen carefully to all instructions. Failure to do so could result in an important safety point being missed. In hillwalking a group will need to produce a route card that is clear and that can be understood by any member of the group. In canoeing, a group will need to keep in close communication with the leader so that they will know when they are likely to enter a difficult section.

Motivation

What motivates us or drives us to do things is normally down to extrinsic rewards or intrinsic motivation.

Extrinsic rewards can help build intrinsic motivation. For example, if a youngster is rewarded for tackling a new challenge in the outdoors through praise from his or her instructor, he or she may get more enjoyment from that activity. If the youngster develops more self-confidence in this way, he or she may feel more able to take on new challenges at home and at school.

Organisations that make use of outdoor activities

You can see that the benefits of participation are considerable. Let's look at a number of organisations to see why they use outdoor activities to develop people's personal and social skills.

The Prince's Trust

This a UK charity that helps young people overcome barriers and to get their lives back on track. Through practical support and training,

---

GLOSSARY

Extrinsic rewards: rewards you get from sources outside yourself – certificates, awards, promotion at work, etc.

Intrinsic motivation: something inside you that drives you on to complete a task or job – a sense of achievement, increased self-respect, realising your ambitions, etc.

mentoring and financial assistance, the trust helps 14–30-year-olds to realise their potential. The trust concentrates its efforts on those who have struggled at school, have been in trouble with the law or are long-term unemployed.

One of the main schemes undertaken by the Prince's Trust is a twelve-week personal development programme. The course is usually delivered through colleges and involves community projects and outdoor activities. Through such activities the participants will benefit in a number of ways:

- Increased intrinsic motivation to tackle all types of tasks.
- Increased self-confidence.
- Improved communication skills, making them more employable.
- Improved teamworking skills which, again, are very important in the workplace.

The Scout Association

The aim of this association is to promote the development of young people so that they achieve their full physical, intellectual, social and spiritual potential as individuals and as citizens.

The association works towards this aim by providing enjoyable and progressive training in a range of activities, including those which take place outdoors. From the age of 6 years onwards, participants have access to many land and water-based outdoor activities, such as canoeing, climbing and sailing.

Participation in such activities helps the Scout Association achieve its aims. Here are some examples:

- Spiritual awareness developed through being closer to nature.
- Teamworking skills encouraged through activities such as hillwalking where you must work as a team.
- Physical development, as many outdoor activities develop both strength and stamina (for example, climbing).

Guides Movement

Girl Guides are usually aged between 10 and 14 years. In the same way as the scouts, being a guide is about belonging to a group, about learning new skills and making new friends whilst helping others. Each guide is encouraged to work towards a series of badges at her own pace.

Guides regularly participate in camping and other outdoor activities. They work in patrols or small groups where they look out for one another. They elect their own leader although everyone shares in the decision-making. The benefits of this participation are similar to those for the scouts, such as teamworking and social skills.

Duke of Edinburgh Award Scheme

The Duke of Edinburgh Award Scheme is a registered charity that provides a series of progressively more challenging awards that encourage young people's personal development. The scheme is open to young people between the ages of 14 and 25 years. There is a clearly defined structure of Bronze, Silver and Gold awards:

- Bronze for those aged 14 and over.
- Silver for those aged 15 and over.
- Gold for those aged 16 and over.

Each level has its own criteria which must be covered in four main sections:

- Participation in a local community project.
- Planning and taking part in a expedition, either on foot, by bicycle or by boat.
- Developing technical skills associated with a hobby or interest.
- Participation in a sport or physical activity.
- Taking part in a residential project (Gold award only).

The scheme is widely recognised amongst employers because of the way it benefits participants in the workplace in terms of the skills listed in Figure 8.8.

It should be clear by now that participation in outdoor activities is recognised as an important activity by many organisations for a variety of reasons, not the least of which are the enjoyment and excitement of taking part!

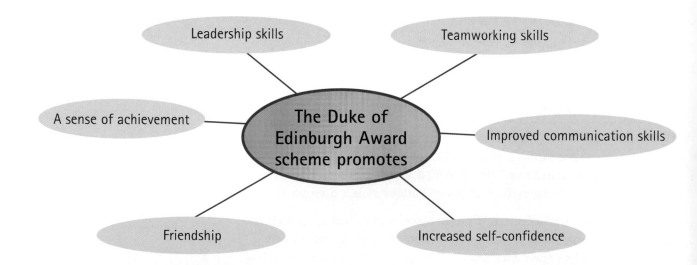

Figure 8.8 *The benefits of participating in the Duke of Edinburgh Award Scheme*

If safety guidelines are met and potential hazards identified in advance, you should have an enjoyable experience. We will now consider some of the main hazards associated with outdoor activities and what you can do to reduce the risk of injury.

ACTIVITY

Your local council is becoming increasingly strapped for cash and is looking at ways of cutting costs. They own a number of outdoor residential centres and are looking at the possibility of withdrawing their financial support for these. You have been asked to give a presentation on the benefits of outdoor activities so that they can weigh up the benefits against costs.

Put together a 10-minute presentation using Microsoft PowerPoint or similar software that shows the benefits of participation for particular groups. You may find it useful to divide your presentation into two parts.

1 An introduction and description of the general benefits of taking part in outdoor activities.

2 A description of the work of three community organisations and the benefits to its members or target group of taking part. You could select three organisations from the following or choose local community groups you know well:

- The Scout Movement.
- The Guide Movement.
- The Prince's Trust.
- The Duke of Edinburgh Award Scheme.

8.4 Identify possible hazards involved in participation in a range of outdoor activities and explain measures used to reduce risk

This section covers

- Inappropriate supervision/tuition
- Poor equipment
- Unforeseen weather conditions
- Illness
- Poor organisation

You will need to identify the potential hazards of taking part in an outdoor activity at an early stage in your planning. There will be general risks and hazards and those that are specific to the activity being undertaken.

Inappropriate supervision/tuition

Anyone who is involved in organising an outdoor activity should check that there are sufficient staff to supervise (Figure 8.9). There are guidelines and/or legal requirements which set out ratios of instructors to participants. These are normally published by the governing body of that sport or activity.

Staff training and qualifications are key areas for organisers to check, particularly if you are using a private or voluntary provider. In particular, you must check the following:

- The staff have the appropriate level of qualification for the activity and for the group's ability level. For example, the BCU has a range of instructor awards for canoeing, whilst the Mountain Leader Training Board oversees awards for leading expeditions. In addition, you would expect the staff to have at least a basic first-aid certificate.
- The staff have local knowledge of terrains, weather and tides so they are not caught out by sudden changes.

Figure 8.9 *Young footballers need adequate supervision if they are to progress*

Poor equipment

When you organise an outdoor activity, you need to make sure that you have the right equipment for the activity and the conditions. For example, when camping at altitude it is important that you select a tent that is suitable, as some may not stand up to the harsh weather conditions. Equipment must also be cleaned and serviced. For example, ropes that have not been cleaned or that have not had their use recorded cannot legally be used for climbing because they may have been weakened.

Equipment also includes clothing. It is important, for example, to take a hat on a mountain expedition as, in colder weather, you can lose up to 60 per cent of your heat through your head. As mentioned earlier, having appropriate footwear and fully waterproof outer garments is essential to being comfortable and could be life saving in adverse weather conditions.

The emergency equipment you need will vary according to the activity, but for all outdoor activities you should have a first-aid kit. A basic first-aid kit may include:

- plasters;
- blister dressings;

- tweezers;
- small-wound dressings;
- bandages;
- sunscreen; and
- painkillers.

CASE STUDY

Care of tents

There are several guidelines that should be followed when looking after tents. A tent should always be left to dry fully before it is put away as leaving it damp may result in a deterioration and weakening of the material. Any dirt or mud should be wiped off the tent, and all the components should be checked and counted.

Flysheets will eventually need reproofing using a waterproof spray, and seams may need to

be sealed before you use the tent (although most are sealed at manufacture). You should also check that you have a repair kit. It may also be useful to have a few spare items, such as ground pegs.

1 What should you do immediately after purchasing a tent and before you use it?
2 Outline three important points concerning the aftercare of tents.

Unforeseen weather conditions

For most outdoor activities that take place in the open countryside, you will need to check the weather conditions. Failure to do so may result in you not enjoying the activity (for example, wearing inappropriate clothing and being soaked because you have not anticipated rain). It can also have more serious consequences because many areas are inhospitable and dangerous in adverse weather conditions.

Hot weather can be exhausting, not only because of the greater heat but also because of the dangerous levels of ultraviolet radiation. Protective clothing is essential: a peaked hat, sunglasses and loose fitting clothes will protect your skin from sunburn. Any exposed skin should be covered by sunscreen and you should drink regularly to avoid dehydration.

Cold weather requires you to wrap up in layers of clothing so that you can trap your body heat. You can dehydrate in cold weather too, so you will need to drink frequently.

It also useful to know what the weather has been like in recent weeks because this can effect ground conditions or the size of rivers and streams – important information if you are planning a walking or canoeing expedition.

Sources of weather forecasts include the following:

- The Internet (the BBC website is useful).
- Television weather reports.
- Radio weather reports.
- Newspapers.
- Telephone weather lines (some are dedicated to specific areas and for certain activities).

Weather in the UK is gloriously unpredictable and can change without warning. You should therefore cover every eventuality in your planning. For example, in summer, it could be a hot day at the bottom of the Snowdon, with tourists in T-shirts and shorts, but at the peak it could still be snowing.

Illness

The risk of illness and injury needs to be considered when you are planning an outdoor activity, particularly in more remote areas. The illnesses that may occur include heat exhaustion or an allergic reaction to an insect bite. A slip or a fall may cause injuries ranging from small cuts and bruises to sprained ankles and broken bones. Most of these will be unforeseen but, with careful planning, need not be life threatening. Carrying a first-aid kit, as already mentioned, will help as long as you are able to identify the common signs and symptoms of such illnesses and injuries and are able to use the kit appropriately.

The ability to summon help may be critical in some situations. Mobile phones are useful for this purpose, but they do have the following drawbacks:

- Some areas have poor coverage, such as hilly and mountainous areas where few people use them.
- Large features, such as mountain slopes, can block signals.
- Mobile phones must be recharged and their batteries can run down more quickly in cold weather.

If you haven't got a mobile phone or it doesn't work, you may have to summon help personally. The normal protocol is to send two people off to the nearest road or habitation to call for help. You must ensure that they have all the information they need. Other team members should remain with the casualty, who may need further first aid and/or reassurance.

ACTIVITY

Wind, rain, fog and lightning are all hazards for outdoor activities. For an activity of your choice, describe how the weather may affect it and explain any safety measures you would take in the event of unforeseen weather conditions.

ACTIVITY

Find out how you would treat the following injuries using equipment from a first-aid kit:

1 A sprained ankle.

2 A fractured leg.

3 A deep cut to the hand.

CASE STUDY

Hypothermia

Hypothermia is the term used to describe what happens when the body loses too much heat and stops functioning properly. It can be brought on by tiredness and exhaustion in both cold and wet conditions. The signs of hypothermia may include the following:

- Numbness of the hands and feet.
- Shivering.
- A pale colour.
- Irrational behaviour and slurred speech.
- Loss of vision.
- Poor co-ordination.

In the later stages, the shivering stops and the person becomes unresponsive and cannot complete the most basic mental tasks.

Obviously it is best to recognise the early signs of hypothermia and to take action immediately. The actions you could take may include a change of clothing or putting the person in a sleeping or survival bag. Warm drinks and food may help as may rest. However, if the person suffering from hyperthermia cannot complete a simple mental task, he or she will not be able to continue. You should seek urgent medical aid.

1 Draw a picture of a hillwalker and label it with the signs of hypothermia.
2 What actions can you take to stop the escalation of hypothermia?

Poor organisation

Forward planning is essential to the success and enjoyment of any outdoor activity. It is certainly true that Prior Preparation and Planning Prevent Poor Performance. We could even go beyond this to say that participation in some outdoor activities may be dangerous or life threatening if the activity is not properly organised beforehand.

Let's consider some examples:

- *Hillwalking*: A group do not bother to check the weather before embarking on a day's walking on Dartmoor. Some members of the group only have clothing that is showerpoof and not fully waterproof. During the walk the temperature drops rapidly and there is torrential rain. The consequences of this may be, at best, that the members of the group come back with a cold, or it could lead to something more serious, such as the onset of hypothermia.

- *Rock climbing*: A group of four climbers have enjoyed a successful day climbing. One member of the group is given the task of returning the equipment to the store. First, he or she must clean it and check it for wear before putting it away for the next trip. The group arrive back late and the group member neglects to clean the equipment or log its use. The potential consequence could be that the rope snaps under pressure the next time it is used.

You will see clearly that organisation is important in terms of planning for the safety of all involved. Remember, planning for the next trip should take place as soon as you have returned from completing an activity, for the reasons given above.

ACTIVITY

Pick two outdoor activities and list all the planning considerations involved in those activities. State the potential consequences if these considerations are ignored. Use the examples given here as a guide.

You should by this stage have a clear understanding of the benefits of participation in outdoor activities and how to take part in them safely. As part of this unit you will participate in at least three outdoor activities. The next section shows you how to log and evaluate your performance.

ACTIVITY

Your council has asked you to promote an awareness of safety measures in outdoor activities in local schools and colleges. To do this you need to write a leaflet that describes the common hazards and measures used to reduce risk. Divide your leaflet into two sections.

1 Describe the hazards associated with at least five outdoor activities (e.g. inappropriate supervision/poor equipment/unforeseen weather conditions).

2 Explain the measures that can be taken to reduce the risk of hazards that cause injury for the five outdoor activities you covered in section 1 (e.g. use of qualified instructors/equipment checks/preparation and planning).

8.5 Take part in three outdoor activities and review own performance

This section covers
- Designing outdoor activity log sheet
- Completing log sheet

Location, date, duration of the activity

Location (attach a map, if appropriate):

Date:

Duration of the activity:

Description of the activity

Instructor(s):

What the activity involved and in what order:

1

2

3

4

5

Unforeseen incidents/events?

How these were overcome:

Techniques learnt

1

2

3

4

5

Safety procedures

1

2

3

4

5

Figure 8.10 *Outdoor activity log sheet*

Equipment used

1
Purpose:

2
Purpose:

3
Purpose:

4
Purpose:

5
Purpose:

Strengths and weaknesses
Those things I was good at:

Those things I was not good at:

Those things I found difficult:

Teamwork skills:

Communication skills:

Social and interpersonal skills
I have benefited in the following ways as a result of taking part in this activity:

Increased confidence

Reason:

Teamwork skills

Reason:

Trust

Reason:

Problem-solving/decision-making skills

Reason:

Organisation skills

Reason:

Leadership skills

Reason:

Communication skills

Reason:

Motivation

Reason:

Figure 8.10 *Continued*

You will need to do some preparation prior to taking part in these activities. You should, for example, design a log sheet so that you can record what you did as part of this activity and where you can make a note of all those things you learnt as a result of participating (see Figure 8.10 above).

You will have to keep this log sheet up to date by completing it as soon as possible after you have participated in the activity. Remember, sooner rather than later is better because the information will be fresh in your mind.

The following is a guide to those things you should include under each heading. Depending on the activity you undertook and what happened whilst you did this, you may need to add more headings to this basic log sheet.

Location, date, duration of the activity, etc.

Under this heading you should say where you undertook the activity (the centre, if appropriate, the exact part of the country, etc. A map may be useful here). You could also add why you chose this particular location. Make sure you include the date and the length of the activity.

Description of the activity

A basic description of the activity you participated in. Who instructed you? What did you do first/second/third, etc.? Were there any unforeseen incidents you had to cope with (for example, you took the wrong route in hillwalking or one particular section of a river was difficult in canoeing)?

Techniques learnt

You should include here a description of some of the main techniques you learnt. This may be how to belay in rock climbing or how to conduct an 'Eskimo roll' in canoeing. You may find a flow chart or series of numbered list points will help you explain this.

Safety procedures

Include any safety points you learnt through doing the activity (for example, planning a detailed route card and checking the equipment for hillwalking).

Equipment used

Make a list of all the equipment you used and its purpose.

Strengths and weaknesses

What parts of the activity were you good at and what parts were you not so good at? Were some skills more difficult than others? Did you work well as part of a group? Did you use effective communication skills? These are some of the questions you could ask yourself in order to analyse your strengths and weaknesses.

Development of social and interpersonal skills

Look back at the section in this unit that explains the benefits of participation in outdoor activities. Have you become more confident as a result of your participation? Has your motivation to meet challenges increased? Have you developed your communication and teamworking skills as a result of your participation? Make sure you enter all this on your log sheet, and try to explain what it was in particular about the activity that developed these skills.

ACTIVITY

Produce a log that describes your participation in at least three outdoor activities. Your log should cover the following areas:

- A description of the activity.
- The location.
- The techniques you learnt.
- The safety procedures.
- The equipment you used.
- Any significant events that occurred.
- Your personal achievements.
- Your strengths and weaknesses.
- The development of your social and interpersonal skills.

TEST YOUR KNOWLEDGE

1. Explain how two outdoor activities can be used for personal development.

2. Describe the work of one community organisation that uses outdoor activities to develop individuals/groups of young people.

3. Give three examples of hazards for the following activities:

   a) hillwalking
   b) canoeing
   c) sailing
   d) rock climbing.

4. Give three examples of safety/accident prevention measures you might take for one outdoor activity.

5. Where can you check the weather before participating in an outdoor activity? Why is finding out about recent weather in the area also important?

6. Describe three basic skills needed to participate in an activity of your choice.

7. List five areas in the UK you can use for hillwalking and rock climbing.

8. What are the important factors to consider in terms of staffing for an outdoor activity?

9. Explain four benefits of participating in a outdoor activities residential course.

10. What factors would you need to consider when reviewing your own performance in an outdoor activity?

Unit 9

Career Planning for the Sports Industry

Introduction

By studying this unit you will gain a more detailed understanding of the employment areas in the sports industry. You will learn about the many sources of careers information that are available in the industry and will find out about how you can progress through various different career routes.

You will also learn how to assess your own skills and achievements so that you chose the most appropriate career. You will study the various stages involved in applying for a job and will practise completing these stages (e.g. filling in application forms and CVs, and planning for and taking part in an interview).

How you will be assessed

For this unit you will produce a portfolio of work that shows you have met all the assessment objectives for the unit. Your portfolio could contain application forms and CVs you have completed, covering letters you have written, video or audio tapes of role plays you have taken part in and witness statements of your performance in interviews.

In this unit you will learn how to:

1. Identify the main areas of employment within a selected sector of the sports industry and describe national trends within the sector
2. Use sources of information to extract information on two career areas within the selected sector
3. Review progression opportunities for the two career areas within the selected sector
4. Assess own personal skills and achievements and analyse implications for progression in the two career areas chosen
5. Describe the steps in identifying job opportunities and the recruitment process of a specific job role
6. Complete written application documentation for a specific job role

⑦ Plan for an interview for a specific job role

⑧ Take part in an interview for a specific job role, presenting personal information effectively and reviewing own performance

9.1 Identify the main areas of employment within a selected sector of the sports industry and describe national tends within the sector

When people talk about employment opportunities in the sports industry, they could have in mind many different occupations. One way of narrowing down all these different types of job is to consider the occupations available in one sector or 'section' of the industry. We can therefore divide the sports industry into categories as follows:

- Sports facilities and activities.
- Health and fitness activities.
- Sports clothing and equipment.
- Sports-related gambling.
- Sports tourism.

Sports facilities and activities

Many people are employed in the provision of sports activities. These include coaches, sports development officers, recreation assistants, supervisors and managers.

Health and fitness activities

This sector has seen tremendous growth in recent years, with an increasing number of people employed as fitness instructors, health and beauty personnel and supervisors/managers of these facilities.

Sports clothing and equipment

There is a market for the sports clothing and equipment needed to play sports and also for 'leisurewear' as people are increasingly wearing sports clothing on a day-to-day basis. Many large chains of sports retailers operate in towns and cities across the UK, and all these outlets need to employ sales assistants, supervisors and managers.

Sports-related gambling

Traditionally, sports gambling was confined to betting shops on the high street, but telephone betting and the Internet have enabled access to gambling at home, and this sector is now attracting an increasing share of the gambling business. Betting shops employ a number of assistants and a manager, whilst the larger Internet-based companies employ teams of telesales/computer operators.

Sports tourism

There is a big demand for live professional sport. People will often opt to stay a night in a hotel or combine a visit to major sports event with their main holiday. Travel companies offer 'packages' that consist of transport, accommodation, tickets and food, and they employ sales people, tour reps and a host of other staff.

CASE STUDY

The growth of the sports industry

SPIRITO, the national training organisation for sports and recreation, conducted a survey of the sports industry and employment within various sectors of the industry. The survey covered those employed directly in sport, fitness and leisure facilities, as well as those employed in professional sport (e.g. athletes, players and coaches). It found that, from a starting point in 1998 of over 255,000 people employed in this sector, a predicted 347,000 people would be employed by 2008. However, the survey did not measure the substantial numbers employed in other sports-related areas (such as sports tourism and retail industries), which are rapidly growing areas of the economy.

A different survey conducted by the government Department of Media, Culture and Sport took a more in-depth look at the industry and found

CASE STUDY

The growth of the sports industry (Contd.)

---

that over 400,000 were employed in the wider industry in 2001. According to this study, employment growth has been between 3 and 4 per cent per year, which is significant compared to other industries where there has been a decrease in the number of people employed (such as in manufacturing).

Many jobs within sports and recreation are described as 'service' jobs as they are providing some form of service to the customer or participant. Service sector jobs are fast replacing other forms of employment in the UK economy.

1 Estimate roughly how many people are currently employed directly in sports and leisure facilities or professional sport in the UK.

2 What is the main problem with the SPIRITO data?

3 How important are service sector jobs to the UK economy?

ACTIVITY

The number and variety of job opportunities for new entrants into the sports industry can often be bewildering. You have therefore been asked to write short guide on career opportunities within a selected area of the sports industry.

Before you write your guide, you should choose one of the following areas to describe:

• Sports facilities and activities.

• Health and fitness activities.

• Sports clothing and equipment.

• Sports-related gambling.

• Sports tourism.

Your guide should cover the main types of jobs available, the employment trends (i.e. growth areas/areas of decline) and any other factors (such as technology) that may effect this job market.

9.2 Use sources of information to extract information on two career areas within the selected sector

Sources of information

You can obtain information on jobs and career opportunities in the sports industry from a variety of sources. A school or college is likely to have a personal adviser who, as part of his or her job, will be able to give students impartial advice on job opportunities. You will also have access to the careers service currently known as Connexions, which can help you through the job-seeking and application process.

Your school or college library and your local public library will have books that give general careers information, and trade journals or periodicals which list current job opportunities. Local and national newspapers are also useful. National newspapers cover different industries on different days of the week. For example, public sector jobs may be covered on Wednesday, including vacancies in the sports/leisure industry. Local newspapers are likely to publish a jobs supplement on one particular day that covers all the jobs available in your area.

You may also contact employers directly to obtain information. That way you are likely to get exact information on what qualifications, knowledge and experience are required for a certain job. Sometimes sending your curriculum vitae (see later in this unit) to employers can reap dividends. An employer may not have any immediate vacancies but will decide to keep your details on record and will then contact you when a job does become available.

Information on jobs

You need to investigate two areas of employment within your chosen sector. This does not necessarily mean specific jobs but general areas where job opportunities exist. For example, every sports centre employs operational staff. These are usually called recreation assistants but may also be called sports centre assistants, leisure attendants and a range of other titles. To get a feel for the kind of work they do, you will need to get details of two or three jobs within each area. Specifically, you need information on the following:

- The range of jobs within each area.
- Job roles and responsibilities.
- The skills needed to work within each area (including qualifications, knowledge and experience).
- The training requirements.
- The types and location of employers.
- Starting packages (pay and conditions of service – e.g. holiday entitlement).

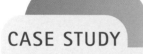

CASE STUDY

Working in leisure/sports centres

Range of jobs

In leisure/sports centres there are a range of jobs for people who are about to work in the sports industry for the first time. Most of these jobs are usually called 'recreation assistants'. The duties may include such general things as cleaning, supervision of sports activities and areas, erecting and dismantling sports equipment and work in the reception area. Other jobs may be more specialised, depending on the employee's experience and qualifications. For example, a sports assistant may be mainly involved in coaching and the supervision of certain sports activities.

Skills and qualifications needed

Successful applicants will normally have specific qualifications, usually including a pool lifeguard certificate, a first-aid certificate and general qualifications such as the OCR National Certificate in sport. At interview they would need to show that they have the following skills and attributes:

- Are able to work as a member of the team.
- Are responsible and punctual.
- Can communicate with the public.
- Display a positive attitude at all times.
- Are able to listen to and act on instructions.
- Possess specific sports coaching skills (this may be desirable rather than essential).

- Are willing to undertake training if they do not have the qualifications listed above.

Types and location of employers

Facilities within both the public and private sectors will have vacancies in this area. The facilities include sports/leisure centres, community recreation centres and health and fitness clubs. Some of these are located in town and city centres, whilst others are sited on the outskirts of towns and will thus not have public transport links.

Starting packages

Pay (according to 2004 figures) ranges from £10,000 to £15,000 per annum. A basic working week is likely to be 37 hours, working on a shift basis to cover the times when the facility is open to the public. A holiday entitlement of 25 days is normal for this type of job. There may also be certain job benefits, such as subsidised private health care and access to the facilities outside work time.

1　What are the typical duties of a recreation assistant?
2　What is the difference between general and specific qualifications?
3　Place in rank order the main skills and attributes needed for the job. You must justify your selection.

ACTIVITY

Using the sources of information discussed in this section, research two career pathways. From these sources, find out for each pathway the following information:

- The range of jobs and the main job roles.
- The skills needed.
- Types and location of employers.
- Starting packages and working conditions.
- Training requirements.

Write up your findings in the form of two reports, one for each career pathway. We will return to these reports later in this unit.

9.3 Review progression opportunities for the two career areas within the selected sector

Work out the career opportunities in each of the areas you have chosen. To do this you will need to consider:

- different progression routes;
- local, national and international opportunities;
- the possibility of transferring the skills acquired in this career to other career areas; and
- the impact of employment tends.

Figure 9.1 shows that, from starting employment as a recreation assistant, you could progress to senior management within the same organisation, transfer to the private sector or leave the industry altogether. The important point to note is that many of the skills obtained (such as teamworking and communication skills) are needed for many different jobs. Once you have developed these skills, you will certainly progress.

However, other factors will affect job prospects. For example, the level of disposable income people have will influence the number of vacancies that become available. If people have less disposable income to spend on sports and leisure, fewer facilities will be built and the job opportunities will thus be reduced.

GLOSSARY

Job opportunity: the possibility of obtaining one specific job.

Career opportunity: a job that has routes that will enable you to progress up the employment ladder to jobs with more responsibility and greater rewards.

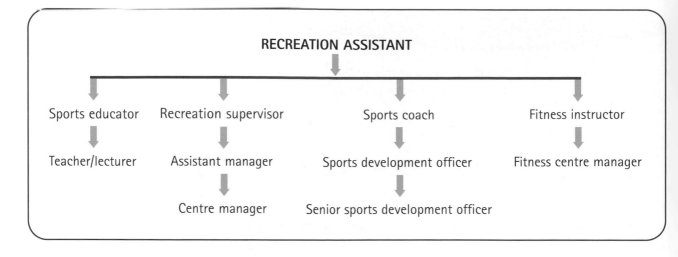

Figure 9.1 *Career routes for a recreation assistant*

ACTIVITY

For the two career pathways you researched in the previous section, add to your reports the potential progression opportunities each pathway offers (include local, national and international opportunities and how each career pathway could lead to jobs in other areas of the sports industry and perhaps further afield).

9.4 Assess own personal skills and achievements and analyse implications for progression in the two career areas chosen

When you consider your career, you must be honest with yourself so that you can decide whether you have the right knowledge, experience, qualifications and skills to work in your chosen area. In most cases these can be developed over time, so it is not essential that you meet all these requirements straightaway.

You should analyse your current skills base and achievements to date, including the following:

- Your interpersonal skills (e.g. assertiveness, appearance/dress, attitude).
- Your communication skills (written, verbal, listening).
- Your ability to complete tasks on time.
- Your ability to work as a member of a team.
- Any formal achievements you may have (e.g. academic qualifications).
- Any informal achievements you have (e.g. through leisure activities/hobbies).

Use the form given in Table 9.1 to record this information. You will then be able to consider what further action you need to take in order to pursue a career in your chosen area. Next, consider how you are going to develop these skills. This may mean taking extra qualifications or undertaking some form of work experience. You will have to make some decisions here. For example, some professional qualifications will incur a cost, and you will have to decide on the timescale you can reasonably expect to obtain these qualifications.

SKILLS/ACHIEVEMENTS	ALREADY HAVE/CAN DO (GIVE DETAILS)	NEED TO DEVELOP (INCLUDING HOW AND THE TIMESCALE)
Interpersonal skills		
Communication skills		
Can complete tasks on time		

Table 9.1 *Analysing your current skills and achievements*

SKILLS/ACHIEVEMENTS	ALREADY HAVE/CAN DO (GIVE DETAILS)	NEED TO DEVELOP (INCLUDING HOW AND THE TIMESCALE)
Can work as a member of a team		
Formal achievements		
Informal achievements		

Table 9.1 *Continued*

ACTIVITY

To make a start on the career ladder, you will have to plan ahead so that you can gain the skills and knowledge you need. Now you have assessed the skills you already possess and your achievements to date, you must analyse these to see how they would help you to progress in two different career areas and to discover which additional skills and experience you must acquire. Use Table 9.2 to help you do this. (The first row has been completed for you to give you an idea of the type of skills needed for a leisure assistant. You can change this depending on the careers areas you have chosen.)

After you have completed this table, draw two career pathway maps (in flow-chart form) that show the opportunities these jobs offer you to develop the relevant skills to move on (if you can, include on these maps the key decision points and the timescales).

CAREER AREA 1:	SKILLS NEEDED (GIVE DETAILS)	SKILLS I ALREADY POSSESS (GIVE DETAILS)
Leisure Assistant	Communication skills	I have gained Key Skill Level 1 Communication whilst at college and I am currently working at Level 2. I use verbal communication skills in my part-time job in a local supermarket and socially and at college (for example, I have given several presentations as part of my course).
CAREER AREA 2:	SKILLS NEEDED (GIVE DETAILS)	SKILLS I ALREADY POSSESS (GIVE DETAILS)

Table 9.2 *Skills and achievements needed for two different careers*

9.5 Describe the steps in identifying job opportunities and the recruitment process of a specific job role

9.6 Complete written application documentation for a specific job role

As you have already seen, there are a number of sources of information you can use to investigate the jobs market. However, when you apply for a specific job, you will most probably have seen it advertised in the local or national press, through a recruitment agency or directly through the employer.

The process of applying for a job is often referred to as the recruitment process. This process has various stages.

Stage 1: Contacting the organisation

First, you will telephone, email or write to the organisation where there is a vacancy to request further information. Some organisations will specify how you should contact them whilst others will not. Remember, this is your first point of contact with the organisation, and first impressions count.

Think about what you are going to say before you contact the organisation. You may be asked to supply the title of the vacancy you would like information on, any job reference number given and details of where you saw the post advertised. Make sure you have this information to hand.

Stage 2: Completing an application form or CV and writing a covering letter

Application form

Application forms vary from organisation to organisation, but you are usually asked to supply the following information:

- Personal details (name, address, telephone number, date of birth).
- Education (details of schools and colleges attended).

- Qualifications (qualifications obtained, level/grade and dates).
- Employment details (previous jobs and/or relevant work experience).
- Hobbies/interests (details of leisure activities).

No matter what information the organisation asks for on its application form, you may find the hints given in Figure 9.2 useful.

1 Read the form thoroughly and make sure you understand every question and the guidance notes.

2 Photocopy the form so that you have a copy to complete as a first draft, which you can check before writing up the original.

3 Be honest but make sure that you provide as much detail as possible.

4 Use an appropriate style of writing, paying attention to any specific instructions (such as filling in the form in a particular colour of ink).

5 Use the personal statement section to sell yourself. Any points made should be relevant to the skills, knowledge and experience required by the job.

6 Use appropriate words and phrases and check your spelling (e.g. avoid street or text language and phrases).

Figure 9.2
Filling in an application form

Curriculum vitae (CV)

You may be asked to send in your curriculum vitae (CV) with the application form. Some employers, on the other hand, do not supply application forms but ask you simply to send in your CV. Whatever you are asked to do, you should make sure your CV includes all those things an employer may need to know. Use Table 9.3 as a guide to writing your CV.

Covering letter

It is usual to send a covering letter with your CV and/or completed application form. This should be addressed to the personnel or human resources manager. Its purpose is to explain which job you are applying for and to give a brief summary of why you think you are suitable. You should include the following information:

- Your address and the date.
- The address of the organisation.
- The job reference number.
- Where you saw the position advertised.
- An opening paragraph explaining where you work at the moment or the course you are currently on and when you expect to complete this.

> **GLOSSARY**
>
> **Curriculum vitae (CV):** a document that lists all those things about yourself an organisation may need to know if it is to consider employing you.

Personal details

Full name (include your title, e.g. Mr, Miss, Mrs, etc.):

Address:

Telephone number (include you mobile phone,
if appropriate):

Email address:
Date of birth:
Age:
Marital status:
Nationality:

Education

School/colleges attended:

Your qualifications:
Academic (e.g. OCR Level 2):

Professional (e.g. a lifeguard certificate):

Employment history

Details of work experience:

Details of your previous and current employment
(list your duties and responsibilities and the dates
you worked for each employer):

Interests and hobbies

References

(It is usual to include at least two references, one
of which (if possible) should be someone you have
worked for. Make sure you ask your referees for
permission to use them before supplying their
names and addresses):

1 Name:
  Address:

  Telephone number:
  Email address:
  The position you held with this employer,
  if applicable:

2 Name:
  Address:

  Telephone number:
  Email address:
  The position you held with this employer,
  if applicable:

Table 9.3 *Writing a CV*

- A second paragraph that gives further details of why are suitable and what skills and knowledge you have developed that meet the requirements of the post.
- A concluding paragraph with details of your availability for interview and that you can be contacted for further information.
- Your signature and your name printed underneath.

Stage 3: Shortlisting candidates

After studying the CVs and/or application forms, the organisation will make a decision about whom they would like to interview for the post. If you are selected for an interview, you will usually be notified in writing of the date and location of the interview.

Stage 4: Preparing for and attending an interview

Not only are interviews a chance for the organisation to learn more about the candidates but also for the interviewee to learn more about the organisation. Depending on the job, the interview may be with just one other person or an interview panel of several people. It may also involve tests and exercises. You will be notified of the form your interview will take before it takes place. You will need to practise your interview technique, so it is likely that your tutor will conduct a mock interview with you in order for you to gain the necessary experience.

Stage 5: Notification

You will be notified either in writing or by telephone if you have been successful. For some jobs this may be almost immediately; for others, you may have to wait, usually about a week. If you are successful in your application, you will be given a start date and any other details you need to know before you begin your new job.

For one job, describe the recruitment process you would go through. This may include the following:

- Where to look for job opportunities.
- Telephoning/writing for an application pack.
- Completion of the letter and application form/CV.
- Attending the interview.

Complete the written documentation for this job. This must include a covering letter and either an application form or a CV.

You must now put together an interview plan for this job that includes the following:

- Questions you may be asked and your responses to these.
- Questions you may want to ask the interviewer.
- Information you must know in advance about the organisation.

9.7 Plan for an interview for a specific job role

Before the interview there are several things you can do to maximise your chances of success.

Plan for your interview well in advance

Make sure you know everything you need to know about the interview and if there is anything you must do to prepare yourself for it:

- How will you get there?
- How long will the journey take?
- Have you got suitable clothing?
- Do you need to buy or clean any clothing?

Prepare your supporting material

Make sure you can get hold of certificates of your qualifications, that you have copies of any written references you have been given and, if appropriate, examples of your work. You may need all these at the interview.

Rehearse your responses to common job interview questions

You can be almost certain that some general question will be asked at the interview. These include the following:

- Why do you want to work for this organisation?
- What are your strengths/weaknesses?
- Where do you see yourself in the future?
- What skills can you bring to the job/organisation?

Prepare the questions that you want to ask during the interview

The questions you will want to ask during the interview may include the following:

- What opportunities exist for promotion?
- Are their opportunities/expectations to work overtime?
- Can you give me further details on pay/holidays/conditions of service?

Note: Don't ask questions about things that were covered in the job details you were sent when you applied for the job. It will look as if you have not read these fully and therefore that you do not understood what the job is about.

Do some research

Research as much information as you can about the organisation you have applied to. For example:

- Who is the head of the organisation?
- How many outlets does it have?
- What is its current turnover?

This information may have been provided in the application pack, in which case you will definitely be expected to have read it.

9.8 Take part in an interview for a specific job role, presenting personal information effectively and reviewing own performance

Being interviewed for a job can be stressful. It is therefore important to practise the skills you will need.

Personal presentation

You should wear clothes that are suitable for the interview. These should be businesslike or at the very least smart casual, depending on the job applied for. You should make sure that you look alert and are well groomed.

Your body language plays a significant part in how you come across to others at an interview. You should avoid putting barriers between yourself and the interviewer (such as crossing your arms, as this indicates a lack of confidence). In general, your posture should be open and relaxed to show that you regard this as a positive experience.

You should establish eye contact with the interviewer as this shows integrity and self-belief and, again, that you are confident in what you are saying. Facial expressions also give out a lot of information about what you are feeling and thinking. For example, if you lie during the interview this may show on your face. Therefore make sure you give an honest account of your previous experience and qualifications as this will increase your chances of looking relaxed and positive.

Tone and manner

You should give as full and detailed answers to questions as possible. You should vary the tone of your voice to emphasise key points and to show that you are enthusiastic. Speaking in a flat, single tone should be avoided as it indicates you are going through the motions and that you are not genuinely interested in what you are saying. This will cause the interviewer to switch off or miss important information.

Use an appropriate manner to answer the questions. The language you choose should be positive and should be language you are comfortable with. Do not attempt to use phrases and words that you do not fully understand or use slang or street language.

GLOSSARY

Body language: the way you stand or sit gives off messages about how you feel about the situation you are in or about the other people around you. You may not be aware your body is sending out these messages, and some of these messages may not reflect how you truly feel. You must, therefore, control your body language.

Supply relevant information

Although your answers should be as full as possible, avoid waffle. Your answers must relate directly to the questions that have been asked. Always present information in a positive light and do not touch on any negative factors or weaknesses unless asked about these. For example, if you are asked about your weaknesses, avoid such phrases as 'Most of the time . . .' or 'Well, sort of . . .' These phrases suggest a lack of confidence and self-belief or that you are lying.

Reviewing your own performance

Whether you are successful or not in the interview, you can learn from the process, which will benefit you in the future. You should be given feedback by the interviewer which will help you the next time around.

Areas you may have to review include the following:

- Your communication skills.
- Your appearance and body language.
- Your responses to questions.

If the interviewer decides that you are not right for the job, do not take it personally. The ability to take criticism of the kind described above and to move on is an attribute many successful people have.

ACTIVITY

You must now take part in, and record your involvement in, a mock interview for a job. You will be graded on your:

- use of an appropriate tone and manner;
- personal presentation;
- presentation of relevant information; and
- ability to review your own performance.

Unit 10

Work Experience in the Sports Industry

Introduction

Work experience provides an opportunity for you to spend a period of time working with an organisation of your choice. Your tutor will help in this process or you may find a placement yourself. Your placement may be for a week or for one day a week throughout the term or year. Remember that your work placement needs to be risk assessed and deemed suitable by your tutor, irrespective of who made the initial contact with the organisation.

Working in an organisation gives you the chance to apply practically some of the skills and knowledge you have learnt and to gain more understanding of the sports industry. Whilst you are undertaking your work experience you will be expected to investigate different aspects of working in that organisation.

How you will be assessed

For this unit you will produce a portfolio of work that shows you have met all the assessment objectives for the unit. This portfolio will be a full record of the work experience you have undertaken. To create this portfolio, you will need to keep a log of your work experience and this unit will give you guidance on how to do this.

In this unit you will learn how to:

1. Describe the purpose and structure of the workplace organisation
2. Review workplace roles within the workplace organisation
3. Describe how to work in a healthy and safe way in the workplace organisation
4. Illustrate how to comply with agreed standards for personal behaviour and presentation in the workplace organisation
5. Plan tasks to be carried out in the workplace
6. Undertake tasks in the workplace, using appropriate skills for work
7. Evaluate performance of tasks

10.1 Describe the purpose and structure of the workplace organisation

To describe the main purpose of your organisation, you will have to look at its mission statement or set of aims/objectives. An organisation's purpose will differ according to whether it is in the private, public or voluntary sectors.

The primary aims of a commercial organisation are likely to be as follows. To:

- maximise profits;
- increase its market share (e.g. have more customers or a bigger share of the overall market than its competitors); and
- provide the best service possible.

The primary aims of a non-commercial organisation are likely to be as follows. To:

- provide the best possible service in a specific locality; and
- cater for as many groups as possible whilst working within an agreed budget (this could include such groups as the unemployed, people with disabilities and older people).

You should also describe the key activities undertaken by your organisation. This may be reflected in the facilities it offers. For example, a sports centre may have a sports hall, squash courts, fitness suite and swimming pool. In order to describe the activities provided, you simply need to look at the programme for each of these areas. Therefore, you may find that the facility offers the following:

- Fitness classes, such as aerobics and circuit training.
- Swimming lessons and sessions aimed at specific groups, such as mothers and toddlers and adults only.
- A squash club and casual sessions.
- A sports hall that offers opportunities to play five-a-side football, basketball, trampolining and badminton, among other sports.

In addition, you may find that the organisation has other activities that support its main operation. These could be fitness advice or the selling of various sports goods and food.

CASE STUDY

Northwich Swimming Pool

Northwich Swimming Pool in Cheshire is run by the local authority and is mainly in the business of providing facilities for swimming. It has a main pool and learners' pool. There is also a health and fitness suite on site with a sauna, sun-beds and weight-training equipment. The organisation's main purpose is to provide opportunities for as many different community groups as possible to enjoy the facilities. Its financial and operational objectives reflect this.

Financial objectives. To:

- keep overhead costs to the minimum;
- increase income from the centre;

- work within specified financial targets; and
- provide a value-for-money service.

Operational objectives. To:

- increase community participation in sport;
- make leisure/sports activities affordable for all;
- promote 'Sport for All'; and
- maximise the use of the facility.

1 **How do Northwich Swimming Pool's objectives differ from those that might belong to a commercial organisation?**
2 **What sort of activities do you think Northwich Swimming Pool may provide for its customers?**

An organisation's structure can be shown in chart form (see Figure 10.1 overleaf). This chart shows clearly how the main staff are organised. You will produce an organisation chart for the facility where you undertake your work experience. Depending on the size of the organisation, you will also need to describe some of the roles of the staff members you have listed on the chart. One way to do this would be to describe a member of staff's role at each level (i.e. operational staff, supervisory staff and senior management).

You will also need to describe the organisation's main customers. For example, a sports centre in the public sector may serve:

- children;
- young adults;
- families;
- single parents;
- older people;
- people with disabilities; and
- different ethnic groups.

You must do more than simply list these groups – you must also explain how they are served by the organisation (for example, through the provision of specialist activities or facilities).

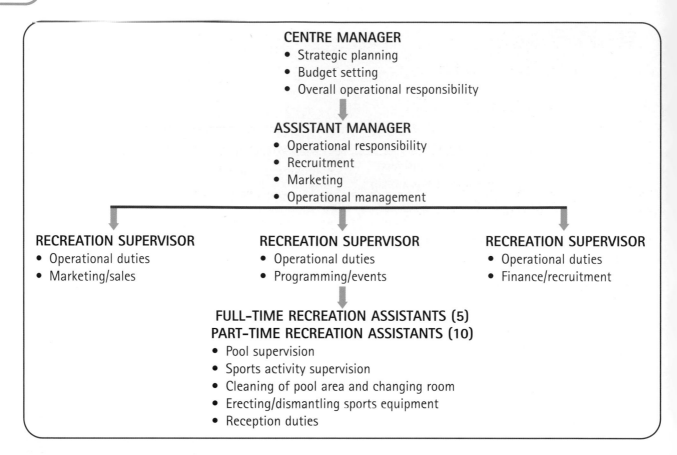

Figure 10.1 *An organisation chart*

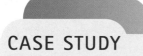

CASE STUDY

Kettering Leisure Village

This local authority facility provides for a wide range of community groups. These include the following:

- *Sports clubs and teams*, through the provision of bookable facilities for team sports that require access to the astro-turf and indoor sports hall.

- *Children*, through the provision of an indoor adventure play area which can be used on a casual basis but can also be booked for children's parties.

- *People with disabilities*, through the provision of ramps/lifts and other arrangements for enabling access to the various sports facilities.

1 What sort of groups might a facility in the private sector (i.e. a commercial organisation) cater for? In what ways might these be different from those catered for by Kettering Leisure Village?

2 What sort of activities would a private sector organisation provide for its customers? Again, in what ways would these differ?

10.2 Review workplace roles within the workplace organisation

When you have described the organisation, you will describe in detail your role within the organisation. For example:

- What tasks have you been given?
- What responsibilities do you have?

The following case study may help you in this.

CASE STUDY

A recreation assistant

Thomas spent two weeks on a work placement as a recreation assistant at his local sports centre.

His roles were to:

- undertake basic administrative tasks;
- help in the setting up and dismantling of sports equipment;
- observe and help in coaching sessions for selected sports;
- help plan and deliver sports activities for a group of children;
- help in completing various cleaning tasks; and
- support other members of the team and provide support where required.

He was responsible for:

- the care of groups of children on sports activity sessions;
- observing health and safety guidelines when setting up sports equipment and undertaking cleaning tasks; and
- carrying out basic administration tasks efficiently and effectively.

1 List all those things Thomas would have to take into consideration when helping to plan and develop a sporting activity for children.
2 What health and safety guidelines might Thomas have had to have followed when setting up sports equipment and undertaking cleaning tasks?

You should also describe the roles of your immediate supervisor or supervisors. To do this, find an up-to-date job description that summarises the role of each member of staff.

You will also describe the way in which your work has contributed to the running of the organisation. For example, by supervising children on a play scheme in a safe manner, you will have made sure that the organisation has met its legal obligation to maintain a safe working environment for all concerned. Similarly, by speaking to customers and telling them where to go for advice, you will have ensured that the organisation maintains a high level of customer service (see Figure 10.2).

In the space below draw a basic structure chart for your organisation.

Describe three main aims of the organisation (e.g. to make a profit).

Describe the main activities/services offered by the organisation (e.g. provision of sports (5-a-side/basketball/squash) and areas, such as fitness suite/sports hall/bar).

Figure 10.2 *Workplace review sheet*

List the main customer groups that use the organisation and their characteristics (e.g. professional couples- tend to have limited spare time but significant disposable income).

Identify one member of operational staff and specify their job title and duties.

Identify one member of supervisory staff and specify their job title and duties.

Figure 10.2 *Continued*

10.3 Describe how to work in a healthy and safe way in the workplace organisation

Both the employer and the employee have responsibilities under health and safety law. The employer has an overall responsibility to 'ensure as is reasonably practicable the health and safety of employees and others using those premises'. The others who have such responsibilities include contractors and students on work experience! This means that the organisation must give you appropriate information and training to enable to carry out your role in a safe way.

All the organisation's employees have a responsibility for health and safety and, for the duration of your work experience, you will be required to operate safely as well. In particular, you must ensure that:

- you do not interfere with heath and safety equipment;
- you receive adequate training/instruction before using equipment or machinery;
- your own safety and the safety of others are not compromised by any shortcuts;
- you are sensibly and safely dressed;
- you report any accidents immediately to a member of staff; and
- all working practices and codes of practice are followed as instructed by the member of staff in charge.

All workplaces have hazards. A hazard (as you learnt in Units 2 and 3) is anything that has the potential to cause harm. You will be made aware of some of these during your induction. You should describe all the major safety hazards in your organisation (See Figure 10.3). It is a legal obligation for every organisation to conduct a risk assessment on its facilities and activities. These assessments will be recorded in writing or on computer and will tell you what the most significant hazards are and how the organisation deals with them. You should concentrate on those hazards that are relevant to your role within the organisation.

You will need to look at the tasks you have been asked to assist with to establish what hazards apply and what you must do to reduce the risk. The precautions may include wearing appropriate personal protective equipment (such as gloves and goggles) when cleaning, or

Record what you have been told about chemicals, dangerous machinery or other hazards in the space below.

What is the fire procedure for your organisation?

What is the dress code for your organisation?

Do you have any personal protective equipment? When are you required to use it? Why?

What written information on health and safety have you seen? (Notices, booklets etc.)

As an 'employee' you have responsibility for the health and safety in the work place of others, such as customers. In the case of a fire or accident, what do you think these responsibilities would be?

Figure 10.3 *Health and safety sheet*

putting up sports equipment (such as a trampoline) in a certain way with a minimum of two people.

In the event of an accident, the organisation will have first-aid facilities, and it must have clearly-laid-down procedures for the treatment and reporting of injuries. You will need to find out what these are. For example, a first-aid procedure may be as follows:

1   Contact reception who will locate the first-aider.
2   The first-aider will report to the scene and will take any action necessary.
3   The first-aider will record the incident. The first-aider and the injured party will sign this document.

10.4   Illustrate how to comply with agreed standards for personal behaviour and presentation in the workplace organisation

Your organisation will also have clearly laid-down rules and guidelines that set out what is required of staff. These are normally known as policies and may include the following:

- An Equal Opportunities Policy.
- A Disciplinary Policy (for the staff).
- A Health and Safety Policy.
- A Customer Care Policy.
- A Data Protection Policy.
- A Staff Induction Manual.

You will need to research these so that you can explain how they impact on jobs within the organisation.
The Disciplinary Policy will set out guidelines on appropriate personal behaviour. The document will include sections on attendance and punctuality, for example, and will explain what will happen if these rules are not followed.

You will need to research what is expected of employees and the consequences if these rules are broken. One important document in this

CASE STUDY

Equal Opportunities Policy

A sports centre will have an Equal Opportunities Policy that applies to the treatment of both staff colleagues and customers. The policy should emphasise that it is everyone's responsibility to treat others fairly. This means no one should discriminate or treat people differently. People may discriminate against others on the grounds of their:

- colour or national origin;
- gender;
- disability or learning difficulties;

- criminal record; or
- sexuality.

1 Give two examples of behaviour that would be considered unacceptable in the light of this policy. Give the reasons for your choices.

2 Give two examples of the type of language that would be considered unacceptable in the light of this policy. Give the reasons for your choices.

respect could be the Staff Induction Manual, which will set out what you are expected to do in terms of your use of language, standard greetings for customers, the wearing of a uniform and so on.

10.5 Plan tasks to be carried out in the workplace

You will perform a variety of tasks during your work placement, and you should keep a record of what you did for each task using the headings below.

Instructions

There may be a set of written instructions for the task which you will be asked to follow, or you may be told what to do. You should make a record of these instructions in the order you did them. The following is an example of cleaning the changing room floor:

1 Put on the appropriate personal protective equipment (gloves and goggles).
2 Make sure any exposed skin is covered.
3 Put out cleaning signs ('Caution: cleaning in progress').
4 Dilute a quantity of cleaning agent in the proportion 3:1 (three parts water to one part agent).
5 Apply using the scrubbing machine. (Make sure the power cable and plug have been checked first.)
6 Rinse off with cold water.
7 Dry and buff the area.

Resources needed

List all the resources you used to complete the task. For the above example this would be:

- personal protective equipment;
- the scrubbing machine;
- a mop and bucket;
- a hose or clean water; and
- a cleaning agent.

Health and safety issues

Make a list of any specific hazards and the precautions that could be taken. For the example of cleaning the floor given above, one hazard would be the danger of the cleaning agent getting on your skin. The precautionary measure you would take is to wear personal protective equipment.

Estimated timescale for completion

Your supervisor should give you guidelines on the amount of time it should take to complete each task.

Policies to be followed

Are there policy documents that need to be referred to before carrying out the task? For the example above, this may be the Health and Safety Policy.

Team members

What are the roles of the other members of the team for this task? For example, putting out an inflatable in a swimming pool may require three or four people:

- *Team member 1*: Watches the pool area and instructs all swimmers to sit on the side whilst the structure is inflated.
- *Team member 2/3*: Inflates the structure and guides it into position in the centre of the pool.
- *Team member 4*: Ties the structure to the side of the pool using ropes and karabiner clips.

Required knowledge and skills

What skills and knowledge do you need to complete the task? This could be considerable for some tasks. For example, coaching children in a sports session may require technical sports skills and knowledge of learning processes, as well as knowledge of health and safety requirements. If you are inexperienced you will only assist in such tasks as you do not yet have all the necessary knowledge and skills to operate alone.

10.6 Undertake tasks in the workplace, using appropriate skills for work

You will be given the opportunity to use and develop many different skills whilst on your work placement. You will need to record how you practised these skills. Some examples are given below.

Teamwork

Many tasks in the workplace can only be undertaken by a team. For example, guarding a pool area requires each individual to monitor the area for which he or she is responsible and, when lifeguards swap shifts, they pass on any information the new guards should be aware of, such as weak swimmers or children misbehaving.

Even if you complete many tasks individually, you are likely to be part of the wider team that operates the facility for the duration of your placement. Team members may include a duty supervisor, a receptionist and other assistants like yourself.

Problem-solving

You may be given tasks you are unsure how to do. To find out, either ask another member of staff or work it out yourself. For example, you may be instructed on how to use specialist machinery, such as a scrubbing machine, but will not get the feel for how it operates until you have used it yourself.

Similarly, a customer may ask for a particular member of staff whom you do not know, so you may have to find out where he or she can be found in the building and if this person is able to speak to the customer concerned.

Communication

You will certainly be called upon to use both your written and oral communication skills. You may have to follow written or oral instructions on how to complete a task or give them yourself. You will get many opportunities to practise these skills, and you should log as many of them as you can.

Information giving

One task you may be given is to pass on details to customers about a change in the programme or you may be asked to relay a message to your supervisor or manager. You should record any situation where you have passed on information to staff or the public.

Seeking guidance

There will be times when you must seek guidance from a fellow member of staff to complete a task. If you are unsure about anything, you must ask for guidance: you will be working in an environment that could prove dangerous if do not follow the set rules and guidelines. For example, you may not know where to look to get information on how to dilute a cleaning agent, which could harm you if you get the dilution wrong. You should record all the occasions when you sought out additional guidance.

Completing tasks in line with requirements

Did you complete all the tasks within the timescale given and to an appropriate standard? If you didn't, were there any reasons why this was not the case? For example, there may have been an emergency elsewhere in the building or you were given other jobs to do that prevented you from completing a task. You should record all the tasks you performed whilst on your placement and give the reasons why any task was not completed.

10.7 Evaluate performance of tasks

It is important to evaluate your performance whilst you are on your work placement. You should ask yourself whether you met the requirements of the role:

● Was you attitude always positive?
● Did you treat all customers with a high standard of professionalism?
● Did you achieve all the tasks set?

These will be your own opinions, but they should be supported by the feedback you receive from your supervisor. Use Table 10.1 as a guide to recording your evaluation of your performance.

YOUR PERFORMANCE	YOUR EVALUATION	YOUR COMMENTS (WITH EXAMPLES, IF APPROPRIATE)
Did you follow the dress/uniform code at all times?		
Did you always attend the workplace on time?		
Did you show a professional attitude to customers?		

Table 10.1 *Evaluating your performance*

YOUR PERFORMANCE	YOUR EVALUATION	YOUR COMMENTS (WITH EXAMPLES, IF APPROPRIATE)
Did you complete all tasks to the required standard?		
Did you complete all tasks on time?		
What skills/knowledge did you learn?		
Were there any skills that were your particular strengths?		
Were there any skills that were your particular weaknesses?		
What improvements would you make if you were undertaking the role again?		

Table 10.1 *Continued*

Bibliography

Sources

AusStats 4177_0 (2000) *Participation in Sport and Physical Activity*. (Australian Bureau of Statistics, see below for website)

Hayward, P. (2000) *Intermediate Leisure & Tourism*. Oxford: Heinemann.

Cox, R. (1994) *Sports Psychology Concepts & Applications* (3rd edition) Iowa, USA: Brown & Benchmark.

Hanin, Y. (1983) *Emotions in Sport*. Champaign, Illinois: Human Kinetics.

Hardy, L. and Fazey, I. (1988) *The Inverted U Hypothesis*. Bass Monograph.

O'Hara, J. (ed.) (1992) *Crowd Violence in Australian Sport. ASSH Studies in Sports History*.

Oxendine, J.B. (1988) 'Emotional Arousal and Motor Performance'. *Quest* 13.

Szymanski, S. and Kuypers, T. (1999) *Winners & Losers*. London: Viking Press

Unger, R. and Crawford, M. (1992) *Women and Gender: A Feminist Psychology*. New York, NY: McGraw-Hill.

Watson, A (2003) from Benedict, J. and Yeager, D. (1998) *Pros & Cons: The Criminals who Play in the NFL*. New York: Warner Books

Further reading

Bean, A. (2000) *A Complete Guide to Sports Nutrition* (3rd edn). London: A & C Black.

Beashel, P. and Taylor, J. (eds) (1996) *Advanced Studies in Physical Education and Sport*. London: Nelson.

Blumstein, A. and Benedict, J. (1999) 'Criminal violence of NFL players compared to the general population', *Chance*, 12: 12–15.

Capranica, L. (2001) *Media Coverage of Women's Sports (Olympic and Non-Olympic Events)*. Rome: Department of Human Movement and Sport Science, IUSM of Rome.

Division of Youth Corrections, Office of Quality Assurance (2003) *Healthy Living: Exercise, Diet and Stress*. CITY, CO: Division of Youth Corrections, Office of Quality Assurance.

Dunning, E., Murphy, P., Waddington, I. and Astrinakis, A.E. (eds) (2002) *Fighting Fans: Football Hooliganism as a World Phenomenon*. Dublin: University College Press.

Godfrey, C. (2004) *Economics of Alcohol and Drugs*. York: Department of Health Sciences, University of York.

Greendale, G.A., Barrett-Connor, E., Edelstein, S. *et al.* (1995) 'Lifetime leisure exercise and osteoporosis: the Rancho Bernardo study', *American Journal of Epidemiology*, 141: 951–9.

Haveman-Nies, A. *et al.* (2003) 'Relation of dietary quality, physical activity, and smoking habits to 10-year changes in health status in older Europeans in the SENECA study', *American Journal of Public Health*, 93: 318–23.

Hodgdon, J. and Beckett, M. (1984) *Prediction of Percent Body Fat for US Navy Men and Women from Body Circumferences and Height.* Reports Nos. 84–29 and 84–11. San Diego, CA: Naval Health Research Center.

Honeybourne. J, Hill M, and Moors H. (1996) *Advanced Physical Education and Sport.* Cheltenham: Stanley Thornes.

Komarniski, R. (2001) *Coping with Shiftwork.* London: Grey Owl Avionic Consultants. Long, J., Hylton, K., Welch, M. and Dart, J. (2000) *An Examination of the Levels of Racism in Amateur Football.* Leeds: School of Leisure and Sports Studies, Leeds Metropolitan University.

Occupational Health Statistics Bulletin (2002/03). London: Office of National Statistics.

Rowe, N. and Champion, R. (2000) *Sports Participation and Ethnicity in England: National Survey 1999/2000.* London: Sport England Research.

Scott, T. (2001) *GCSE PE for Edexcel* (2nd edn). Oxford: Heinemann.

Scottish Schools Adolescent Lifestyle and Substance Use Survey (2002) (National Health Service for Scotland, see below for website).

Second IOC World Congress on Sports Sciences (1991) *Psychological Skills Training.* Barcelona, 26–31 October.

Sport England (2002) *Adults with a Disability and Sport: National Survey, 2000–2001.* London: Sport England.

Yuhasz, M.S. (1974) *Physical Fitness Manual.* London, Ontario: University of Western Ontario.

Useful websites

Please see www.heinemann.co.uk/hotlinks (express code 9406P) for links to the following websites.

Australian Bureau of Statistics provides national statistics on many topics including social trends and sport.

Central Council for Physical Recreation speaks and acts to promote, protect and develop the interest of sport and physical recreation for all. It is completely independent of any form of government control and has no responsibility for allocating funds.

Future Foundation predicts and defines social trends and provides information on analysis of the market in the UK.

Health and Safety Executive for UK provides information and publications on health and fitness.

National Health Service for Scotland provides information on health in Scotland including survey results on fitness and health.

OCR (Oxford, Cambridge and RSA) provides information relating to the many vocational qualifications and specifications supported by the examining body.

Sport England provides details on funding, providers/coaching services and participation initiatives.

UK Sport covers elite level sports initiatives and links to governing bodies and other sites.

Index